Privacy in the 21st Century

Privacy in the 21st Century

*Issues for Public, School,
and Academic Libraries*

Helen R. Adams, Robert F. Bocher,
Carol A. Gordon, and Elizabeth Barry-Kessler

Foreword by Judith Krug

LIBRARIES
UNLIMITED
A Member of the Greenwood Publishing Group
Westport, Connecticut • London

Library of Congress Cataloging-in-Publication Data

Privacy in the 21st century : issues for public, school, and academic libraries / by Helen R. Adams . . . [et al.] ; foreword by Judith Krug.
    p. cm.
  Includes bibliographical references and index.
  ISBN 1–59158–209–1 (pbk. : alk. paper)
  1. Library surveillance—United States. 2. Confidential communications—Library records—United States. 3. Library users—Legal status, laws, etc.—United States. 4. Privacy, Right of—United States. I. Adams, Helen R., 1943– II. Title: Privacy in the twenty-first century.
  KF4858.L5P75 2005
  342.7308'58—dc22   2004063832

British Library Cataloguing in Publication Data is available.

Library of Congress Catalog Card Number: 2004063832
ISBN: 1–59158–209–1

First published in 2005

Libraries Unlimited, 88 Post Road West, Westport, CT 06881
A Member of the Greenwood Publishing Group, Inc.
www.lu.com

Printed in the United States of America

The paper used in this book complies with the Permanent Paper Standard issued by the National Information Standards Organization (Z39.48–1984).

10 9 8 7 6 5 4 3 2 1

Copyright Acknowledgments

This publication is designed to provide legal information for a library setting. This information is NOT provided as a substitute for legal advice. If legal advice or expert assistance is required, the services of a competent legal professional should be sought.

The author and publisher gratefully acknowledge permission for the use of the following material:

Code of Ethics for the American Library Association; ALA Policy on Confidentiality of Library Records; ALA Policy Concerning Confidentiality of Personally Identifiable Information About Library Users; Privacy: An Interpretation of the Library Bill of Rights; and Resolution Reaffirming the Principles of Intellectual Freedom in the Aftermath of Terrorist Attacks © Copyright 1997, 1998, 1999, 2000, 2001, 2002, 2003, 2004 American Library Association. These documents may be reprinted and distributed for non-commercial and educational purposes only, and not for resale.

Model Privacy Audit and Guidelines/University of California Libraries' Systemwide Operations and Planning Advisory Group (SOPAG) Privacy Policy Task Force. This material is used with permission of the University of California and copyright of the source material is the Regents of the University of California.

Helen R. Adams:
To my husband Ed who has always supported my projects and to Jake, the German shepherd who faithfully stayed with me throughout hours of writing.

Robert Bocher:
To my family and my colleagues in the Wisconsin library community.

Carol Gordon:
To my colleagues at Boston University and M.I.T. who wittingly and unwittingly have helped me to morph from a school library media specialist to an academic librarian.

Elizabeth Barry-Kessler:
To Jill Barry-Kessler, Fred and Joan Kessler, and my teammates in the Team Management and Leadership Program, for their support of this and all of my endeavors.

Special Dedications

To U.S. Senator Russ Feingold (Wisconsin) for trying to amend Section 215 of the USA PATRIOT Act to protect library records, both when it was first considered and subsequently; for being the only member of the Senate to vote against the law; and for being a consistent, strong supporter of intellectual freedom issues.

To the American Library Association Office for Intellectual Freedom staff including Judith Krug, Deborah Caldwell-Stone, Beverley Becker, and Don Wood and to the ALA Intellectual Freedom Committee for their tireless efforts to preserve privacy and confidentiality in school, public, and academic libraries across the United States.

To the American Library Association Washington Office including Executive Director Emily Sheketoff, Director of the Office of Government Relations Lynne Bradley, the rest of the ALA Office of Government Relations staff, outside counsel from Leslie Harris & Associates and from Jenner & Block, and former ALA staff member Claudette Tennant, for their front line fight at the federal level to protect privacy in all types of libraries.

Contents

Foreword

Privacy is the issue of the moment in librarianship, brought forward by relentless changes in technology, law, and social attitudes. Whether it is the question of adopting Radio Frequency Identification Devices (RFIDs) to track book inventory, devising policy to deal with law enforcement inquiries under the USA PATRIOT Act, or addressing a library user's concerns about the use of her personal information, each day finds librarians confronting new questions and new challenges concerning privacy and confidentiality.

Protecting user privacy has long been an integral part of the mission of libraries and librarians. Librarians recognize that privacy is essential to the exercise of free speech, free thought, and free association and, therefore, essential to democracy. Without privacy, the right of every citizen to seek out and receive information anonymously, free from any government interference, is meaningless.

Yet, privacy appears to be one of the most confused and confusing issues in librarianship. Even with the guidance provided by the American Library Association through its policy "Privacy: An Interpretation of the Library Bill of Rights," questions abound about the legal basis for keeping library records confidential, minors' rights to privacy, records retention policies, and privacy and national security.

But librarians cannot afford to be confused or misinformed about privacy. When a person uses a library, he entrusts the library with his personal information—information about what he chooses to read, view, or listen to, a thumbnail sketch of his intellectual habits. Librarians must take their responsibility to protect this information seriously, and learn to be effective guardians of their users' privacy. Appreciating the history of privacy and intellectual freedom, recognizing what constitutes a privacy violation, and understanding the librarian's legal and ethical duties are all necessary components of this learning process.

That is why I welcome the publication of *Privacy in the 21st Century: Issues for Public, School, and Academic Libraries*. It provides librarians with a solid grounding in the theory and practice of privacy and guidance in developing policies to protect users' privacy and confidentiality in every library environment, and it amplifies and expands the efforts of the American Library Association and its Office for Intellectual Freedom to educate librarians about protecting users' privacy rights. It is an indispensable resource for any member of the library community who is committed to preserving library patrons' Constitutional right to access information free from any fear of government intimidation or reprisal.

Judith F. Krug, Director
American Library Association
Office for Intellectual Freedom
Chicago, Illinois

Introduction

The purpose of this book is to gather in a single volume information and further resources on privacy and confidentiality for public, school, and academic librarians. It will also serve as a valuable reference for K–12 administrators and other educators. For those unfamiliar with the American Library Association (ALA) intellectual freedom resources relating to privacy, we have described them as well as reprinted key documents in the appendices. We have also detailed the considerable work of the ALA to lead the efforts to retain those civil liberties following September 11, 2001 and the passage of the USA PATRIOT Act. The authors acknowledge that because the subject of privacy touches all types of libraries, this has resulted in some aspects of privacy being discussed in several different areas of the text. Terms associated in many contexts with privacy and confidentiality are defined in the Glossary.

For purposes of this book, the authors use the ALA definitions of privacy and confidentiality.

"In a library, the right to privacy is the right to open inquiry without having the subject of one's interest examined or scrutinized by others."[1]

"Confidentiality exists when a library is in possession of personally identifiable information about users and keeps that information private on their behalf."[2]

One of the strengths of the book is the broad and varied background of its authors. Helen Adams is an experienced school library media specialist in Wisconsin and former American Association of School Librarians president. Robert Bocher is a state public library consultant for the Wisconsin Department of Public Instruction and chair of the American Library Association E-rate Task Force. Dr. Carol Gordon is head of the Pickering Educational Resources Library at Boston University and an associate professor in the School of Education. Elizabeth (Liza) Barry-Kessler is an attorney formerly employed at the Center for Democracy and Technology and at Leslie Harris and Associates in Washington, DC, where she worked on privacy and other intellectual freedom issues. She now works for Earthlink, Inc.

Another strength of the book is that it gives a wide range of general privacy information related to state and federal privacy laws as well as laws relating to library and public records. Additionally, it addressses specific privacy issues by type of library—public, school, and academic.

We want to thank Judith Krug, director of the ALA Office for Intellectual Freedom, for providing the Foreword for this book and for being a strong advocate and visionary force for intellectual freedom. The authors wish to acknowledge the assistance of the ALA Office for Intellectual Freedom for granting permission to reprint its documents relating to privacy and confidentiality. Thank you to Debra Caldwell-Stone, executive director, American Library Association, Office for Intellectual Freedom, and Beverley Becker, associate director, American Library Association, Office for Intellectual Freedom, for their review of sample policies and audit guidelines.

Thanks to Jim Dempsey, executive director of the Center for Democracy and Technology, for arranging for the use of the center's newly revised "Standards for Government Access to Papers, Records, and Communications" chart.

Thanks also to George Hall, program assistant, Public Library Development Team, Wisconsin Department of Public Instruction; Mary Minow, librarian, attorney, and founder of LibraryLaw.com.; Dr. Carrie Gardner, assistant professor of Library and Information Science at Catholic University of America; Dr. Barbara A. Fiehn, assistant professor, Northern Illinois University; Jeff Gibson, technology director for the Wisconsin Rapids (Wisconsin) School District; Steve Day, technology coordinator, Montello (Wisconsin) School District; Sanata Lau, technology coordinator, Port Edwards (Wisconsin) School District; Stephen Sanders, K–12 technology consultant, Wisconsin Department of Public Instruction; and Rebekah Anderson, marketing manager for 3M Library Systems for their generous giving of time and information to add to the content and facilitate the publication of this work.

Notes

1. American Library Association Office for Intellectual Freedom, "Questions and Answers on Privacy and Confidentiality," http://www.ala.org/ala/oif/state mentspols/statementsif/interpretations/questionsanswers.htm (accessed July 26, 2004).

2. Ibid.

CHAPTER 1

An Overview of Privacy in the United States

Introduction

Privacy protection in the United States is a somewhat bewildering array of various laws and policies at both the federal and state levels. Privacy law, which forms the foundation of privacy protection, is complex, inconsistent, difficult to interpret, and occasionally frustrating. One way of thinking about it is to compare it to a quilt put together by a group of quilters—and being constantly worked on by new members of the sewing circle. In this context, there is one broad, mostly consistent layer, which is federal law, including constitutional law. This provides the foundation, but even it is subject to inconsistent court rulings from different federal appellate court circuits—like quilters with distinct styles. Then there are fifty different state legal systems, each unique unto itself and each reflecting the development of privacy law in its own context.

In this chapter, we will provide an overview of this patchwork quilt. Many of the topics addressed briefly in this chapter will be more fully developed in subsequent chapters.

The Origins of Our "Right to Privacy"

Although the word "privacy" never appears in the U.S. Constitution, several important privacy protections are clear in the Bill of Rights. For example, the Fourth Amendment protects people's right to be "secure in their persons, houses, papers, and effects, against unreasonable searches and seizures." Additionally, the First Amendment's protection of freedom of religion and freedom of speech is understood to protect the privacy of individual beliefs.

The first articulation of a right to privacy under the U.S. Constitution was made in a now famous *Harvard Law Review* article written by Louis Brandeis and Samuel Warren in 1890, entitled, "The Right to Privacy."[1] In this article, the authors describe various ways in which laws governing various aspects of life have evolved as both society and technology have changed, and they argue for the similar evolution of legal protection of individual privacy. Brandeis later became a justice of the U.S. Supreme Court. There, he wrote the dissent in *Olmstead v. United States*, arguing that the Founding Fathers "sought to protect Americans in their beliefs, their thoughts, their emotions and their sensations. They conferred, as against the government, THE RIGHT TO BE LET ALONE—the most comprehensive of rights and the right most valued by civilized men" (emphasis in original).[2]

Penumbra of Privacy Rights

In 1965, the Supreme Court held in *Griswold v. Connecticut*[3] that the "right to privacy" was a complex one, emanating from a variety of Constitutional guarantees. This case addressed the question of whether or not a married couple had a protected right to privacy in making decisions about using birth control. The justices found that this right was protected by the Fourteenth Amendment's guarantee of the right to equal protection and due process of law. The Court used this case as an opportunity to describe a broad theory on the protection of privacy.

Writing for the court, Justice William O. Douglas explained that "specific guarantees in the Bill of Rights have penumbras, formed by emanations from those guarantees that help give them life and substance. . . . Various guarantees create zones of privacy."[4] Another way of describing this is to observe that while privacy rights are not the central focus of any amendment to the Constitution, there are, as shown in the following list, privacy rights associated with several sections of the Bill of Rights.

- *First Amendment:* Protection of the freedom to associate necessarily protects privacy in one's associations;

- *Third Amendment:* Prohibition against the quartering of soldiers "in any house" in time of peace without the consent of the owner protects privacy in the home;

- *Fourth Amendment:* The "right of the people to be secure in their persons, houses, papers, and effects, against unreasonable searches and seizures" clearly protects individual privacy;

- *Fifth Amendment:* The "Self Incrimination Clause" enables citizens to create a zone of privacy which government may not force citizens to surrender to their detriment;

- *Ninth Amendment:* The enumeration in the Constitution, of certain rights, shall not be construed to deny or disparage others retained by the people;

- *Fourteenth Amendment:* The dual rights of due process of law and equal protection under the law have been held to protect individual rights to privacy, especially in the area of sexual or marital activity that some states have criminalized (including the right to contraception, interracial marriage, abortion, and consensual sexual activity).

In 1967, only two years after *Griswold*, the Supreme Court began to back away from the idea that a fully articulated right to privacy could be found under the Constitution. In *Katz v. United States*, Justice Stewart noted that "the protection of a person's general right to privacy—his right to be let alone by other people—is, like the protection of his property and of his very life, *left largely to the law of the individual States*"[5] (emphasis added). In his concurring opinion in *Katz*, Justice Harlan articulated a test which today remains part of most legal analysis related to Constitutional protections of privacy. He said, "There is a twofold requirement, first that a person have exhibited an actual (subjective) expectation of privacy and, second, that the expectation be one that society is prepared to recognize as 'reasonable.'"[6]

Subsequent Supreme Court decisions have provided some guidance to what may be considered a "reasonable expectation of privacy" and thus protected by the Constitution. For example, in *Roe v. Wade*[7] the Court found that a woman's right to have an abortion was a protected privacy right. By contrast, in *California v. Greenwood*[8] the Supreme Court held that people do not have a privacy right regarding their garbage once it has been taken out to be thrown away. More recently in 2003, in *Lawrence v. Texas*,[9] the Supreme Court held that states can no longer criminalize same-sex consensual sexual activity, because such laws violate individuals' right to privacy.

Privacy rights have also evolved from the common law in many states. There are four distinct "privacy torts," or injuries to privacy, that are recognized in some U.S. states. They are: (1) intrusion upon an individual's seclusion or solitude, (2) public disclosure of private facts, (3) placing an individual in a false light highly offensive to a reasonable person, and (4) unpermitted use of a person's identity for commercial gain. Generally, prohibitions against these behaviors also create a private right of action for one private individual to make a legal claim against another private individual or business. The authoritative article on this topic is a 1960 law journal article, "Privacy," by William Prosser.[10]

Federal Privacy Protections

Privacy Act of 1974

Most federal protections to your privacy are based on laws that have been passed by Congress over the past several decades. One of the first, and still most important federal statutes related to privacy, is the Privacy Act of 1974.[11] This was the first effort to regulate any government's collection, maintenance, use, and dissemination of personally identifiable information (PII). Personally identifiable information refers to information specific enough (e.g., full name, home address, email address, library patron record) to enable someone to identify an individual. One of the primary subjects addressed by the Privacy Act was the government's collection of PII and the use of computer technology to share such information across federal agencies. It also established the concept of "fair information practices" which continue to inform the debates on public and private sector privacy today.

The fair information practices initially addressed by the Privacy Act include:

- *Openness and Transparency:* People should be aware that records are being created and kept. There should be no secret record collection.
- *Review and Correction:* People should have access to records related to themselves, and should have the opportunity to correct mistakes in those records. The Privacy Act gave this right to U.S. citizens and resident aliens, but not to foreign visitors.
- *Collection Limitations:* The government should not collect personally identifiable information it does not need.
- *Relevant, Accurate, Complete, and Timely:* Personally identifiable information should only be collected if it is relevant, accurate, complete, and timely.
- *Use Limitations:* Personal data should only be used for purposes related to the reason for which they were collected.
- *Limitations on Sharing Information:* Personally identifiable information should only be shared across agencies with the express permission of the person.

Many of the original principles were implemented inconsistently from agency to agency, and over time, some have changed significantly. For example, in the wake of the September 11, 2001, attacks, there is far greater support than in the past for agencies, especially the intelligence and law enforcement agencies, to share information.

Since the Privacy Act of 1974, nearly all federal efforts to protect, or limit, individual privacy rights have focused more on specific privacy concerns rather than broad privacy rights. For example, there has been legislation on financial privacy, health care privacy, and credit report privacy. Of special interest to the library community has been the legislation on educational records and on children's privacy.

Consumer Privacy Laws

The federal government has addressed a number of consumer privacy concerns over the last thirty years, including protecting the privacy of our video rental records and our pictures and addresses held by state driver's licensing agencies. The most recent legislation addresses protections related to consumer financial information and medical and health-related information.

Federal Protection on Disclosure of Financial Information

The issue of privacy in relation to financial information is often listed near the top of consumers' concerns. A 2003 poll commissioned by the Consumer Federation of California found that 67 percent of those surveyed said that privacy of their financial records is a major or important concern to them and 74 percent supported "opt-in" policies for companies that share their customers' financial information.[12] There have been instances in which financial institutions used their customers' personally identifiable information for questionable purposes. For example, in 1999 the Minnesota attorney general settled a lawsuit against U.S. Bancorp for sharing customer account information with third parties, who then used the information for marketing nonfinancial products and services.[13]

In the area of federal protections a number of laws include language related to privacy and protecting a consumer's financial information. These laws include the Electronic Fund Transfer Act, the Right to Financial Privacy Act, the Fair Credit Reporting Act, and the Gramm-Leach-Bliley Act (GLBA).[14] Of these laws, GLBA is the most recent and probably the best known from a consumer perspective.

More formally known as the Financial Modernization Act (Public Law 106-102), GLBA passed Congress and was signed into law in November 1999. The act removed federal statutory language prohibiting the merger of certain financial institutions, like banks and insurance companies.* With mergers now allowed under GLBA, there was concern that the new mega-financial institutions and all of their units or "affiliates" would now have

---

Opt-in: The term commonly used where you have the choice on whether and how any of your PII will be used. In other words, you are in control of your PII and anyone wanting to use it must ask your permission. This is the current European Union's standard for the protection of its citizens' PII.

Opt-out: The opposite of opt-in is opt-out, where any PII you make available on paper, via the web, and so forth, can be used in any manner, unless you specifically "opt-out" and request that it not be used. Unfortunately opt-out provisions may not be available on a web site or paper form where you are entering PII. Of course if no opt-out provision is given, you always have the option not to continue using the web site or service.

---

*Prohibitions against such mergers were passed as part of a New Deal legislation to address financial abuses that some felt contributed to the Wall Street Crash of 1929 and the subsequent Great Depression.

many millions of customers and access to all their financial data. In part to address this concern the following privacy provisions were incorporated into Title V of the act.[15]

- With limited exceptions, financial institutions can disclose a customer's personal information to a third party only upon notifying consumers, and allowing them the option to prevent such disclosure (an "opt-out" provision).
- Financial institutions cannot disclose a consumer's access number or code to a nonaffiliated third party for use in marketing to consumers.
- Financial institutions must ensure the security and confidentiality of customer financial records and information and protect against unauthorized access to such information.
- At least once annually financial institutions must in a "clear, conspicuous, and accurate statement"[16] notify their customers of the institution's privacy policies. (Unfortunately, the dense, legalistic style in which many privacy notices are written often discourages consumers from fully reading or understanding their financial privacy rights.)

In addition to the jargon-filled privacy notification, there have been criticisms that GLBA does not go far enough in protecting consumer rights, or that it has too many loopholes. For example, the law does not prevent any unit or "affiliate" of a financial corporation from sharing information among all other affiliates. If a credit card company merges with an insurance company it is not too unrealistic to see implications of the insurance unit of the now combined company having access to a customer's credit card purchases of health-related products or services.[17] In part to address the less than comprehensive privacy protections in GLBA, the law does not override state laws that provide more stringent privacy protections of a consumer's financial information. Several states, including California, Connecticut, and North Dakota, have passed legislation providing stronger protections.[18] In 2001 the North Dakota legislature replaced a previous pro-privacy opt-in law with a weaker opt-out law. Protests from consumer groups resulted in a successful statewide referendum in June 2002 when 72 percent of voters supported repealing the weaker opt-out law.[19]

Federal Protection on Disclosure of Health and Medical Information

Along with the protection of their financial information, consumers are concerned about the protection of their personal health information and medical records. One of the key federal protections that address this issue is the Health Insurance Portability and Accountability Act (HIPAA, PL 104-191). Passed in 1996, HIPAA provided federal privacy protections related to personally identifiable information in a patient's medical records or other health-related records, regardless of the format of such information. HIPAA set a baseline federal standard for the protection of consumer health and medical information that, until the law's passage, did not exist on a nationwide basis.[20] Among the types of personal information HIPAA defines as "Protected Health Information" are individual names, street addresses, email addresses, telephone and fax numbers, Social Security numbers, full-face photos, biometric identifiers (e.g., finger and voice prints), and any medical record identification numbers and health plan member numbers.[21] The law covers medical clinics, hospitals, other health care providers, and health insurers.

Although passed in 1996, the language in the law allowed for a long rulemaking process before its privacy provisions finally went into effect in April 2003.[22] As part of this process more than 52,000 comments were received from the health care profession and consumer rights and privacy groups.[23] While there are always some specific exceptions, in general health care providers covered under the law must do the following.[24]

- Notify patients of their rights under the new privacy regulation, including the right to review and obtain a copy of all their medical records and to correct errors in their records.
- Take reasonable steps to ensure that communications with the patient are confidential.
- Have administrative, technical, and physical safeguards to prevent the misuse of a patient's health information.
- Obtain an individual's permission (opt-in) before disclosing a patient's medical information for marketing purposes.

To provide better control of medical records, HIPAA's passage has helped accelerate the trend toward digitizing patients' medical records, the benefits of which were even noted in the President's 2004 State of the Union address.[25] However, digitization has also increased privacy concerns, in part because some transcription of medical records is being outsourced to other countries. There has already been at least one instance in which a Pakistani woman transcribing medical records in Karachi threatened to post confidential patient records on the Internet unless she received a raise.[26] (Outsourcing is not prohibited by HIPAA.) In relationship to the outsourced processing of medical and other information (e.g., a person's financial data), Representative Edward J. Markey (D-Massachusetts), who co-chairs the Congressional Privacy Caucus, noted, "There is no assurance that privacy will be protected when personal data is transferred to offshore companies that are beyond the reach of U.S. law enforcement."[27]

Genetic testing is another medically related privacy issue that has reached the public's attention in recent years. Genetic testing offers many benefits, including the ability to determine one's susceptibility or likelihood of contracting genetically based diseases. Within HIPAA's privacy regulations, genetic information is treated like all other "Protected Health Information."[28] However, HIPAA does not address such issues as employment discrimination based on an employee's DNA, or the refusal of an employee to take such a test. Federal oversight in this area is the responsibility of the Equal Employment Opportunity Commission (EEOC). In February 2001 the EEOC went to court to ask that the Burlington Northern Santa Fe Railway Company stop genetic testing of its employees who had filed claims for work-related injuries. The EEOC said that employment decisions based on the results of genetic testing violated the Americans With Disabilities Act. As part of a settlement of the case, the railroad agreed to stop DNA testing of employees and agreed to not retaliate against any worker who refused such testing. This was the first settlement of a case based on genetic testing in the workplace.[29] As more illnesses are found that have a genetic predisposition, the issue of protecting a person's DNA will become even more important.

Federal Privacy Laws of Particular Interest to Libraries

While laws like GLBA and HIPAA have a very broad impact, several federal laws address privacy issues in a narrower context and with a more direct impact on the library community. Some of these are listed below.

Family Education Rights and Privacy Act (FERPA)

The Family Education Rights and Privacy Act of 1974[30] provides parents, and students who have reached adulthood, the right to review their educational records, have errors corrected, and grant schools permission to use the records for purposes outside of a predetermined list of reasons a school would need to share student records. Public library records are not considered educational records under FERPA; however, it is uncertain whether school library records are considered "educational records." The Department of Education web site contains considerable information on FERPA compliance.[31]

Electronic Communications Privacy Act (ECPA)

The Electronic Communications Privacy Act of 1986 (ECPA)[32] represented the federal government's first major attempt to take existing telephone wiretap laws[33] and update them to incorporate computer and wireless communications. ECPA was an attempt to balance both individual privacy and the government need to use wiretapping as a tool in criminal investigation. It authorized wiretapping of electronic communication such as email, but required that a law enforcement agent seeking such a wiretap show probable cause and obtain a warrant before collecting the information.

Children's Online Privacy Protection Act (COPPA)

While it is difficult to accurately determine how the privacy of children and young adults is faring, online privacy for children age twelve and under has increased significantly since 2000. This is because of the Children's Online Privacy Protection Act (COPPA), passed by Congress and signed by the President in 1998. The law is targeted at commercial web sites that collect personally identifiable information from young web site visitors. These sites, as required by COPPA, must:

- Post a privacy policy,
- Provide notice of data collection practices,
- Get verifiable consent from parents to collect personal information from children,
- Allow parents to review the information collected, revoke their consent and/or request deletion of the collected information, and
- Establish procedures to safeguard the confidentiality and integrity of the data.[34]

Although the law was signed in October 1998, the Federal Trade Commission (FTC) was given time to formulate rules to implement the law's provisions. These rules became effective on April 21, 2000. Shortly thereafter (July 2000) the FTC announced that it was sending email notices to many children's web sites reminding them that they must comply with COPPA if they collect personally identifiable data from children age twelve and under.

Nonprofit organizations, including libraries, are not subject to COPPA's requirements. So if your library offers email reading lists or reading clubs, for example, you do not need to obtain verifiable parental consent before children can participate. But during deliberations on the law, librarians still found themselves debating its provisions. For example, while committed to children's privacy, librarians know that many children use the Internet in the library without close parental supervision. This makes it very difficult for young users to obtain the "verifiable parental consent" needed to use some popular and valuable online resources. Where it might be easy for a child using the Internet in the family room at home to get parental consent, a child using the Internet at the library is in a very different position. Librarians will have to either identify alternative online resources or help the child obtain the required parental permission. Staff need to have materials readily available that help explain to children, parents, and the broader community the privacy provisions in COPPA.

By April 2001, the FTC reported its first settlements for violations of COPPA.[35] Since then the FTC has continued to monitor web site compliance with the law. In April 2002, the FTC released "Protecting Children's Privacy Under COPPA: A Survey of Compliance." For this report, the FTC examined the data collection practices of 144 web sites directed toward young children. It found that at least 90 percent posted privacy policies stating whether the site collected personally identifiable information from children under thirteen, how the information was used, and whether it was shared with third parties. Findings show that the types and amount of information collected have decreased since the act went into effect. However, full compliance with the act has not been achieved because only about one half of sites inform parents of their right to review their child's information, have it deleted, or deny further collection of their children's personal information.[36]

The FTC has continued to charge commercial web sites with COPPA violations and levy substantial fiscal penalties. In February 2003, the FTC announced that Mrs. Fields Cookies and Hershey Foods would pay civil penalties of $100,000 and $85,000, respectively, for collecting personal information from children without procuring parental consent. Violations not withstanding, the online privacy of young children has definitely improved and commercial web sites have retreated from the aggressive and sometimes underhanded data collection tactics of the pre-COPPA days.

Neighborhood Children's Internet Protection Act (NCIPA)

The Neighborhood Children's Internet Protection Act[37] was originally proposed as an alternative to the mandatory Internet filtering requirements of the Children's Internet Protection Act (CIPA). However, not only did CIPA pass but NCIPA's community-oriented provisions were incorporated into the final law.

One of the provisions NCIPA requires is that schools and libraries participating in the E-rate program must have Internet Safety Policies which address, among other things, the "unauthorized disclosure, use, and dissemination of personal identification information regarding minors." Additionally, those policies must be discussed in a public meeting before they are finalized. Schools must also indicate how they will "monitor" student Internet use. The law notes that schools are not required to monitor students electronically, although neither are they prohibited from electronic monitoring of student Internet activity. (Public libraries are not required to monitor Internet use under NCIPA.) For more information on this, see issue 3, the "Student Privacy in the District's AUP" section in Chapter 5.

The USA PATRIOT Act

Passed in the immediate wake of the September 11, 2001 attacks on the United States, the Uniting and Strengthening America by Providing Appropriate Tools Required to Intercept and Obstruct Terrorism Act of 2001 (the "USA PATRIOT Act")[38] made significant changes to many of the privacy protections in existing law. The act passed 357–66 in the House of Representatives and by 99–1 in the Senate. Senator Russ Feingold from Wisconsin was the only senator to vote against the bill.

Unlike the overwhelming majority of other laws related to privacy passed in recent years that increase privacy—most notably HIPAA[39] and COPPA[40]—the USA PATRIOT Act reduces the privacy rights of ordinary people, instead of expanding them. The Act is a complex and far reaching law[41] that changed over one hundred sections of fifteen existing federal statutes. In part because of this, reading the act itself, taken out of the context of the other effected statutes, is frustrating and confusing. It is probably more useful to read an analysis of the act rather than the act itself.

While coming under considerable criticism, some sections of the act were supported by law enforcement officials and civil libertarians alike. When problems with the law are debated, advocates of the law often point to those sections that had broad support or were uncontroversial. For example, one generally uncontroversial area was Section 206. This section permits investigators to obtain a wiretap order associated with a person, rather than a phone number. This change means that when a person purchases a new cell phone or uses a pay phone, the law enforcement agency does not have to get another wiretap order, which was required under the previous statute.

Here are the provisions in the USA PATRIOT Act that were the biggest changes from previous federal law.

• Permits "roving" surveillance—that is, surveillance orders attached to specific people, not necessarily specific locations or telephone numbers;

• Allows application for Foreign Intelligence Surveillance Act (FISA) surveillance or a search order if gathering foreign intelligence is a significant reason for the application rather than the reason;

• Authorizes pen register and trap and trace device orders for email as well as telephone conversations;

• Permits secret FISA court to order access to any "tangible thing," rather than only business records held by lodging, car rental, and locker rental businesses;

• Prohibits U.S. financial institutions from maintaining "correspondent accounts" for foreign banks;

- Creates new customer identification and record keeping standards, especially for foreign customers;
- Encourages financial institutions and law enforcement agencies to share information concerning suspected money laundering and terrorist activities;
- Prohibits laundering the proceeds from cyber crime or supporting a terrorist organization;
- Provides explicit authority to prosecute overseas fraud involving American credit cards;
- Allows confiscation of property located in this country for crimes committed in violation of foreign law;
- Creates new federal crimes for terrorist attacks on mass transportation facilities and for offenses involving biological weapons;
- Creates new federal crimes for harboring terrorists and for affording terrorists material support;
- Creates new federal crimes for conducting the affairs of an enterprise which affects interstate or foreign commerce through the patterned commission of terrorist offenses;
- Creates new federal crimes for fraudulent charitable solicitation;
- Authorizes "sneak and peek" search warrants;
- Permits nationwide execution of warrants in terrorism cases;
- Allows the attorney general to collect DNA samples from prisoners convicted of any federal crime of violence or terrorism.

See the section on the USA PATRIOT Act in Chapter 3, where its impact on libraries is discussed in more detail.

The Federal Trade Commission

The Federal Trade Commission (FTC) is the federal agency with primary responsibility for consumer privacy. This is considered part of the agency's overall consumer protection mission and also stems from explicit authority under statutes such as the Gramm-Leach-Bliley Act, the Fair Credit Reporting Act, and the Children's Online Privacy Protection Act.

The FTC's privacy agenda, as of October 2001, includes the following:[42]

- Creation of a national Do Not Call list
- More aggressive enforcement against spam email
- Helping victims of identity theft
- Putting a stop to "pretexting" the collection of PII under false pretenses
- Encouraging accuracy in credit reporting and compliance with the Fair Credit Reporting Act
- Enforcing corporate privacy statements or policies

- Increasing enforcement and outreach related to children's online privacy (e.g., COPPA)
- Encouraging consumer privacy complaints
- Enforcing telemarketing sales regulations
- Restricting the use of "preacquired" account information
- Enforcing the Gramm-Leach-Bliley Act
- Holding workshops on emerging technologies

Anyone with a phone probably knows that in 2003 the FTC did launch the national Do Not Call list. By March 21, 2004, approximately nine months after registration opened, there were already 58.4 million telephone numbers registered on the Do Not Call list.[43]

Congress also passed the CAN-SPAM Act of 2003 (Controlling the Assault of Non-Solicited Pornography and Marketing Act), which requires commercial email to be identified as an advertisement, including valid return addresses for both physical and electronic mail, provides consumers with the ability to "opt out" of future email, and prohibits deceptive subject lines and false or deceptive email header information. The FTC provides information and guidance on the CAN-SPAM Act for businesses and consumers at http://www.ftc.gov/bcp/conline/edcams/spam/index.html (accessed May 10, 2004).

In addition to enforcing privacy laws, the FTC enforces corporate privacy policies. When a company creates a privacy policy, the FTC considers it an "unfair or deceptive" trade practice when the company violates its own policy. Recently, the agency took action against Tower Records for exposing personal customer information on its web site, in conflict with its stated privacy policy.[44]

The FTC also has the responsibility to explore emerging technologies that may have the potential to impact consumer privacy. In April 2004, the FTC conducted a workshop on "spyware."[45] Loosely defined, spyware is computer software that collects information about a computer user, without that user's knowledge, and shares that information with another entity. Depending on how the spyware works, it may pose privacy, security, and functionality risks for consumers' PC's. All users of the web and providers of web access, like libraries, need to be aware of the privacy issues related to spyware on Internet workstations. This is covered in more detail in Chapter 2.

Another area of the FTC's responsibility that is of particular interest to many librarians is enforcement of the Children's Online Privacy Protection Act (COPPA), which was discussed earlier in this chapter. The FTC's Kidz Privacy web site, http://www.ftc.gov/bcp/conline/edcams/kidzprivacy/, does not have a section designated specifically for librarians, but the information found under teachers is helpful.

As can be seen from these examples, and from the FTC's Privacy Agenda list, the agency has broad legal authority in the area of consumer privacy. If a citizen or library patron has a question related to the use of their PII for commercial purposes, the FTC is an excellent place to begin their research. The FTC's web site includes a considerable amount of useful information and links to more focused sites like the National Do Not Call Registry. Depending on the nature of the privacy issue, another resource that may be helpful is your state's consumer protection office.

State Privacy Protection

All states have a state government–level consumer protection office, often under the state's attorney general, that has some level of authority over consumer privacy issues. In some cases, this authority will be limited to investigating identity theft or other fraudulent acts that invade consumer privacy. Most of these offices provide print and web-based information resources on consumer privacy issues.

In addition to state consumer protection offices, many states have specific state statutes addressing some aspects of privacy. For example, in the state of Washington, there is an anti-spam law making it "illegal to send unsolicited commercial email that has been addressed in a false or misleading way."[46] Not only do individuals feel that their privacy has been invaded when they receive spam email, but it can be designed to manipulate consumers into inadvertently providing personal information, leading to possible identity theft and related criminal activity.

Other states have specific laws regulating different kinds of technology with privacy implications. Wisconsin and several other states require that telephone companies offering "Caller ID" also offer a consumer the ability to block their number from appearing when they make a call, either on a per-call or a per-line basis. In Wisconsin, all consumers must be allowed to block calls from showing up in Caller ID.[47] Utah has passed a law[48]—which is under injunction and cannot be enforced at the time of this writing[49]—requiring that anyone putting spyware on a consumer's computer give notice, obtain consent, and provide the consumer with a means to uninstall the spyware.

State laws vary considerably in how they define and address privacy issues. For example, most state attorneys general have advice on their web sites on how to avoid identity theft[50] and Internet scams.[51] Libraries should consider asking their State Libraries to partner with those consumer protection agencies to provide consumer protection educational materials tailored to their specific state laws and consumers' concerns.

Privacy in the Workplace

The privacy protections afforded directly or indirectly by the Constitution or federal and state laws are very much circumscribed while you are at work. Plainly stated: While working, you have far fewer privacy (and other) rights than you do while not at work. Employers, including libraries, have considerable latitude to make certain their employees are not just on the job, but are engaged in proper work-related activities. It is not just wasting time that is an issue, but the employee is using communication tools (e.g., telephones, computer workstations) that are owned by the employer, and thus the employer has considerable liberty to craft policies on how such communication tools are to be used.

As a normal course of business, all employers should have clear policies that state what employees can and cannot do with technology and technology-related communication tools. It is incumbent upon employees that if they are not certain what types of activities are allowed, like occasional personal use of email or the telephone, they should ask management. Using a public library as an example, the library board may have a policy that says staff, during their work hours, are to use the web or email only for work-related purposes. Obviously, when the employee's work ends he or she can just walk over to a public Internet workstation in the library and be free of the board's on-the-job restrictions.

More traditional forms of communication, like telephones, have been subject to employer scrutiny for many years. With very few exceptions, your employer may monitor your phone calls and all of us have heard the automated message when making a call that the call may be monitored for quality assurance purposes. Phone billing systems can be specific enough to list each number an employee has called and the time, date, and duration of each call. Such monitoring can also apply to voice mail and the use of fax machines.

Over the past decade many companies (and libraries) have found it essential to their business success and the provision of services to provide their employees with Internet workstations which have access to the web and email. However, Internet access has increased management concerns about employees engaged in non-work-related web surfing or sending personal emails when they should be doing other productive work. A 2003 survey by the American Management Association showed that 52 percent of employers monitor their employees' email and 22 percent have terminated an employee for violating the company's email policy.[52] Employers do have a vested interest in ensuring that employee use of email or the web does not in some manner misrepresent the company or its products, or compromise proprietary information or trade secrets.

The right that employers have to ensure that technology and communication resources are used properly has generally been upheld in the courts. Several cases have also recognized that employers have a justifiable right to electronically monitor employees.[53] The federal Electronic Communications Privacy Act (ECPA) does not allow a person to "intentionally intercept, endeavor to intercept, or procure any other person to intercept or endeavor to intercept, any wire, oral or electronic communication." However, this prohibition is narrowed considerably by several exceptions, including one allowing such interception by employers during the normal course of conducting business.[54]

One of the ironies about ubiquitous employee Internet access is that while it only takes one click of a mouse to visit a non-work-related web site, it is almost as easy for management to monitor such activities. Once computer desktop workstations moved into a networked environment, it opened the employee's activities on the workstation to intrusive and relatively easy scrutiny by management. In a networked environment there are monitoring tools available that can track each keystroke made on the desktop PC, every web site visited, and every email sent and received. Monitoring tools can also view files held not just on networked drives but on desktop workstation drives too. Even files on pen or thumb drives that an employee connects to their workstation's USB port can be monitored over the network. Network monitoring tools enable employers to examine exactly what activities the employees are engaged in with or without the employees' knowledge. And, depending on how the network is configured, such monitoring can be done in another office just down the hall, or halfway around the world.

Conclusion

For a topic as seemingly intuitive as privacy, both the average citizen and especially librarians must be aware that the laws are complex, often vague, and vary in what they protect and that there are differences in federal and state protections and even differences from one state to another in the level of consumer privacy protections. We hope this overview of privacy protections and issues will be a valuable reference for librarians trying to do the right thing within their library and trying to educate library users, staff, and our communities.

Notes

1. Samuel Warren and Louis Brandeis, "The Right to Privacy," *Harvard Law Review* 193, 1890.

2. *Olmstead v. United States*, 277 U.S. 438 (1928).

3. *Griswold v. Connecticut*, 381 U.S. 479 (1965).

4. Ibid.

5. *Katz v. United States*, 389 U.S. 347, at 350–351 (1967).

6. Ibid. at 361.

7. *Roe v. Wade*, 410 U.S. 113 (1973).

8. *California v. Greenwood*, 486 U.S. 35 (1988).

9. *Lawrence et al. v. Texas*, No. 02–102, argued March 26, 2003, decided June 26, 2003, http://a257.g.akamaitech.net/7/257/2422/26jun20031200/www.supreme courtus.gov/opinions/02pdf/02-102.pdf (accessed August 1, 2004).

10. William Prosser, "Privacy," *California Law Review* (1960).

11. 5 U.S.C. §552(a).

12. Richard Holober, "Statement by Richard Holober, Executive Director Consumer Federation of California," http://www.consumerfedofca.org/news_privacy_031203.html (accessed April 1, 2004).

13. "Minnesota Attorney General and U.S. Bancorp Settle Customer Privacy Suit," http://www.ag.state.mn.us/consumer/Privacy/PR/pr_usbank_07011999. html (accessed April 2, 2004).

14. Loretta Nott, "Financial Privacy: An Economic Perspective," Congressional Research Service, February 25, 2003, #RL31758, http://www.epic.org/privacy/glba/RL31758.pdf (accessed April 2, 2004).

15. "In Brief: The Financial Privacy Requirements of the Gramm-Leach-Bliley Act," Federal Trade Commission, http://www.ftc.gov/bcp/conline/pubs/bus pubs/glbshort.htm (accessed April 12, 2004).

16. "In Brief: The Financial Privacy Requirements of the Gramm-Leach-Bliley Act," Federal Trade Commission, http://www.ftc.gov/bcp/conline/pubs/bus pubs/glbshort.htm (accessed April 5, 2004).

17. Beth Givens, "Financial Privacy: The Shortcomings of the Federal Financial Services Modernization Act," http://www.privacyrights.org/ar/fin_privacy.htm (accessed April 8, 2004).

18. M. Maureen Murphy, "Financial Privacy Laws Affecting Sharing of Customer Information Among Affiliated Institutions," Congressional Research Service, February 27, 2003, #RS21427.

19. Tena Friery, "Privacy Alert: North Dakota Votes for 'Opt-In' Financial Privacy," Privacy Rights Clearinghouse, June 21, 2002, http://www.privacyrights. org/ar/nd_optin.htm (accessed April 9, 2004).

20. "Protecting the Privacy of Patients' Health Information," U.S. Department of Health and Human Services, http://www.hhs.gov/news/facts/privacy.html (accessed April 6, 2004).

21. "Standards for Privacy of Individually Identifiable Health Information; Final Rule," *Federal Register*, Vol. 67, No. 157, August 14, 2002, http://www.hhs.gov/ocr/hipaa/privrulepd.pdf (accessed May 28, 2004).

22. Compliance Dates for Initial Implementation of the Privacy Standards, 45 *Code of Federal Regulations*, Title 45, §164.534, http://a257.g.akamaitech.net/7/257/2422/05dec20031700/edocket.access.gpo.gov/cfr_2003/octqtr/pdf/45cfr164.534.pdf (accessed May 2, 2004).

23. Ibid.

24. "Protecting the Privacy of Patients' Health Information," U.S. Department of Health and Human Services.

25. "State of the Union Address," The White House, January 20, 2004, http://www.whitehouse.gov/news/releases/2004/01/20040120-7.html (accessed April 2, 2004).

26. David Lazarus, "Outsourced UCSF Notes Highlight Privacy Risk: How One Offshore Worker Sent Tremor Through Medical System," *San Francisco Chronicle*, March 28, 2004, http://www.sfgate.com/cgi-bin/article.cgi?f=/c/a/2004/03/28/OFFSHORE.TMP (accessed April 4, 2004).

27. "Markey Investigates Corporate Off-Shoring of Personal Privacy Rights," February 23, 2004, http://www.house.gov/markey/Issues/iss_privacy_pr040223. pdf (accessed April 6, 2004).

28. "Privacy of Genetic Information," National Human Genome Research Institute, http://www.genome.gov/10002336 (accessed April 6, 2004).

29. Sarah Schafer, "Railroad Agrees to Stop Gene-Testing Workers," *Washington Post*, April 19, 2001, http://www.washingtonpost.com/ac2/wp-dyn/A34877-2001 Apr18?language=printer (accessed April 6, 2004).

30. 20 U.S.C. §1232(g).

31. http://www.ed.gov/policy/gen/guid/fpco/ferpa/index.html (accessed April 25, 2004).

32. Various sections of 18 U.S.C.

33. Also codified in various sections of 18 U.S.C.

34. "Protecting Children's Privacy under COPPA: A Survey of Compliance," April 2, 2002, Federal Trade Commission, http://www.ftc.gov/os/2002/04/cop pasurvey.pdf (accessed August 10, 2003).

35. "Protecting Children's Privacy under COPPA: A Survey of Compliance," April 2002, ii (accessed August 10, 2003).

36. "Protecting Children's Privacy under COPPA: A Survey of Compliance," April 2002, I (accessed August 10, 2003).

37. 47 U.S.C. 254.

38. More than ten areas of the U.S. Code were amended by the USA PATRIOT Act. An unofficial version of the law can be found at http://www.epic.org/privacy/terrorism/hr3162.html (accessed April 25, 2004).

39. Health Insurance Portability and Accountability Act of 1996.

40. Ibid. at note 16.

41. Analysis by various legal scholars, http://www.abanet.org/irr/hr/winter02.html, particularly the article by former chief of staff to President Clinton, John Podesta, http://www.abanet.org/irr/hr/winter02/podesta.html (both accessed April 25, 2004).

42. "Privacy Agenda," Federal Trade Commission, http://www.ftc.gov/opa/2001/10/privacyagenda.htm (accessed August 5, 2004).

43. "FTC Amends Telemarketing Sales Rule Regarding Access to National Do Not Call Registry," Federal Trade Commission, http://www.ftc.gov/opa/2004/03/tsrdncscrub.htm (accessed August 5, 2004).

44. "Tower Records Settles FTC Charges," Federal Trade Commission, April 21, 2004, http://www.ftc.gov/opa/2004/04/towerrecords.htm (accessed August 6, 2004).

45. "Spyware Poses Risk to Consumers," Federal Trade Commission, April 29, 2004, http://www.ftc.gov/opa/2004/04/spywaretest.htm (accessed August 6, 2004).

46. The Office of the Attorney General, Washington, http://www.atg.wa.gov/junkemail/ (accessed August 1, 2004).

47. Wis. Stat. Ann. 196.207 (Regulation of Public Utilities).

48. Utah Stat. Ann. Tit. 13 Ch. 40 (Spyware Control Act).

49. "Utah Judge Freezes Anti-Spyware Law," Stephanie Olsen, *CNET News.com*, June 22, 2004, http://news.com.com/2100-1024_3-5244151.html (accessed August 1, 2004).

50. See, for example, Florida, http://myfloridalegal.com/identitytheft (accessed August 1, 2004); Vermont, http://www.atg.state.vt.us/display.php?pubsec=4&curdoc=693 (accessed August 1, 2004); and Nebraska, http://www.ago.state.ne.us/content/id_theft_info.html (accessed August 1, 2004).

51. See, for example, New Mexico, http://www.ago.state.nm.us/know/know_scamalerts.htm (accessed August 1, 2004); Maryland, http://www.oag.state.md.us/Press/2004/072804.htm (accessed August 1, 2004); and Kentucky, http://ag.ky.gov/news/2003rel/Internetfraud.htm (accessed August 1, 2004).

52. "New Survey on Workplace E-Mail Reveals Disasters in the Making," American Management Association, May 28, 2003, http://www.amanet.org/press/amanews/Email_Survey2003.htm (accessed April 4, 2004).

53. Amy Rogers, "You Got Mail But Your Employer Does Too: Electronic Communication and Privacy in the 21st Century," *Journal of Technology Law and Policy*, Vol. 5, Issue 1, Spring 2000, http://grove.ufl.edu/%7Etechlaw/vol5/issue1/email.html (accessed June 1, 2004).

54. Ibid.

CHAPTER 2

Privacy and Emerging Technologies

Introduction

> Numerous mechanical devices threaten to make good the prediction that "what is whispered in the closet shall be proclaimed from the housetops."
>
> —Samuel D. Warren and Louis D. Brandeis,
> "The Right to Privacy," *Harvard Law Review* (1890)

It has been well over a century since this privacy alert on technology was voiced in Samuel D. Warren and Louis D. Brandeis' now famous article in the *Harvard Law Review*.[1] And certainly in the last several decades technology has become even more inexorably intertwined with privacy issues. In fact, simply substituting the word "technological" for "mechanical" makes this quote very appropriate over one hundred years later and what is whispered in today's closets may be published online for the amusement or titillation of a worldwide audience, not merely the residents in your neighborhood.

A specific example of the complex relationship between privacy and technology has been the Internet and its dramatic rise as a mass communications medium. In 1993 a *New Yorker* cartoon showed a dog in front of a monitor surfing the Internet with the caption, "On the Internet nobody knows you're a dog." Unfortunately, with today's technology it is not too difficult for anyone on the Internet to know who you are, human or otherwise.

In Chapter 1 we reviewed the foundation of privacy in America, starting with Constitutional protections and then looking at specific legislation and its impact on privacy in general and more specifically in areas like children's privacy and privacy in the workplace. In this chapter we will review the recent impact of technology on privacy beginning with a number of federal programs, and then continuing with a look at the impact of the Internet and several other technologies.

Federal Programs and Privacy Issues

The federal government is the single largest collector of personal information on American citizens. This fact alone is enough to raise privacy concerns. Within the past several years a number of federal programs have been announced, some in a rather low-keyed fashion, which have raised concerns among privacy advocates, civil libertarians, and the general public. There has always been a fine line between the federal government's need to collect personally identifiable information (PII) and its sometimes overzealousness to invasively monitor citizen activity. This line has become much more visible since September 11, 2001, and many of the federal programs listed in the following text have become equally more visible.

From the federal government's perspective, the report *Safeguarding Privacy in the Fight Against Terrorism,* released in 2004, recommends that the President appoint a committee within the federal government to ensure consistency in efforts to safeguard privacy in the context of national security, and that the President also appoint an external panel to advise the President on issues of privacy in the same context.[2]

Most federal programs that collect and analyze PII are based on large-scale data mining. From the crime preventive perspective, the follow-up data analysis is then designed to reveal suspect activity on everything from the filing of false income tax statements to possibly engaging in terrorist activities. A recent General Accounting Office (GAO) report[3] identified 199 data mining projects conducted by fifty-two different federal agencies. Of these projects, 122 (61 percent) of them collected or used personally identifiable information in some manner. (Neither the Central Intelligence Agency nor the National Security Agency responded to the GAO data mining survey.)

The protection of one's PII and the security of the government's or any organization's data systems are intimately linked. The greater the security, the more likely that your PII will be protected from unauthorized access or use. Another GAO report on the security of information collected and maintained by federal agencies showed that many agencies lack programs for staff training related to data security, and many agencies have no meaningful system in place to monitor or detect unauthorized system access or intruders.[4]

Obviously, a great amount of PII collected and retained by the federal government is used to support a very wide variety of programs that raise no real privacy issues. At the same time, however, there are a number of federal programs that have been criticized by privacy advocates and civil libertarians for their potential abuse of privacy or misuse of personally identifiable information. Below is a synopsis of several of the better-known programs in this area.

Terrorism Information Awareness (TIA) and LifeLog

The Terrorism Information Awareness program was a project being developed by the Defense Advanced Research Projects Agency (DARPA), the main research arm of the U.S. Defense Department. In the late 1960s and early 1970s DARPA played a critical role in funding the development of "ARPANET," one of the first packet switched networks. ARPANET eventually evolved beyond the military and research spheres to become the Internet. (And the rest, as they say, is history.) The Terrorism Information Awareness program was first known as the Total Information Awareness program. Officials decided that the word "Total" had a rather Orwellian ring to it and the name was changed in May 2003.[5] In addition to name problems, it also did not help the program's reputation that John Poindexter, former national security advisor to President Reagan who was involved in the Iran Contra scandal, was a key figure in the early stages of the project. He resigned from the TIA project in August 2003.[6]

TIA was basically a research and development program with the goal of accumulating, managing, and analyzing vast quantities of information to ultimately identify possible threats to national security and to detect and defeat terrorist networks. In 2003 DARPA Director Tony Teather said the TIA initiative was "designed as an experimental, multi-agency prototype network that participating agencies can use to better share, analyze, understand, and make decisions based on whatever data to which they currently have legal access."[7] Senator Ron Wyden (D-Oregon), a member of the Senate Intelligence Committee and a key opponent of the program, said that TIA was the "biggest spying and surveillance overreach in America's history."[8] In September 2003, as part of a defense appropriation measure, Congress did not include funding to continue the TIA program as it was initially conceived.[9] However, DARPA can continue research for "processing, analysis, and collaboration tools for counterterrorism" when such tools are deployed or implemented for military operations overseas, or for foreign intelligence activities conducted overseas or wholly against non-U.S. citizens.[10]

LifeLog was another of DARPA's research projects. LifeLog was intended to use the increasing power of personnel digital assistants to record every activity that a person did during a given day including phone calls, emails, and the recording of all conversations and movements by a digital video recorder worn on your person (e.g., around your neck, on your belt). This would be an all-knowing "electronic diary" and its intent was to help people better organize and manage their time.[11] While DARPA's focus was more on LifeLog's application to enhancing military command and control, its ability, in theory, to track and record your every movement and activity 24/7 (24 hours a day, 7 days a week) raised obvious privacy concerns. The project was cancelled in 2004.

Novel Intelligence from Massive Data (NIMD)

The NIMD project is sponsored by the Advanced Research and Development Activity (ARDA) center, which was created by the federal government's "Intelligence Community."[12] The Intelligence Community consists of federal executive branch agencies who have responsibility for the protecting the country from foreign security threats. Members of the community include the Central Intelligence Agency, Defense Intelligence Agency, Department of Homeland Security, Federal Bureau of Investigation, and National Security Agency. NIMD started in 1998 and its work focuses on avoiding "strategic surprise" such as unforeseen events that impact national security, like the terrorist attacks of September 11, 2001.[13] The word "novel" is used to indicate the use of techniques and analytical software tools to scrutinize massive amounts of data to detect new, "novel" patterns of suspicious activity not previously known. The assumption is that some of this activity may indicate possible threats to national security. The analysis includes data from structured files, like passenger databases, to information in less structured formats like audio recordings, maps, equations, and chemical formulas. The data are "massive" simply because of the amount of information to be analyzed and the fact that ARDA estimates that intelligence data sources subject to review by NIMD are increasing at a mind boggling rate of four petabytes (2 to the 50th power or 1,125,899,906,842,624 bytes) per month.[14]

Multistate Anti-TeRrorism Information eXchange (MATRIX)

One of the newest data mining initiatives to raise concerns among privacy advocates is the MATRIX program. Of interest, the program was based on data held by a private company in Florida working with the Florida state government on a tool to identify possible terrorists. The company offered to share its data with the U.S. Department of Justice after September 11, 2001, and subsequently the company received $12 million in federal funds to continue developing the program.[15] The initial purpose of MATRIX has expanded to become more of a tool used by state law enforcement officials. This program combines information about individuals from government databases and private-sector data repositories. It is then possible to search through millions of records and to make a judgment if a resulting response identifies possible terrorist or other criminal activity.[16] Critics and privacy advocates are quick to point out that while Congress decommissioned the Total Information Awareness program, it appears that the MATRIX program may be taking its place. Barry Steinhardt, director of the American Civil Liberties Union's (ACLU) Technology and Liberty Program, stated, "In essence, the government is replacing an unpopular Big Brother initiative [i.e., TIA] with a lot of Little Brothers."[17] Of the thirteen states that participated in the MATRIX pilot program only five remained as of June 2004. Privacy issues were a key factor in the decision by many of the participating states to eventually withdraw from the program.[18]

Computer Assisted Passenger Prescreening System II (CAPPS II)

The Computer Assisted Passenger Prescreening System is a program, known as CAPPS I, deployed in the late 1990s. The CAPPS system flagged ten of the nineteen September 11, 2001 hijackers but all, obviously and tragically, were able to eventually board their flights.[19] At the time of the September 11, 2001 hijackings, only passengers checking bags were selected by CAPPS for additional scrutiny, and that further scrutiny only entailed having one's checked baggage screened for explosives or held off the plane until the person had boarded. The baggage of the hijackers held no detectable explosives and they all boarded their flights.

The newer version of the program, CAPPS II, was being developed by the Transportation Security Administration (TSA) and was specifically authorized by Congress as a result of September 11, 2001. The program was to expand the types of information now routinely collected as part of creating a Passenger Name Record (PNR) for each person who travels. The additional information would include who you are traveling with, where you are staying, and if you are sharing lodging with someone else.[20] The program proposed to use the PNR data from a variety of sources to authenticate air passengers' identities and conduct an assessment to analyze whether any given passenger poses a security risk or threat. In testimony before the National Commission of Terrorist Attacks Upon the United States (9-11 Commission) a TSA official admitted that as CAPPS II was currently configured about 14.5 percent of airline passengers would be targeted for further screening.[21]

In addition to assessing the security risk of any given passenger, CAPPS II was to also determine whether a passenger has any outstanding federal or state criminal warrants or possible visa violations.[22] It is this "mission creep" that has raised additional concerns that the program will turn into a much broader surveillance system that could eventually track anyone using any type of public transportation.[23]

Under an appropriations bill passed in October 2003, Congress required the GAO to develop a report on CAPPS II, including addressing privacy concerns with the "technological architecture of the system." The report, issued in February 2004, found that the Transportation Security Administration had not addressed some key issues including several related to airline passenger privacy.[24] For example, GAO noted that there was still a need to address the security of passenger data, how long specific passenger data will be retained, and the ability of passengers to correct inaccurate information. In addition, the report stated that "As the program evolves, it will ultimately be up to policymakers to determine if TSA has struck an appropriate balance between protecting personal privacy and other public policy interests."[25] Initial specifications for the program called for passenger data to be retained for 50 years. After receiving many comments critical of this and other characteristics of the program, the 50-year retention period was removed from the final regulations. Continued development of CAPPS II was slowed because some air carriers refused to provide needed passenger data because of privacy concerns. Conversely, several airlines did turn over to the Transportation Security Administration databases containing several million passenger records.[26] In August 2004 the CAPPS II program was replaced by a new program called Secure Flight. Unlike the broader CAPPS II program, Secure Flight will focus more on identifying possible terrorist suspects.[27] In November 2004 all major airlines operating in the United States turned their June 2004 domestic passenger flight records over to the TSA for initial testing of the Secure Flight program. Because of privacy concerns, the airlines had questioned the TSA's order, which it issued in early November, but all airlines did comply.[28]

DCS1000 (Also known as Carnivore)

The FBI, following proper legal procedures, has the statutory authority to intercept or tap electronic communications, including voice telephone and Internet communications.[29] In relation to the interception of Internet communications, considerable attention has been focused on the FBI's DCS1000 program. This program, formally known by the rather foreboding moniker "Carnivore," was initiated in the late 1990s. (The federal government and its contractors seem to be tone deaf in creating names for some of these programs. Terms like "*Total* Information Awareness" and "*Carnivore*" will, by their very nature, raise suspicions. And Carnivore's predecessor was "Omnivore.") DCS1000 is used whenever Internet service providers (ISP) have been issued a court order for specific information, such as an email address in an email "To:" line, and for whatever reason the ISP is unable to comply with the order.[30] The DCS1000 program has the ability to intercept almost any type of Internet traffic—from emails to chat room conversations to web pages—visited by an ISP's customers.

The DCS1000 system consists of both hardware and software that federal agents typically install in an ISP's facilities. There the system intercepts Internet packets based on specific filtering parameters that are determined by the type of information referenced in the court order.[31] When properly configured the DCS1000 filtering parameters will only intercept traffic that the program is authorized to collect. But as an Illinois Institute of Technology report noted, "While the system . . . can perform fine-tuned searches, it is also capable of broad sweeps, potentially enabling the FBI to monitor all of the network's communications."[32] In this regard there have been some documented cases in which the system inadvertently collected information from individuals who were not in any manner part of an FBI investigation. After one such incident an FBI attorney noted that the agency must avoid intercepting innocent third-party communications but also stated, "I am not sure how we can proceed to test [Carnivore] without inadvertently intercepting the communications of others, but we really need to try."[33] Most ISPs can now track this activity and DCS1000 is used less often.

The Internet

From a technology perspective, the Internet must be addressed in any discussion on privacy. While it is no longer a new or emerging technology, the Internet has become the underlying technology and medium used for considerable private and public communications, and for the continuing development of new and innovative applications that have privacy implications, like library virtual reference services. As shown in the following sections, in a relatively few short years the Internet has infused itself into mainstream American life.

A Snapshot of Internet Use

Many surveys have been done over the past decade that highlight the dramatic rise in Internet use in the home, at work, and in libraries. One of the early (1997) studies conducted by the National Telecommunications and Information Administration (NTIA) showed that 18.6 percent of all U.S. households had computers and were using "Online Services."[34] Many of these early studies asked about access to "online services" which included services such as America Online (AOL). AOL initially was a proprietary and not an open, Internet-based service. Many citizens also had accounts with other proprietary services, like CompuServe, which were "online services" but not true Internet-based services.

By 2001 more than half of the country's population (143 million, about 54 percent) were using the Internet at home, at work, or at other locations like the local public library.[35] One of the more recent studies showed that 74.9 percent of Americans have Internet access at home, although not all were regular users.[36] Kenneth Cassar from Nielsen//NetRatings observed, "In just a handful of years, online access has managed to gain the type of traction that took other media decades to achieve."[37]

While there are still socioeconomic disparities in access to and use of computers and the Internet, those disparities have decreased. Of the African American families surveyed, 71 percent reported owning a computer, up from 39 percent in 2000, and 69 percent of Hispanics acknowledge computer ownership.[38] In low-income families, computer ownership rose from 45 percent in 2000 to 65 percent in 2002.[39]

An even more dramatic increase has been the deployment of broadband Internet access to the home. For example, in 2004, 24 percent of all adult Americans had broadband Internet in their residence, an increase of 60 percent from March 2003.[40] Residential broadband access presents many privacy issues and threats that are not present in the more traditional dial-up mode of Internet access. See the "Internet Threats to Privacy" section later in this chapter where some of these issues are explored.

A Snapshot of Internet Use by Children and Young Adults

We are now entering a time when the first generation of Americans are reaching their early adulthood having grown up with Internet access. The perspective they have of the Internet or the use of other communication technologies like cell phones and instant messaging is very different from the perspective that their parents have. Below are some interesting statistics and viewpoints that reflect the Internet generation.

In March 2003, the Corporation for Public Broadcasting issued its "Connected to the Future" report comparing American children's Internet use in 2000 and 2002. Researchers found that children's use of the Internet increased significantly in the past two years with 65 percent of American children ages two to seventeen accessing the Internet from school, home, or some other location. This was a 59 percent growth rate from 2000, when 41 percent of children went online from any location.[41] Two other statistics show dramatic growth in Internet use by children and their families. In 2000, 64 percent of households with at least one child between the ages of two and seventeen had a computer; by 2002, 83 percent were computer owners.[42] Internet access also rose during this two-year period from 46 percent to 78 percent in households with at least one child.[43] Those youth ages two to seventeen surveyed for "Connected to the Future" reported averaging 5.9 hours per week in online activities including exploring sites; communicating with others via email, chat rooms, and instant messaging; playing games; downloading music, videos, and graphics; and doing homework.[44] As many as 64 percent of teenagers reported using the Internet at least weekly for general learning, homework, or research.[45]

Use of the Internet for homework was corroborated by findings in "Digital Disconnect: The Widening Gap between Internet-Savvy Students and Their Schools," a report released in August 2002 by the Pew Internet and American Life Project. Students surveyed described many different ways they use the Internet to help them do schoolwork. They use the Internet as virtual textbooks and reference libraries, tutors, study groups, guidance counselors, and lockers where they can store school-related materials.[46] A high school girl described her affinity for the Internet this way: "Life without the Internet would be odd. I've grown used to using it in school since we got it four years ago. I almost take it for granted sometimes. It can make schoolwork easier, but every now and then it will set you back. Like everything in life, it has its advantages and disadvantages."[47] Students like the Internet because of its obvious advantages over school and public library access. The Internet is available 24/7 and can be used at the convenience of the student. Another high school girl said, "The Internet is basically, like, your local library times a thousand. [The material is] instantly available wherever there's a computer."[48]

Use of the Internet was also confirmed by a June 2001 Pew Internet and the American Life survey, "Teen Life Online: The Rise of the Instant Message Generation and the Internet's Impact on Friendship and Family Relationships." "Part 3: Teens and Their Schools" reported that 71 percent of teenagers online used the Internet for their latest school report. Only 25 percent used primarily school and public library sources, and only 4 percent relied on both equally.[49] The survey's statistics mirror the observations of many school library media specialists and public librarians. Students with Internet access at home rely less on library resources.

In addition to school work, the Kaiser Family Foundation found in its "Generation Rx.com: How Young People Use the Internet for Health Information" study released in December 2001 that young adults use the Internet for checking sports scores, shopping, communicating in chat rooms, downloading music, and looking up health information. Seventy-five percent used the Internet to search for health information at least once, and 39 percent reported they "changed their behavior" because of the information obtained.[50]

The reports cited in the preceding paragraphs give a picture of the increasing importance of the Internet and use of computers by youth of all ages. While parents and educators once worried about the number of hours children spent watching television, teenagers now spend slightly more time daily with digital media, defined as video games and non-Internet computer use, than watching television by an average of twenty-four minutes per day.[51] In fact, a study completed in April 2002 found that 33 percent of youth between the ages of eight and seventeen chose to use the Internet over watching television, listening to the radio, or talking on the telephone.[52] Given children's fascination with technology in any form, it does not take a crystal ball to predict the increased importance of computers and the Internet in the lives of American youth. Parents also play a large role with their children in the use of computers and the Internet. Of the parents surveyed for the Corporation for Public Broadcasting report "Connected to the Future," 81 percent believe "the Internet is valuable to their children's learning."[53] This led the researchers in that study to conclude the Internet has moved from "nice to have" to a "must-have."

Internet Threats to Privacy

The Internet has attained the status as a mass medium, viewed by both adults and young people as an essential communications tool of daily life.

Along with ubiquitous Internet use has come—unfortunately—Internet abuse. This abuse takes on many forms from the release of computer viruses that spread worldwide in a matter of hours to malware or spyware that prey on innocent or unsuspecting Internet users to co-opt their identity and invade their privacy.

While concerns about government use and possibly abuse of technology to compromise citizen privacy is certainly an issue, most individuals have a far greater chance of having their privacy compromised by simply sitting at their desktop workstations or home PCs (personal computers) and cruising the Internet. These fears have been well documented in several surveys that show a very high percentage of consumers are concerned about possible wrongful use of any PII they submit while online. One study indicated that 92 percent of consumers were concerned and 67 percent were "very concerned" about misuse of their PII.[54]

Temporary Internet Files and Web Cookies

Every time you visit a web site, that web page and other information about the site are retained on the PC's hard drive. As you continue to cruise the Internet these files build a "history" of where you have been during your session on the web. Unless specific steps are taken by you, or your browser is configured to regularly delete the history, these files are stored on the hard disk until the disk space allocated to them is filled. This can easily be several weeks, several months, or more.

And then there are cookies. Cookies are small text files stored on your hard drive. Cookies can record when you last visited a given web site and other information. Many times you will not be aware that a cookie is being placed on your PC or when, at some later time, that cookie on your PC is accessed by a remote server. Cookies often serve a valuable service. For example, they also serve as a mechanism some web sites use to enable you to customize a service, like MyYahoo, to your particular needs or record items that you have purchased through a web shopping site.[55]

There are justifiable concerns about privacy and the storage of temporary Internet files, including cookies. There are Internet marketing and advertising companies that use cookies to build user profiles. When you then go to another web site that is working with the marketing company, you may see customized ads on the screen targeted at products or services you are interested in. While specific names and email addresses are generally not collected, there are concerns that enough information may be collected, even indirectly, over a long enough time to identify who is using the workstation. In probably the best known case involving the use of cookies for creating targeted web ads, DoubleClick, an Internet marketing firm, was subject to an investigation from ten states' attorneys general regarding its use of cookies and other information it collected from unsuspecting web users. A settlement was reached in 2002 in which DoubleClick admitted no wrongdoing but did agree to state on its web site how it was using the information it was collecting.[56] In the early days of the web it was often recommended that users refuse cookies or set their browser to warn you when a remote site was trying to place a cookie on your PC. With the pervasiveness of cookies the user option to always refuse them is not realistic. Web browsers offer a minimal amount of cookie management options and there are many free and shareware programs that can be used to better manage cookies and, as a result, help to preserve your privacy. In any locations (for example many libraries) where different people use the same workstation, the browser should be set to delete temporary files and cookies upon its closing, and the PC's security settings should be configured to prevent access to such files.

Entering PII on a Web Site

With the growing use of the web for business and virtual shopping, many people have become accustomed to entering their name, address, and email as part of requesting information on a product or registering to use a given web site. Furthermore, many of us readily enter our credit card information as part of completing an online purchase. At a minimum, to help protect your privacy, a web site asking for any PII should have a clearly stated policy on how it will use the information you have provided and what measures have been taken to help ensure that the information you have entered is secure. Most web browsers, including Internet Explorer and Firefox, have icons on the screen that indicate if the site requesting entry of PII is operating in a secure mode. Unfortunately, even a privacy statement or use of site security may not tell the whole story about what is done with the PII you enter. For example, a 2004 study done by the Customer Respect Group found that 95 percent of the companies they surveyed had privacy statements, but 21 percent said they still share users' PII with unaffiliated third parties without asking permission.[57] Truste and BBOnLine (Better Business Bureau) are two programs sponsored by the business sector that are self-regulatory attempts to assure consumers that the participating businesses respect their privacy. Consumers should look for the icons from these or similar organizations on commercial web sites that market services or products online.

Many Internet start-up companies that found themselves in financial difficulties when the Internet bubble burst realized that their most valuable asset was their customer database, and some were all too willing in their financial desperation to sell this information. In July 2000 the Federal Trade Commission filed a complaint in federal district court to prevent Toysmart.com, which had filed for bankruptcy, from selling its personal customer information. The FTC claimed that Toysmart.com was violating its own privacy statement which said that customer information would never be shared with any third parties.[58] In early 2001 an agreement was reached in which the parties involved agreed that Toysmart's customer list would be destroyed.[59]

Internet Spyware

Concerns about temporary files and cookies have been voiced since the mid-1990s, but a more recent concern is having your privacy compromised by tracking programs that are downloaded and installed on your PC, often without your permission or knowledge. These programs are often generically called "spyware" or sometimes "adware" because of their ability to track your Internet surfing habits. The terms "spyware" and "adware" are often used interchangeably, but there is a difference between them. Spyware is software loaded on your PC without your knowledge. It operates in the background collecting information about your surfing habits, which it may then send to another entity without your knowledge or consent. Adware often gives consumers relevant and at times valuable information on given products and services. Any programs installed by legitimate adware companies make their installation optional, and they can be easily removed from the PC by consumers. In addition to being extremely annoying, spyware is some of the more invasive and insidious violators of privacy. As these programs track where you have been on the web, they then send that information to a remote server without your knowledge. Typically, the server then sends you a pop-up ad window that appears on your screen based on the sites you are visiting or have just visited. For example, if you are in the market for a used auto and are visiting several auto web sites, you may suddenly see a context-sensitive pop-up window on your screen advertising other auto web sites or perhaps a site for low-interest auto loans. Other spyware programs will arbitrarily change your home page and in some instances make it almost impossible to change it back.

The amount of PII that spyware collects can differ with each program. Many companies with such programs claim to not collect or misuse your PII, but in most instances it is impossible to verify such claims. Any company with a program that automatically installs itself on your PC without your knowledge or permission and then asks that you trust that they will not collect or misuse your PII has a real credibility problem.

Spyware applications are often bundled with freeware or shareware applications downloaded from the Internet. Some of the most popular programs, like music sharing programs, are notorious for including spyware. In many instances, once you install the program you really want, the spyware program will be also be automatically loaded onto your hard drive. Sometimes just visiting a web site or clicking on a link that looks of interest will result in spyware being installed. This is often referred to as a "drive-by download."

For the uninitiated citizen on a home PC, spyware can be a very real and annoying problem. Once a PC is infected with spyware it may be possible to remove it using the Windows Add/Remove Programs option, but not all spyware will be listed in the Add/Remove directory. Sometimes it will be necessary to load Windows in Safe mode and then delete the offending program and its associated files. Of course this assumes you know what files to remove. It can also require editing the Windows registry settings. Neither of these procedures are realistic tasks for most users. There are commercial and freeware programs available to help detect and remove spyware once it has been installed. Most libraries have installed software, like Fortres, or hardware, like Centurion Guard, that can help to either prevent the installation of spyware or eliminate it upon rebooting the workstation. Whether in a library setting or at home, it is necessary to always take obvious security measures, like installing and properly configuring a firewall. These measures used in combination with commercial or freeware programs developed to prevent the installation of spyware or detect its presence and the use of other programs to block pop-ups will help keep problems to a minimum.

Like email spam, spyware has caught the attention of legislators at both the federal and state levels. Several bills were introduced in the 108th Congress that address spyware. In March 2004 Utah became the first state to pass legislation targeted at spyware. The Spyware Control Act prohibits installation of software that records where a user has been on the web or the sending of any personal data to other companies without the user's consent.[60] As noted in Chapter 1, this law is currently not being enforced because of legal action brought against it by an Internet advertising firm.[61] The possibility of fifty different state laws regulating spyware raises concerns for many Internet businesses. Because of the global nature of the Internet, state laws are difficult for businesses to comply with and for governments to enforce, and there are Constitutional prohibitions against states interfering with interstate commerce.

Email

Any information sent via email over the Internet should never be assumed to be private or protected in any manner from being read by others. Email encryption software is available but very few consumers use it. In most states, public-sector employees' emails are public records, subject to the state's open records laws. (This applies to many libraries.) Whether email is a public record or not, caution is advised when dealing, via email, with such topics as personnel issues and patron complaints. Depending on how your email is managed (in house, outsourced, etc.), it is possible that email sent between staff will never traverse the public Internet. While this affords some degree of privacy, caution is still advised.

There are also privacy concerns that the popular free email services will harvest patron information for targeted advertising or other more nefarious purposes. In the spring of 2004 the popular search engine Google announced it was starting its own free "Gmail" email service available to anyone. The service proposed to scan the text of emails to target advertisements to Gmail users. Over thirty organizations stated their concerns about privacy issues and in May 2004 the Electronic Privacy Information Center asked the California attorney general to investigate Google's email service for possible violations of the state's statute that addresses confidential communications.[62]

In another blow to any assumption of email privacy, in June 2004 a federal district court declared that privacy protections found in the 1968 federal Wiretap Act do not extend to email. The court said that the act's protections relate to eavesdropping on "live communications" (e.g., phone conversations) and they do not cover communications, such as email messages, which are stored even temporarily on a server.[63] Mark Plotkin, partner in a Washington, DC, law firm, stated, "What the courts are telling us is that unless the Wiretap Act is changed, email should be viewed as public communication that anybody could potentially view."[64] This is another example of the law failing to keep up with the technology.

Another aspect of email and privacy is the increasing number of fraudulent emails designed to deceive the receiver to reveal some personally identifiable information. This can easily lead to becoming a victim of an Internet scam and even identity theft. Bogus online sales and auctions are a common ruse used by scammers. Very few users of email have escaped getting any variety of emails commonly known as the Nigerian scam ("Hello, I am Ajaka Dusabe, son of the late potentate . . ."). The Nigerian scam is so popular it is often known as the 419 scam, which is the section of the Nigerian criminal code that addresses fraud. This scam has been in existence for over twenty years, starting as a postal and fax scam and moving more recently to email. Real people have lost real money as a result of this scam. Most scams are obvious, but an increasingly sophisticated practice, commonly called "phishing," often uses more subtly deceptive claims to get people to respond. It has been estimated that over 50 million U.S. residents have received bogus emails asking them to reveal some of their PII, and direct fraud related to phishing attacks exceeded $1 billion in 2003.[65] Common sense and a healthy level of skepticism are useful in helping to prevent such frauds.

Privacy and Technology: A Sampling of Particular Issues

It is a common maxim that technology is neutral. It is the specific implementation or use of any given technology that determines if it provides dramatic benefits to individuals and society or if it poses threats to the same. This is certainly true in relation to technology and privacy. The following is a brief description of three technologies, (1) radio frequency identification, (2) global positioning systems, and (3) biometrics, and their potential impact on one's privacy.

Radio Frequency Identification (RFID)

As its name implies, Radio Frequency Identification uses the frequency spectrum (e.g., radio waves) to transfer data on an item or product that is stored in a small microchip that is usually physically attached to the item or product. Similar to a uniform product barcode, the data stored on the chip usually include information that describes the product, for example, a serial or model number, manufacturer, date and place of manufacture, and shipping information. RFID tags are activated by an electronic reader and the transponder on the tag then sends the reader its data.[66] Most RFID tags are passive. That is, they have no embedded power source that is constantly transmitting data. Instead, they transmit data only when they detect a request from the receiving device, the transceiver. Passive tags often cannot be read unless the transceiver is within several feet of the tag. Active RFID tags can be read from several hundred feet and are most often used on a larger scale, for example, to track shipping containers or railroad cars.

In the library world, passive RFID tags are being increasingly used to replace barcodes on books and other items in the library's collection. One benefit is that, unlike barcode scanners, there is no need to properly align the item to be checked out or checked in. RFID technology also makes it possible to implement automated materials sorting systems. The increasing use of RFID in libraries has caught the attention of privacy advocates. In October 2003 the Electronic Frontier Foundation (EFF) sent a letter to the San Francisco Public Library stating its concerns as the library planned to move forward with implementing RFID. The memo states, in part, that the "EFF is very concerned that the Library may not have fully considered the privacy and civil liberties implications of implementing RFIDs."[67] The library community should be concerned about attempts to increase the range of RFID technology used in libraries, beyond the physical limits needed to conduct regular library business. Additional concerns are warranted if more than the barcode number is stored on the tag. (See Chapter 4 for more information on RFID use in public libraries.)

It does not take too much imagination to see the privacy implications of RFID technology, for example, the use of active RFID tags embedded in products remaining active after a purchase. In an Orwellian scenario, and assuming lack of adequate safeguards, it would then be possible for government or marketers to track at a considerable distance what you have purchased, where it is at any given time, and what is being used for long after the item leaves the place of purchase. In 2004 a bill was introduced in the California legislature (SB1834) to address some of the consumer privacy issues that are implicit with use of RFID. The bill passed in the state senate but did not pass in the assembly.[68]

Global Positioning Systems (GPS)

Global Positioning Systems are used in a wide range of products. Originally developed by the U.S. Department of Defense for precision targeting of Soviet missile silos,[69] over the past decade GPS has become widely available in the commercial market and to consumers. The technology is commonly sold to replace compasses for hikers and campers and to enable mapping and roadside assistance programs in cars. It is being phased in to new cellular phones to enable more precise "Enhanced 911" capability. But what, exactly, is GPS?

A GPS unit is an electronic device that can determine your approximate location (within around 6–20 feet) on the planet. Coordinates are normally given in Longitude and Latitude. You can use the unit to navigate from your current location to another location. Some units have their own maps, built-in electronic compasses, voice navigation, depending on the complexity of the device.

GPS devices do not actually broadcast your location. The satellites using radio frequencies actually broadcast *their* position. Your GPS unit then takes that information and triangulates where you are.[70]

Although GPS devices themselves do not broadcast their location, they can be tracked. For example, businesses with fleet security concerns can install GPS devices in their vehicles and track location and distance traveled, either in real time or through logs. This can be done covertly, so that the driver or other vehicle users are never aware of it.[71] GPS devices are also sold embedded in colorful watches designed to help parents know where their children are.[72]

The new hobby/sport of geocaching is possible because of the easy availability and affordability of GPS devices. Participants hide a collection of inexpensive (and weather-resistant) items in a "cache" and then post the cache's coordinates to a geocaching web site. Other enthusiasts then travel to the site, which is often remote, and take a "prize" to commemorate their trip.

In many ways, GPS technology benefits citizens. If a person witnesses a car accident or otherwise needs to call 911 from an unfamiliar location, having a precise location available via GPS can be a life saver. Being able to get directions when lost in the car is also valuable to many consumers.

On the other hand, there are consumer concerns about its use as well. At present, it is not being used by law enforcement agencies to catch speeders, but the potential is certainly there. It is equally easy to imagine it being installed in a car by an abusive spouse to "keep tabs" on his or her family members, perhaps even after a court has issued a protective order.

Biometrics

Biometrics is the broad term for all technology that identifies people by their physical characteristics—fingerprints, retina or iris scans, hand geometry readers, facial and voice recognition technology, even typing rhythm patterns or the force profile of your steps as you walk.[73] Biometrics is not yet widely known—in fact, a 2002 public opinion survey found that approximately half of Americans were familiar with biometric technology.[74] It became somewhat better known in public discourse as a result of the 2001 Super Bowl, in Tampa, Florida. The Tampa police set up "Facefinder" technology to scan the faces of the 100,000 fans who attended Super Bowl XXXV and compare their faces against a database of criminal suspects.[75]

In the immediate aftermath of September 11, 2001, there was widespread interest in the idea of creating a "national ID card" with biometric technology incorporated into the ID. This idea alarmed civil libertarians and privacy advocates across the political spectrum. While there is widespread support for effective efforts to prevent future terrorist activity, there is conflict and skepticism about whether a national ID card would be an effective tool toward that end. Conservative columnist William Safire issued the following warning about a national ID, particularly one incorporating biometric identification technology:

> Beware: It is not just an efficient little card to speed you through lines faster or to buy you sure-fire protection from suicide bombers. A national ID card would be a ticket to the loss of much of your personal freedom. Its size could then be reduced for implantation under the skin in the back of your neck.[76]

There are practical as well as philosophical concerns with a national biometric ID card. Experts estimate that fingerprint technology—which has the longest track record of any biometric technology—has an error rate of between 1 and 3 percent.[77] This was made very evident in May 2004 when, based on a misread fingerprint, the FBI mistakenly arrested a Portland, Oregon, resident as a material witness in the March 2004 train bombings in Madrid, Spain. What the FBI initially said was a 100 percent match turned out to be based on a "substandard" copy of the single print.[78] Facial recognition technology is nowhere near as accurate as fingerprints, with a Department of Defense study concluding that "the Visionics system correctly recognized individuals a mere 51 percent of the time."[79] Even the iris-scanning technology tested by the Department of Defense inaccurately identified 6 percent of the individuals tested.[80]

Assuming conservatively that a national ID card is implemented with only a 1 percent error rate, with a present population of almost three hundred million[81] that means there would be nearly 3 million people whose official national ID card contained errors. That could lead to dramatic results: 3 million people being denied entry into airplanes, 3 million people denied Social Security benefits, just to name a few possibilities. As anyone who has ever attempted to correct an error in their credit report or on their taxes is aware, correcting mistakes in bureaucratic records can be a time-consuming, difficult, and frustrating task.

Adoption rates of biometric technology continue to accelerate. In August 2004, the State Department announced that beginning in spring 2005 it will implement "electronic identification chips in U.S. passports that will allow computer matching of facial characteristics."[82] This controversial decision was criticized by leading experts, even within the federal government. "'I don't think there's a debate,' said Charles L. Wilson, who supervises biometric testing at the National Institute of Standards and Technology, an arm of the Commerce Department. 'Fingerprints are much better.' "[83] Wilson's team recently found that "With face recognition, if the pictures are taken under controlled circumstances with proper illumination, angles and facial expression, the accuracy rate was 90 percent."[84] Although that is considerably higher than the 51 percent accuracy of facial recognition technology found earlier by the Defense Department, it also reflects controlled testing circumstances, not the chaotic realities of immigration offices in major airports and border crossings. Criticism of the State Department decision also came from James L. Wayman, director of biometric identification research at San Jose State University in California, who commented, "Facial recognition isn't going to do it for us at large scale. . . . If there's a 10 percent error rate with 300 people on a 747, that's a problem."[85]

Private employers and organizations are also implementing biometric technology in a number of different ways. For example, in New York, banks are required to obtain fingerprints of all employees with access to a securities exchange; Children's Hospital of Columbus, Ohio, uses digital fingerprint technology to identify doctors;[86] and tobacco vending machines have been deployed in Utah using fingerprints to try to prevent underage customers from purchasing tobacco.[87] Alone, most of these applications of biometric technology seem sensible or convenient. However, according to Chris Hoofnagle of the Electronic Privacy Information Center, "Most of these [biometric] applications seem harmless at the start, but then there are new applications. Soon you have full-force Big Brother watching over you."[88]

At the present time, there are no laws in place to help prevent the misuse of biometric data in the United States. However, business writer Jane

Black proposed that four key principles be incorporated into a "Biometric Bill of Rights"—Scope, Access, Storage, and Segregation of Data,[89] or "SASS." In brief, these principles are defined as follows.

- *Scope:* Biometric ID should be used only in ways known to and approved by the individual, and the individual should be able to opt-out of any expanded use in the future.
- *Access:* Biometric information should be kept within the original organization unless a court order requires its release to law enforcement agents.
- *Storage:* Biometric information should be destroyed or discarded when it is no longer necessary, particularly when a person leaves the organization using the biometric data in question.
- *Segregation of Data:* Biometric data, regardless of the use, should always be stored separately from personally identifiable information such as name, address, medical data, or financial data.

While there are no bills pending in Congress to create a national Biometrics Bill of Rights, it is an intriguing idea, and organizations considering incorporating biometrics into their security and authentication procedures would do well to design their systems with the above principles in mind.

The Future of Technology and the Fourth Amendment

The lust to take advantage of the public's fear of terrorist penetration by penetrating everyone's private lives—this time including the lives of U.S. citizens protected by the Fourth Amendment—is gaining popularity.[90]

—William Safire

Mr. Safire was specifically criticizing efforts to create a national ID card, but his comments certainly apply to broader law enforcement efforts to obtain data through all technological means available. Fortunately, popularity of an idea is not the final factor for determining whether or not it is legally permissible. The Fourth Amendment to the U.S. Constitution protects us against unreasonable searches and seizures: "The right of the people to be secure in their persons, houses, papers, and effects, against unreasonable searches and seizures, shall not be violated, and no Warrants shall issue, but upon probable cause, supported by Oath or affirmation, and particularly describing the place to be searched, and the persons or things to be seized."

Exactly what uses of technology constitute "unreasonable searches and seizures" has recently been clarified—somewhat—by the U.S. Supreme Court in *Kyllo v. US*, 533 U.S. 27 (2001). There, the Court held that using thermal imaging technology to measure the heat radiating from a house was a search, and thus could not be done constitutionally by law enforcement officers without a search warrant. In the past, the Supreme Court has found that it is reasonable to fly over someone's home and observe activity inside a fenced yard without a warrant[91] and to search garbage left at the curb[92] but that any kind of physical intrusion into the home requires a warrant.[93] The Court noted in its Kyllo decision, "Where, as here, the Government uses a device that is not in general public use, to explore details of the home that would previously have been unknowable without physical intrusion, the surveillance is a 'search' and is presumptively unreasonable without a warrant."[94]

What is troubling, however, is the distinction "a device that is not in general public use." It suggests that the Court will be sympathetic to an ever-shrinking zone of personal privacy, determined by what privacy-invasive devices are popular and commercially successful. This is a frightening and frustrating standard for determining such important public policy and such important personal rights.

Conclusion

We opened this chapter with a quotation about the ways in which technological advances are reducing privacy—a quotation dating back to 1890. In the last 115 years, technology that reduces privacy has continued to develop, in turn changing what the law calls our "reasonable expectations of privacy." Given the advances in biometrics, RFID, and GPS technology—and the shrinking costs of producing this kind of technology—we must expect these changes to continue, in ways that are not just difficult to predict but are even difficult to imagine.

While it is too soon to predict how that will change librarianship, it is clear that there will be dramatic impacts on individuals as consumers and citizens. The technology may be confusing to ordinary people, at least initially, but just as the Internet has gone from being an obscure and difficult-to-explain technology used mostly by academics and the military to being a mainstream technology used daily in most schools and libraries, so too will these technologies become part of the fabric of daily life. In order to protect personal information, these technologies must be deployed intelligently and consciously with well-established safeguards. People need to understand what they do, and make informed choices about their use.

Notes

1. Samuel Warren and Louis Brandeis, "The Right to Privacy," *Harvard Law Review* 193, 1890.

2. "Safeguarding Privacy in the Fight Against Terrorism," report of the Technology and Privacy Advisory Committee, Department of Defense, March 2004, http://www.sainc.com/tapac/TAPAC_Report_Final_5-10-04.pdf (accessed May 28, 2004).

3. "Data Mining: Federal Efforts Cover a Wide Range of Users," General Accounting Office, May 2004, http://www.gao.gov/new.items/d04548.pdf (accessed June 1, 2004).

4. "FY 2001 Report to Congress on Federal Government Information Security Reform," Office of Management and Budget, http://www.whitehouse.gov/omb/inforeg/fy01securityactreport.pdf (accessed June 1, 2004).

5. "Safeguarding Privacy in the Fight Against Terrorism," report of the Technology and Privacy Advisory Committee, Department of Defense, March 2004, http://www.cdt.org/security/usapatriot/20040300tapac.pdf (accessed June 1, 2004).

6. "Pentagon Spy Office to Close," *Wired News*, September 25, 2003, http://www.wired.com/news/privacy/0,1848,60588,00.html?tw=wn_story_related (accessed April 10, 2004).

7. Statement by Dr. Tony Tether, Director, Defense Advanced Research Projects Agency, submitted to the Subcommittee on Terrorism, Unconventional Threats and Capabilities, House Armed Services Committee, United States House of Representatives, March 27, 2003, http://www.darpa.mil/body/NewsItems/pdf/hasc_3_27_03final.pdf (accessed April 10, 2004).

8. "Wyden, Dorgan Continue Call for Closure of 'Terrorism Information Awareness' Program," Media Zone Speeches/Statements of Senator Ron Wyden, July 31, 2003, http://wyden.senate.gov/media/speeches/2003/07312003_tia_statement.html (accessed April 6, 2004).

9. William New, "Congress Funds Defense, Kills Terrorism Information Awareness," Daily Briefing, GOVEXEC.Com, http://www.govexec.com/dailyfed/0903/092503td1.htm, September 25, 2003 (accessed April 8, 2004).

10. "Conference Report on H.R. 2658, Department of Defense Appropriations Act, 2004," *Congressional Record*, September 24, 2003, H8500-H8550, http://www.eff.org/Privacy/TIA/20031003_conf_report.php (accessed April 9, 2004).

11. "LifeLog," Information Technology Processing Office, Defense Advanced Research Projects Agency, http://www.darpa.mil/ipto/Programs/lifelog/index.htm (accessed June 1, 2004).

12. "Safeguarding Privacy in the Fight Against Terrorism," report of the Technology and Privacy Advisory Committee, Department of Defense.

13. "Novel Intelligence from Massive Data," Advanced Research and Development Activity, http://www.ic-arda.org/Novel_Intelligence/index.html (accessed May 23, 2004).

14. Ibid.

15. John Schwartz, "Privacy Fears Erode Support for a Network to Fight Crime," *New York Times*, March 15, 2004, http://www.nytimes.com/2004/03/15/technology/15matrix.html?ex=1086580800&en=85a758cc68dea460&ei=5070&ei=5040&en=ca0c1ef27dac1b4a&ex=1080018000&partner=MOREOVER&pagewanted=print&position= (accessed May 20, 2004).

16. "Matrix Defined," http://www.matrix-at.org/matrix_defined.htm (accessed June 3, 2004).

17. "What Is the Matrix? ACLU Seeks Answers on New State-Run Surveillance Program," American Civil Liberties Union, October 30, 2003, http://www.aclu.org/Privacy/Privacy.cfm?ID=14257&c=130 (accessed April 17, 2004).

18. "More States Back Out of MATRIX," *EPIC Alert*, volume 11.06, March 24, 2004, http://www.epic.org/alert/EPIC_Alert_11.06.html (accessed June 2, 2004).

19. *9/11 Commission Report*, National Commission on the Terrorist Attacks Upon the United States (New York: Norton, 2004), p. 451.

20. "CAPPS II: Government Surveillance via Passenger Profiling," Electronic Frontier Foundation, http://www.eff.org/Privacy/cappsii/concern.php (accessed June 1, 2004).

21. "DHS Deputy Secretary Questioned About Passenger Profiling," *EPIC Alert*, volume 11.03, February 11, 2004, http://www.epic.org/alert/EPIC_Alert_11.03.html (accessed April 30, 2004).

22. "CAPPS II at a Glance," U.S. Department of Homeland Security, Transportation Security Administration, February 20, 2004, http://www.tsa.gov/public/display?theme=5&content=0900051980088d91 (accessed April 7, 2004).

23. "The Seven Problems with CAPPS II," American Civil Liberties Union, April 6, 2004, http://www.aclu.org/Privacy/Privacy.cfm?ID=15426&c=130 (accessed June 1, 2004).

24. "Computer-Assisted Passenger Prescreening System Faces Significant Implementation Challenges," General Accounting Office, February 2004, http://www.gao.gov/new.items/d04385.pdf (accessed April 6, 2004).

25. Ibid.

26. "Northwest Airlines' Disclosure of Passenger Data to Federal Agencies," Electronic Privacy Information Center, April 30, 2004, http://www.epic.org/privacy/airtravel/nasa/ (accessed June 2, 2004).

27. Aliya Sternstein, "TSA launches Secure Flight," FCW.com, August 27, 2004, http://www.fcw.com/fcw/articles/2004/0823/web-tsa-08-27-04.asp (accessed November 24, 2004).

28. Ryan Singel, "Airlines Cough Up Passenger Data," *Wired News*, November 24, 2004, http://www.wired.com/news/privacy/0,1848,65822,00.html?tw=wn_tophead_1 (accessed November 24, 2004).

29. "Internet and Data Interception Capabilities Developed by FBI," testimony of Donald M. Kerr, Assistant Director, Laboratory Division, FBI, before the U.S. House of Representatives, Committee on the Judiciary, Subcommittee on the Constitution, July 24, 2000, http://www.fbi.gov/congress/congress00/kerr072400.htm (accessed April 14, 2004).

30. "Carnivore Diagnostic Tool," testimony of Donald M. Kerr, Assistant Director, Laboratory Division, FBI, before the U.S. Senate, Committee on the Judiciary, September 6, 2000, http://www.fbi.gov/congress/congress00/kerr090600.htm (accessed June 1, 2004).

31. "Independent Technical Review of the Carnivore System: Final Report," Illinois Institute of Technology Research Institute, December 8, 2000, http://www.epic.org/privacy/carnivore/carniv_final.pdf (accessed April 8, 2004).

32. Ibid., pp. 1–3.

33. "FBI's Carnivore System Disrupted Anti-Terror Investigation," Electronic

Privacy Information Center, May 28, 2002, http://www.epic.org/privacy/carnivore/5_02_release.html (accessed April 20, 2004).

34. "Falling Through the Net II: New Data on the Digital Divide, National Telecommunications and Information," National Telecommunications and Information Administration, 1998, http://www.ntia.doc.gov/ntiahome/net2 (accessed May 29, 2004).

35. "A Nation Online: How Americans Are Expanding Their Use of the Internet," National Telecommunications and Information Administration, 2002, http://www.ntia.doc.gov/ntiahome/dn/index.html (accessed May 25, 2004).

36. "Three out of Four Americans Have Access to the Internet," Nielsen// Netratings, March 2004, http://www.nielsen-netratings.com/pr/pr_040318.pdf (accessed May 20, 2004).

37. "Broadband Adoption at Home Grows Strongly in Winter Months of 2003 & 2004," Pew Internet and American Life Project, April 19, 2004, http://www.pewtrusts.com/news/news_subpage.cfm?content_item_id=2314&content_type_id=7&page=nr1 (accessed August 12, 2004).

38. "Connected to the Future," Corporation for Public Broadcasting, 3, http://www.cpb.org/pdfs/ed/resources/connected/03_connect_report.pdf (accessed August 10, 2004).

39. "Connected to the Future," Corporation for Public Broadcasting, 4, http://www.cpb.org/pdfs/ed/resources/connected/03_connect_report.pdf (accessed August 10, 2004).

40. Ibid.

41. "Connected to the Future," Corporation for Public Broadcasting, 2, http://www.cpb.org/pdfs/ed/resources/connected/03_connect_report.pdf (accessed August 9, 2003).

42. Ibid.

43. Ibid.

44. Ibid.

45. Ibid.

46. "Digital Disconnect: The Widening Gap Between Internet-savvy Students & Their Schools," Pew Internet and American Life Project, August 14, 2002, http://www.pewinternet.org/reports/toc.asp?Report=67 (accessed July 21, 2003).

47. "Metaphor 3: The Internet as Virtual Study Group," "Digital Disconnect: The Widening Gap Between Internet-savvy Students & Their Schools," Pew Internet and American Life Project, August 14, 2002, http://www.pewinternet.org/reports/toc.asp?Report=67 (accessed August 12, 2003).

48. "Metaphor 1: The Internet as Virtual Textbook and Reference Library," "Digital Disconnect: The Widening Gap Between Internet-savvy Students & Their Schools," Pew Internet and American Life Project, August 14, 2002, http://www.pewinternet.org/reports/toc.asp?Report=67 (accessed August 12, 2003).

49. "Teenage Life Online: The Rise of the Instant Message Generation and the Internet's Impact on Friendships and Family Relationships, Part 3: Teens and Their Schools, Research for Papers and Projects—From Dewey to dot-com," Pew Internet and American Life Project, June 2001, http://www.pewinternet.org/reports/reports.asp?Report=36&Section=Reportlevel1&Field=Level1D&ID=143 (accessed February 28, 2004).

50. Victoria Rideout, "Generation Rx.com: How Young People Use the Inter-

net for Health Information," Kaiser Family Foundation Survey, http://www.kff.org (accessed August 11, 2003).

51. "Connected to the Future," Corporation for Public Broadcasting, 4.

52. "Statistical Research: US Kids Choose Internet over Other Media," NUA, April 8, 2002, http://www.nua.ie/surveys/?f=VS&art_id=905357821&rel=true (accessed August 11, 2003).

53. "Connected to the Future," Corporation for Public Broadcasting, 7 (accessed August 10, 2003).

54. "Privacy Online: Fair Information Practices in the Electronic Marketplace," Federal Trade Commission, May 2000, http://www.ftc.gov/reports/privacy2000/privacy2000text.pdf (accessed May 23, 2004).

55. "The Cookie Concept," http://www.cookiecentral.com/content.phtml?area=2&id=1 (accessed June 1, 2005).

56. "DoubleClick Loses Its Cookies," *Wired News*, August 26, 2002, http://www.wired.com/news/business/0,1367,54774,00.html (accessed April 5, 2004).

57. "19 Entertainment and Media Firms Ranked on How They Treat Online Customers in Winter 2004 Online Customer Respect Study," Customer Respect, February 24, 2004, http://www.ivapp.com/offer/cust_respect/collateral/Media_CRI_Winter_PR_2004.pdf (accessed June 1, 2004).

58. "FTC Sues Failed Website, Toysmart.com, for Deceptively Offering for Sale Personal Information of Website Visitors," Federal Trade Commission, July 10, 2000, http://www.ftc.gov/opa/2000/07/toysmart.htm (accessed April 4, 2004).

59. "Toysmart Bankruptcy Settlement Ensures Consumer Privacy Protection," January 11, 2001, Office of New York State Attorney General Eliot Spitzer, http://www.oag.state.ny.us/press/2001/jan/jan11a_01.htm (accessed April 3, 2004).

60. John Borland, "States Join Spyware Battle," *CNET*, March 4, 2004, http://news.com.com/2100-1024_3-5170263.html?tag=nefd_top (accessed April 9, 2004).

61. Jay Lyman, "Utah Anti-Spyware Law Suspended by Judge," *TechNewsWorld*, June 24, 2004, http://www.technewsworld.com/story/34728.html (accessed August 14, 2004).

62. Letter to Attorney General Lockyer, May 3, 2004, http://www.epic.org/privacy/gmail/agltr5.3.04.html (accessed May 7, 2004).

63. Matt Hicks, "Wiretap Ruling Could Signal End of E-Mail Privacy," *eWeek*, July 1, 2004, http://www.eweek.com/article2/0,1759,1619520,00.asp (accessed August 1, 2004).

64. Ibid.

65. "Gartner Study Finds Significant Increase in E-Mail Phishing Attacks," May 6, 2004, http://www4.gartner.com/5_about/press_releases/asset_71087_11.jsp (accessed August 4, 2004).

66. "Radio Frequency Identification (RFID) Systems," Electronic Privacy Information Center, June 23, 2004, http://www.epic.org/privacy/rfid/#history (accessed July 1, 2004).

67. Lee Tien, "Privacy Risks of Radio Frequency Identification 'Tagging' of Library Books," Electronic Frontier Foundation Memo, October 1, 2003, http://www.eff.org/Privacy/Surveillance/RFID/20031002_sfpl_comments.php (accessed April 10, 2004).

68. "California RFID Legislation Rejected," *RFID Journal*, July 5, 2004, http://www.rfidjournal.com/article/articleview/1015/1/1/ (accessed July 7, 2004).

69. "Why Did the Department of Defense Develop GPS?" http://www.trimble.com/gps/dod.html (accessed July 18, 2004).

70. "Frequently Asked Questions about Geocaching," emphasis in the original, http://www.geocaching.com/faq/ (accessed July 18, 2004).

71. For example, "Active, Real-Time Tracking," http://mightygps.com/mightygpstrackingsolutions.htm (accessed July 18, 2004); http://www.trackyourtruck.com/ (accessed July 18, 2004); http://www.midadirect-track.com/ (accessed July 18, 2004).

72. "GPS Locator for Kids," http://www.wherifywireless.com/prod_watches.htm (accessed July 18, 2004).

73. BioPassword, http://www.securityconfig.com/resources/authentication/biopassword.htm (accessed August 1, 2004).

74. "Biometrics Awareness Still Low," *Federal Computer Week*, Dibya Sarkar, November 6, 2002, http://www.fcw.com/geb/articles/2002/1104/web-survey-11-06-02.asp (accessed August 1, 2004).

75. "Snooper Bowl?" Associated Press, http://abcnews.go.com/sections/scitech/DailyNews/superbowl_biometrics_010213.html (accessed August 1, 2004).

76. William Safire, "Threat of National ID," *New York Times*, December 24, 2001, http://query.nytimes.com/gst/abstract.html?res=F4071EF63C550C778EDDAB0099 4D9404482 (accessed August 1, 2004).

77. "Ins and Outs of Biometrics," *USA Today*, January 27, 2003, http://search.epnet.com/direct.asp?J0E188926089303&db=afh (accessed July 22, 2004).

78. Todd Murphy, "'100 Percent' Wrong: How the FBI's Arrest of Suspected Terrorist Brandon Mayfield Unraveled," *Portland Tribune*, May 28, 2004, http://www.portlandtribune.com/archview.cgi?id=24586 (accessed August 15, 2004).

79. "Scanning Tech a Blurry Picture," Declan McCullagh and Robert Zarate, *Wired News*, February 16, 2002, http://www.wired.com/news/politics/0,1283,50470,00.html (accessed August 1, 2004).

80. Ibid.

81. The United States Census Bureau Population Clock, http://www.census.gov/population/www/ (accessed August 1, 2004).

82. "Passport ID Technology Has High Error Rate," *Washington Post*, A01, August 6, 2004.

83. Ibid.

84. Ibid.

85. Ibid.

86. "Ins and Outs of Biometrics."

87. "Biometrics, Evidence, and Personal Privacy," Information Systems Security, July/August 12, 2003, issue 3, http://search.epnet.com/login.aspx?direct=true&db=f5h&an=10093756 (accessed July 22, 2004).

88. Jane Black, "Towards a Biometric Bill of Rights," *Business Week Online*, November 14, 2002, http://search.epnet.com/direct.asp?an=7914465&db=afh (accessed August 1, 2004).

89. Ibid.

90. Safire, "Threat of National ID."

91. *California v. Ciraolo*, 476 U.S. 207 (1986), *Florida v. Riley*, 488 U.S. 445 (1989).

92. *California v. Greenwood*, 486 U.S. 35 (1988).

93. *Silverman v. United States*, 365 U.S. 505 (1961).

94. *Kyllo v. US*, 533 U.S. 27 (2001).

CHAPTER 3

Privacy and Libraries in a Changing World

Introduction

> If the lady from Toledo can be required to disclose what she read yesterday and what she will read tomorrow, fear will take the place of freedom in the libraries, bookstores, and homes of the land.
> —*United States v. Rumely*, 345 U.S. 41, 58 (1953)
> (Douglas, J., concurring)

Libraries in the United States have been evolving since the first library was established at Harvard University in 1638.[1] There have been many political and social events that affected the development of libraries and shaped the core values of librarianship espoused by the American Library Association (ALA), other library associations, and their members. Recently surveillance of and requests for the confidential library records of patrons by law enforcement agents have again become major topics of concern in the library community. With concerns surrounding Section 215 of the USA PATRIOT Act, it is appropriate that the origins of library patron privacy and confidentiality be examined and measured against the current broader threat to privacy and civil liberties in general.

Confidentiality and Privacy: Patron Protections in Libraries

Patron privacy in the use of a library's resources and services is supported by three types of protections: (1) state library privacy statutes, (2) ALA policies and pronouncements on privacy, and (3) individual library policies addressing privacy issues.

State Library Privacy Statutes

There is no federal law that is specifically directed at protecting a patron's privacy when using a library's resources and services. However, as noted in Chapter 1, there are court cases and language associated with broad privacy rights in various sections of the Bill of Rights, for example, the Fourth Amendment's language prohibiting unreasonable searches and seizures.[2] Privacy is also addressed in some specific federal statutes like the Family Education Rights and Privacy Act (FERPA). But for most librarians and patrons their strongest claim of library privacy protection will be based on their respective state statutes. Forty-eight states have statutes related to library privacy and confidentiality and two states (Hawaii and Kentucky) have attorneys general's opinions upholding, to some degree, the privacy rights of patrons.[3] In most instances state laws cover libraries funded in whole or in part with public funding. Private and corporate libraries generally do not come under state library law privacy protections, although they may have their own privacy policies. For those libraries covered by state statute, it is essential that all staff and the libraries' governing boards have a thorough understanding of their state's library privacy statute and how it applies to their library. ALA policy statements on privacy and the library's own policy notwithstanding, it is a state's library privacy statute that offers the strongest *legal* protection to patron privacy when patrons are using the library.

Statutory language and protections in each state differ somewhat, but a common theme of most state statutes is that they define (1) what is protected, (2) who is protected, and (3) when protected information can be released to or viewed by others, including law enforcement authorities.

What Is Protected?

Libraries provide resources and services. The differentiation between a library's "resources" and its "services" is somewhat arbitrary. Resources can generally be thought of as providing for tangible items, like the library's collection. Examples of services include the provision of reference, photo copy machines, or a public bulletin board. Providing public Internet access probably falls somewhere in the middle between resources and services.

Ideally, privacy statutes should cover patron use of a library's resources or services regardless of their format or delivery mechanism. Such broad protections are reflected in the ALA policy on confidentiality that refers not just to circulation records but also to "other records identifying the name of library users."[4] Unfortunately, many states lack the ideal statute that encompasses all library use. Historically, most state statutes were drafted with explicit or implied language that focused on protecting the privacy of circulation transactions. This language leaves open questions on the law's applicability to patron use of a library's resources beyond the traditional circulation function. (See the later section, "Statutory Interpretation.") An example of this is found in the Connecticut library privacy statute that says, "personally identifiable information contained in the circulation records of all public libraries shall be confidential."[5] This language does not include the more inclusive language, as does the law in New York, which says that patron privacy is covered under a variety of circumstances that include but are not limited to "[r]ecords related to the circulation of library materials, computer database searches, interlibrary loan transactions, reference queries, requests for photocopies of library materials, title reserve requests, or the use of audio-visual materials, films or records."[6]

Another service offered by many public libraries is the use of their meeting room facilities to organizations such as community service clubs. Generally the names of the people from the outside organization who reserve the room or the names of those in attendance are a matter of public record and may not come under the protection of a state's library privacy law.

Who Is Protected?

While ensuring the privacy of all patrons, regardless of age, may be the ideal, it is not always the law or even library policy. Who is covered by state statutes does differ by state, and most often this difference is reflected in lower privacy thresholds accorded to children. This directly affects K–12 school media centers and public libraries. For example, the library statute in Ohio states, "If a library record or patron information pertaining to a minor child is requested from a library by the minor child's parent, guardian, or custodian, the library shall make that record or information available to the parent, guardian, or custodian."[7] Wisconsin was one of the more recent states to pass a similar statute in 2004. About fourteen states have some type of statutory language allowing parents or guardians access to their children's circulation records.[8] (For more discussion on this issue, see the "Privacy and Children" section in Chapter 4.)

When Protected Information Can Be Released

It cannot be overemphasized that all staff must be well informed about the circumstances under which information protected by statute can be released, who can release it, and to whom such information can be released. In addition to the release of juvenile information under some circumstances, state statutes very often describe other circumstances in which protected information can be released to others. Most laws state that information regarding patron use of the library can be released to the patron, to others with the consent of the patron, or by court order. Another common clause in statutory language is the ability of library staff to access confidential patron information as part of their regular work responsibilities. One could reasonably interpret this to include the transfer of such information to another library, if needed, for interlibrary loan or other library purposes.

Since passage of the USA PATRIOT Act, there has been considerable discussion in the library community about the relationship between the expanded powers of federal law enforcement authorities and the privacy protections afforded under state statutes. State library privacy laws routinely allow law enforcement access to protected patron information with a court order or in some cases with just a subpoena. Among its many changes to existing federal laws, the USA PATRIOT Act lowers the threshold for obtaining a court order from "probable cause" to being a "suspect of a current investigation." Senator Russ Feingold (D-Wisconsin), the only senator to vote against the USA PATRIOT Act, tried to amend the bill so that the law would not preempt existing state privacy laws. This amendment failed.[9] The act still requires that law enforcement officers obtain such an order; law enforcement officers who demand a patron's records without a proper court order risk having the evidence resulting from such a search declared inadmissible in any formal legal proceeding because it was obtained as a result of an illegal search. In this regard, state legal protections are still valid.

Most state statutes do not list any penalties for violation of the state's library privacy law. If a patron believes his or her confidentiality or privacy has been violated in relation to legal protections offered under state law, the proper recourse in most states is to initiate a civil action against the library or its governing body.[10]

Open Records Statutes and Privacy Statutes

Most states have broad open records laws that almost always cover libraries receiving public funding. The intent of open records legislation is to provide citizens with as much information as possible about the workings of their government. In a library setting, open records cover the vast majority of documents produced by, and actions taken by, staff and the library's governing body. State open records statutes often have a clause exempting the disclosure of information that is specifically protected by other statutory provisions, such as library patron privacy language. Under these circumstances any information produced in response to a public records request must first be reviewed to ensure that it does not contain information protected under the state's library privacy law. If such information is present it must be removed before complying with the open records request.[11]

Statutory Interpretation

What is covered, who is covered, and the circumstances of coverage are often open to legal interpretation. Because of this, library staff must closely examine their state's library privacy law, especially in relation to the use of electronic resources including the Internet. If a state's library privacy law is not broad enough or has not been updated to reflect patron use of electronic resources, then staff and patrons must rely on the interpretation of existing statutory language established in the pre-Internet age. Such interpretations are problematic and more susceptible to challenge. It may be difficult, or require a liberal interpretation of the statutes, to claim that legal protections crafted in pre-Internet times also cover Internet use or the use of other electronic resources.

To hold any legal weight, a determination that general statutory language covers specific uses of library resources must be made by legal counsel. Staff should first seek the advice of the library's own counsel. If local counsel is uncertain about the privacy protections, especially interpretations based on general or vague statutory language, then the next step is to get an opinion from the state library agency. The Wisconsin State Library has given such an opinion in relation to its state library privacy statute.[12] The Wisconsin statute in question states that information "[i]ndicating the identity of any individual who borrows or uses the library's documents or other materials, resources or services may not be disclosed except by court order."[13] In response to questions from the state's library community, the state library opined that the phrase "or other materials, resources or services" included use of electronic databases and the Internet. Furthermore, this interpretation also provides privacy protection for any patron login information, residual files residing on the workstation, and patron Internet sign-up sheets. If the state library is uncertain about statutory interpretation, the next step is to get an opinion from the state's attorney general.[14] (One of the responsibilities of the attorney general is to interpret state statutes.) Since an interpretation of the law by the attorney general then applies to all libraries in the state covered by the statute, it is strongly recommended that any such request be initiated or coordinated through the state library agency. Finally, if the legal opinion from the attorney general questions whether existing statutory language protects some uses of library resources (e.g., Internet), then the state's library community should consider seeking legislation to make such protections explicit.

In an example of a local legal interpretation related to Internet use, in January 2003 the St. Louis Public Library released to the FBI two weeks of Internet sign-up sheets from one of its branch libraries. The FBI had made a verbal request for the information. It did not have a court order. Library staff assumed such information was a public record. After an editorial on this subject appeared in the St. Louis *Post Dispatch* and based on advice of its legal counsel, the library changed its policy shortly after this incident to declare that Internet sign-up sheets now had the same protection as circulation records.[15]

ALA Policies and Pronouncements on Privacy

In addition to state privacy laws, the American Library Association has adopted several important policy statements that reflect its strong support for privacy and confidentiality related to patron use of a library's resources and services. While the ALA's policy statements do not hold legal authority, the association's positions on patron privacy and many other issues have been widely endorsed and supported by the library profession and by library governing authorities. These policy statements are instrumental in helping to support local library policies on privacy. For example, many library governing bodies have adopted ALA language on library privacy. Furthermore, some of the ALA policy language on privacy has been incorporated into state statutory protections. Listed in the following paragraphs, in chronological order, are summaries of several important statements including: (a) the "Code of Ethics of the American Library Association," (b) the "ALA Policy on Confidentiality of Library Records," (c) the "ALA Policy Concerning Confidentiality of Personally Identifiable Information about Library Users," and (d) "Privacy: An Interpretation of the Library Bill of Rights." The complete text of these documents is reprinted in Appendix I.

The Code of Ethics of the American Library Association (1939, 1995)

Originally adopted in 1939 and revised in 1995, the code of ethics encompasses a wide variety of issues including the responsibility of librarians to protect the privacy of library patrons. Article Three states: "We protect each library user's right to privacy and confidentiality with respect to information sought or received and resources consulted, borrowed, acquired or transmitted."[16]

The ALA Policy on Confidentiality of Library Records (1971, 1986)

The policy on confidentiality was originally adopted in 1971 and was further revised in 1986 by the ALA Council.[17] The policy includes three core elements that it recommends be implemented by libraries. These include (1) adopting a policy which recognizes that any records identifying the names of library users are confidential, (2) advising all staff on the circumstances under which such records can be released and to whom, and (3) making certain that any request by law enforcement to access such records is properly issued. This latter point means that library management will consult with legal counsel to determine if the process, court order, or subpoena is proper.

Policy Concerning Confidentiality of Personally Identifiable Information about Library Users (1991, 2004)

In 1991, the ALA Council adopted a policy on the confidentiality of personally identifiable information (PII) about library patrons.[18] The policy is broad in its coverage, stating, "Confidentiality extends to 'information sought or received, and materials consulted, borrowed, acquired or transmitted' (*ALA Code of Ethics*), and includes, but is not limited to, database search records, reference interviews, circulation records, interlibrary loan records, and other personally identifiable uses of library materials, facilities, or services." The ALA's policy recognizes that law enforcement authorities can have legitimate reasons to seek access to confidential patron records related to library use, but it also notes that there are legal mechanisms to follow when seeking such access. Furthermore, it notes, "The government's interest in library use reflects a dangerous and fallacious equation of what a person reads with what that person believes or how that person is likely to behave. Such a presumption can and does threaten the freedom of access to information."[19] The policy was updated in June 2004 and now includes the definition of privacy and confidentiality from "Privacy: An Interpretation of the Library Bill of Rights."

Privacy: An Interpretation of the Library Bill of Rights (2002)

The most recent policy statement relating to privacy and confidentiality from the American Library Association was approved in 2002.[20] This privacy statement is intended to help librarians preserve their patrons' privacy following the terrorist attacks of September 11, 2001, and privacy concerns related to subsequent passage of the USA PATRIOT Act in October 2001. This privacy interpretation of the Library Bill of Rights speaks to the importance of maintaining patron privacy and confidentiality in *all* types of libraries. After defining the difference between privacy and confidentiality in a library context, the policy statement emphasizes the need for privacy to ensure that patrons feel comfortable seeking information without having their request for information questioned or known by others.

There are several other ALA statements and declarations that address issues of privacy, at least to some extent. For example, in 2003 the ALA published "Principles for the Networked World." Among the principles this document includes is one that succinctly defines privacy as "The freedom to choose the degree to which personal information is monitored, collected, disclosed, and distributed."[21] It addresses the need for patron privacy protections in a networked environment, including the right of patrons to be fully informed about privacy policies and their privacy rights, and to have location independent access to information without having to forfeit their privacy. As an example, patrons should feel confident when placing an item on hold from a remote site (e.g., home) that any transmittal of information will be done over a secure network and that the information will remain confidential.

Individual Library Policies Addressing Privacy Issues

Information on developing library policies on privacy and confidentiality can be found in the respective chapters on school, academic, and public libraries and in Appendix III.

Law Enforcement Interest in Libraries

As previously noted, law enforcement agencies have legal means to access library patron records. During the Cold War, U.S. government agencies showed a special interest in library use. For example, in 1970 the Senate Subcommittee on Investigations requested the Alcohol, Tobacco and Firearms Division (ATF) of the Internal Revenue Service (IRS) to "initiate a broad program to investigate suspected users of explosives."[22] Part of the program involved looking at library circulation records to determine who was reading about explosives or guerilla warfare. The American Library Association notified its members that requests were being made for library records without court orders or subpoenas. Libraries had a powerful supporter in Senator Sam Irvin (D-North Carolina), who wrote to the secretary of the treasury, "Throughout history, official surveillance of the reading habits of citizens has been a litmus test of tyranny."[23] The issue was resolved by guidelines agreed upon between the ALA and the IRS that recognized the right of patron privacy as well as the government's responsibility for conducting criminal investigations.

The FBI's Library Awareness Program

The next interest in what patrons were reading occurred under the FBI's Library Awareness Program, which operated from 1973 through the 1980s. Under this program the FBI conducted secret surveillance of unclassified scientific publications in public and academic libraries. The program had two purposes: "1) To restrict access by foreign nationals, particularly Soviet and East Europeans, to unclassified scientific information; and 2) To recruit librarians to report on any 'foreigners' using America's unclassified scientific libraries."[24]

Librarians first became aware of the program through a *New York Times* article in September 1987 that detailed a visit by FBI agents to Columbia University. The article was based on information provided by the American Library Association, which had received a letter from Paula Kaufman,

Columbia's director of Academic Information Services. In her letter she stated: "They [the FBI] explained that they were doing a general 'library awareness' program in the city and that they were asking librarians to be alert to the use of their libraries by persons from countries hostile to the United States, such as the Soviet Union, and to provide the FBI with information about these activities."[25]

From inquiries by the ALA, it first appeared that the program was focused solely on libraries in the New York City area; however, it was later learned that the program was also being implemented in San Francisco and Washington, DC. In 1987, the Intellectual Freedom Committee of the ALA prepared a statement on the FBI's program and "warned that libraries are not 'extensions of the long arm of the law or of the gaze of Big Brother,' and it defined the role of libraries 'to make available and provide access to a diversity of information, not to monitor what use a patron makes of publicly available information.' "[26]

In 1988 Congressional hearings found many witnesses testifying against the program and noting that any appearance of librarians assisting law enforcement agents by reporting on the actions and use of libraries by library patrons, foreign born or not, would have serious impact on the intellectual freedom of library users and the credibility of librarians. It was also pointed out that acceding to law enforcement requests would violate the ALA Code of Ethics. Representative Don Edwards (D-California), chairman of the House Subcommittee on Civil and Constitutional Rights, spoke for many concerned with the abuse of civil liberties inherent in this program, telling FBI Assistant Director James Geer,

> What disturbs some of us about this program is the FBI's apparent failure to recognize the special status of libraries in our society. . . . [T]he FBI should recognize that libraries and books and reading are special. In our nation libraries are sacred institutions, which should be protected and nurtured. Going into libraries and asking librarians to report on suspicious users has ominous implications for freedom of speech and privacy. Everybody in this country has a right to use libraries and they have the right to do so with confidentiality.[27]

Librarians protested the FBI's program with impassioned letters and policy statements. Judith Keogh from the Pennsylvania Library Association stated in a letter to FBI Director William S. Sessions, "Libraries must uphold the rights of patrons to pursue information without the fear that library staff will 'spy' on them to any government agency. . . . Librarians are employed to serve the needs of their patrons, not to act as agents for the government."[28] In 1988, the ALA Government Documents Round Table (GODORT) passed a "Resolution in Opposition to FBI Library Awareness Program" that called for "immediate cessation of the FBI Library Awareness program and all other related visits by the Bureau to libraries where the intent is to gain information, without a court order, on patrons' use."[29] Interestingly, in 1989 FBI officials revealed that they had also conducted investigations of librarians and others who had protested the program.[30]

Through the efforts of the American Library Association, the American Civil Liberties Union, the People for the American Way, and other groups; public and academic librarians; Congress; and the media, the program became a public relations problem for the FBI. Political satirist Mark Russell poked fun at the FBI's concern for library users with foreign-sounding names and accents, joking, "So far they've arrested Henry Kissinger, Zbigniew Brzezinski, and Michael Dukakis."[31]

The Library Awareness Program did have at least one positive result. By the time the program ended in the late 1980s, the majority of states and the District of Columbia had passed library confidentiality laws to protect the records of library patrons and require a subpoena or court order for the release of such records to law enforcement agents. In effect, these laws protected not only patrons but also libraries and librarians.

A detailed account of the Library Awareness Program is available in the book *Surveillance in the Stacks* by Herbert Foerstel published by Greenwood Press in 1991.

The USA PATRIOT Act

The Uniting and Strengthening America by Providing Appropriate Tools Required to Intercept and Obstruct Terrorism Act of 2001, also known as the USA PATRIOT Act, was enacted on October 26, 2001, following the terrorist attack of September 11. The USA PATRIOT Act changed the way libraries are required to handle certain inquiries from the FBI—and it has implications for patron privacy that are dramatic and distressing. The act amounts to a "shopping list" of enhanced authority that federal law enforcement agents have been seeking for years, and in some cases decades. Some of the provisions are not too controversial, but others tip the delicate balance of protecting security and liberty, far away from the side of liberty.

How the USA PATRIOT Act Was Passed

In Michael Moore's controversial film, *Fahrenheit 9/11*, Representative John Conyers (D-Michigan) memorably explains to Mr. Moore—using the tone of voice ordinarily reserved for reminding not-too-swift children of things they have been told before—that members of Congress do not read the bills they vote on, and specifically, that they did not read the USA PATRIOT Act before voting on it. While this may have been a slight exaggeration, it was not news to the people who followed the bill as it was being considered by Congress. Lobbyists for the ALA and other concerned civil liberties and privacy advocates had difficulties obtaining copies of the bill, and "many Senators complained that they didn't have enough time to read it."[32]

In the same film, Representative Jim McDermott (D-Washington) describes the USA PATRIOT Act as a "wish list" of legislative changes that the law enforcement community had been seeking for years. In an op-ed published the day before the USA PATRIOT Act was passed, Morton H. Halperin, who served in the Johnson, Nixon, and Clinton administrations in the Department of Defense, the State Department, and the National Security Council, described the USA PATRIOT Act this way:

> The administration simply dusted off every proposal it had on the shelf, many of which had been defeated previously. It wrapped the old proposals into a new bill and sent the bill up to Congress without new interagency review, demanding that it be passed immediately. When the House Judiciary Committee unanimously reported a bill with some safeguards, the administration successfully pressured the House leadership to abandon the bill and adopt most of the far worse Senate measure. The final text was drafted in a secret and closed informal conference. No conference report or committee reports exist to explain the bill's meaning. This is a dangerous way to legislate the delicate balance between national security and civil liberties.[33]

This kind of lawmaking was possible because of the climate of fear and horror present after the September 11, 2001, attacks on the United States. Those feelings, of course, are perfectly understandable. In the aftermath of September 11, 2001, many Americans expressed a strong willingness to sacrifice some civil liberties in the name of national security. For example, in a survey conducted by National Public Radio, the Kennedy School, and the Kaiser Family Foundation in November 2001, large majorities of Americans supported giving law enforcement broader authority to engage in tactics such as examining people's Internet activity (82 percent) and student educational records (76 percent).[34] Library records were not specifically addressed in the poll. These numbers are especially distressing in light of respondents' awareness of the potential for these expanded powers to be abused. In this regard, 65 percent of those surveyed expected that given this expanded authority law enforcement officials would use it against innocent people.[35]

A year after the terrorist attacks, researchers updated this poll and found that "a small but statistically significant number of Americans have shifted towards the civil liberties side of the issue since last year."[36] However, the majority still felt it was necessary for the average person to give up some rights and liberties in order to curb terrorism.[37] This poll did not explore law enforcement powers in the same depth as the previous year's poll.

What the USA PATRIOT Act Does

The USA PATRIOT Act is an immensely complicated and far-reaching law. It changes law related to telecommunications privacy, money laundering, foreign intelligence, immigration, and criminal activity and the procedures law enforcement agents and courts must follow for implementing those changes.[38] It would be inappropriate to assume that all provisions in the act are uniformly criticized by privacy advocates. For example, some sections were supported by law enforcement officials and civil libertarians alike. When the problems with the law are debated now, this fact is often overlooked. Advocates of the law point to those sections of the law that were uncontroversial, such as Section 206, which permits intelligence investigators to obtain a wiretap order associated with a person, rather than a phone number, so that when that person purchases a new cell phone or uses a pay phone, the law enforcement agency does not have to go through the process of getting a new wiretap order.[39]

The area of the law that has generated the most interest in the library community is Section 215, which amended the Title V of the Foreign Intelligence Surveillance Act of 1978 (FISA).[40] The two key sections that affect Title V of the Foreign Intelligence Surveillance Act of 1978[41] are 501(a)(1) and 501(d):

501(a)(1) [The FBI] may make an application for an order *requiring the production of any tangible things (including books, records, papers, documents, and other items)* for an investigation to protect against international terrorism or clandestine intelligence activities, provided that such investigation of a United States person is not conducted solely upon the basis of activities protected by the first amendment to the Constitution. (emphasis added)

501(d) No person shall disclose to any other person (other than those persons necessary to produce the tangible things under this section) that the Federal Bureau of Investigation has sought or obtained tangible things under this section.

These two sections are issues for libraries for two main reasons:

Tangible Things and Records. In Section 501(a)(1) of the USA PATRIOT Act, libraries must produce any "tangible thing" requested by law enforcement agents under a FISA court order. For libraries, giving up any record or "tangible" item with personally identifiable information about patrons creates a serious conflict with the profession's code of ethics and core principles of Intellectual Freedom. Additionally, the term "records" may be broader than libraries realize. It can include *any* type of record that is routinely created in the course of doing business. For example, if libraries use personally identifiable means for providing Internet access

through a cardswipe device, individual patron login, or Internet workstation sign-up lists, they are creating a record of Internet access linked with
patron personally identifiable information.

Notice Restrictions. Section 501(d) prohibits staff in an organization,
such as a library, that has been subpoenaed from disclosing that fact to
anyone other than their attorney and "supervisory staff charged with responding to law enforcement inquiries, especially when library policy explicitly states that only the director or head librarian or counsel is
designated to respond to law enforcement inquiries on behalf of the library. There are two reasons for this: first, the PATRIOT Act cannot eliminate or erase the constitutional right to counsel; second, the PATRIOT
Act itself permits the recipient of an order to notify 'all persons necessary'
to produce the documents."[42] If the library does not have a legal counsel,
it may call the ALA Office for Intellectual Freedom and ask to speak to
legal counsel at the Freedom to Read Foundation. When calling, library
staff should *not divulge to OIF staff why conversation with the Foundation's legal
counsel is requested.*

Library staff may not alert the patron to the law enforcement inquiries.
There are some good reasons for this—if a customer is under investigation
for purchasing suspicious amounts of dangerous chemicals, and the chemical company announced that it was being investigated for selling dangerous chemicals to suspected terrorists, the target of the investigation would
probably quit purchasing from them. Constitutional law is very clear that
criminal suspects may be given "delayed notice" that they have been under
surveillance or that records or evidence belonging to them has been
seized. Law enforcement agents have a well-founded fear that suspects
would try to destroy evidence against them if they knew they were under
suspicion. However, this provision in the USA PATRIOT Act takes that concept to a whole new level of secrecy.

Some libraries have attempted to address this issue by placing notices
alerting patrons that the library may, at some point in time, be subject to
a FISA Court subpoena of library records; and if that should ever take
place, the library will not be permitted to inform patrons that their records
have been released to the FBI. While this does give patrons the opportunity to protect their own privacy, it also may alarm them unnecessarily and
discourage them from using the library.

There are other troubling aspects to the USA PATRIOT Act. For example, previously law enforcement agents investigating terrorism suspects
could only subpoena library records and otherwise engage in surveillance
of someone if they could demonstrate to a judge that they had a "probable cause" to believe that the person was a spy or an agent of a foreign
power.[43] The new standard is that agents investigating terrorism may request those records if they are "sought for an authorized investigation"[44]
of foreign intelligence activity. This standard essentially permits law enforcement to "fish" for evidence anywhere they choose to authorize an in-

vestigation, regardless of whether or not there is any evidence to support that choice.

The scenario library and civil liberties advocates imagined when this was proposed is one in which a library in a community with a high concentration of Arab or Arab American residents is faced with requests for Internet activity or circulation records for all patrons. In the past, if a law enforcement agent had probable cause to believe that an agent of a foreign power was improperly using library resources to spy or plan criminal or terrorist activity, the agent could have obtained a warrant to seize those records, and the library would properly have cooperated. But in that case, only particular, targeted records related to the suspect would have been requested and provided.

Under the USA PATRIOT Act, a warrant can be obtained to seize any records that are sought for an authorized investigation. Incidentally, if the law enforcement agent finds evidence of some other criminal activity unrelated to terrorism or to the authorized investigation for which the records were sought, the agent is free to pursue the newly discovered suspect activity. The concern here is law enforcement agents may investigate many residents of a particular neighborhood, even if they have no reliable evidence that a specific crime has been committed. Instead of searching for that evidence in order to open a criminal investigation, they might open a pretextual investigation of foreign intelligence activity, and under the lower standard, seize evidence to create a criminal case they could not have legitimately pursued before the act was passed.

There is good news in the USA PATRIOT Act for librarians: Section 215 was passed with a "sunset" provision, meaning that it will expire on December 31, 2005, unless Congress takes action otherwise. There is also bad news for librarians. Proponents may either extend Section 215 or make it a permanent part of the law.

ALA's Response to the USA PATRIOT Act

The American Library Association and its members reacted quickly to Section 215 of the USA PATRIOT Act and have remained steadfast in their fight to preserve the confidentiality of library records and to protect the privacy of patrons. Its actions can be seen through its documents—resolutions, policy statements, tool kits, and press releases—and its web pages.

ALA Council and Intellectual Freedom Committee Documents

On January 23, 2002, the ALA Council approved the "Resolution Reaffirming the Principles of Intellectual Freedom in the Aftermath of Terrorist Attacks." Beginning with Benjamin Franklin's stirring words, "They that can give up essential liberty to obtain a little temporary safety deserve neither liberty nor safety" and resolving that the ALA "encourages libraries and their staff to protect the privacy and confidentiality of the people's lawful use of the library, its equipment, and its resources" (Policy 52.4, "Policy on Confidentiality of Library Records"), the Council voted to send the resolution to the President, the U.S. Attorney General, and members of both Houses of Congress.[45]

The ALA Council further emphasized the importance of patron privacy by adopting the "Privacy: An Interpretation of the Library Bill of Rights" statement on June 19, 2002. The Council's actions and the language of the document reaffirmed that "The library profession has a long-standing commitment to an ethic of facilitating, not monitoring access to information."[46] The full text of these statements appears in Appendix I.

Previously endorsed by many divisions and units within the ALA, the ALA Council adopted the "Resolution on the USA PATRIOT Act and Related Measures That Infringe on the Rights of Library Users" on January 29, 2003. Forty-nine state library associations have either endorsed the ALA's resolution or adopted similar statements. The resolution encourages all librarians "to educate their users, staff, and communities about the process for compliance with the USA PATRIOT Act . . . and about the dangers to individual privacy and the confidentiality of library records resulting from those measures."[47]

The Intellectual Freedom Committee of the ALA tirelessly continued its work of defending patron privacy, and the ALA's Office for Intellectual Freedom and the ALA Washington Office web pages have extensive information on privacy and the USA PATRIOT Act. In September 2003, the ALA "Privacy Tool Kit" was posted on the ALA Intellectual Freedom web site (http://www.ala.org/oif). A very extensive resource, it does the following:

- Provides background on the ALA's historical efforts to protect privacy and confidentiality.
- Explains state and federal privacy laws.
- Details how a privacy audit is conducted and supplies sample privacy and confidentiality policies.
- Recommends procedures for law enforcement visits.

Sections continue to be posted and reviewed for currency.

The Privacy Subcommittee of the ALA Intellectual Freedom Committee revised the "Policy Concerning Confidentiality of Personally Identifiable Information about Library Users," and the ALA Council adopted the changes in June 2004. In reality, the work of the ALA Intellectual Freedom Committee and the Privacy Subcommittee will never be completed. In addition, the more traditional intellectual freedom issues, such as censorship, have not been eliminated and continue to be monitored as the ALA committees work on the latest threats to intellectual freedom. The ALA staff and its member volunteers have done an excellent job of keeping librarians, library trustees, and the general public aware of the threats to civil liberties inherent in the USA PATRIOT Act.

Monitoring the Use of the USA PATRIOT Act in Libraries

Dr. Leigh Estabrook, director of the Library Research Center at the University of Illinois, Urbana-Champaign, conducted two surveys to determine the effects of September 11, 2001, and the USA PATRIOT Act on public libraries. The first survey, entitled "Public Libraries Response to the Events of September 11th," was conducted in December 2001. Sent to 1,503 public libraries, it included questions on the USA PATRIOT Act and library surveillance. A total of 4.1 percent, or 85 libraries, of those responding answered affirmatively to the question "Have authorities (e.g., FBI, police) requested any information about your patrons pursuant to the events of Sept. 11th?"[48]

In October 2002, the second University of Illinois, Urbana-Champaign survey polled directors of 1,505 of the 5,094 public libraries serving over 5,000 persons. The following results were reported in "Public Libraries and Civil Liberties: A Profession Divided" written by Dr. Leigh S. Estabrook. Of the 911 libraries that responded, at least 545 libraries were visited in the last year by local and federal law enforcement officials who asked for borrowers' records, including 178 visits from the FBI. It is important to note that fifteen libraries indicated that they did not answer some questions because they were unable to do so legally. Nearly 60 percent of respondents felt the gag order placed on libraries was an abridgement of First Amendment rights.[49]

The California Library Association Intellectual Freedom Committee surveyed its members during the summer of 2003 and received data from 344 public, academic, school, and special libraries as well as library schools. Fourteen libraries indicated FBI agents had formally contacted them for patron record information.[50]

The ALA plans to conduct its own survey of U.S. libraries to determine how often federal agents have used the USA PATRIOT Act to access patron records. According to Emily Sheketoff, executive director of the ALA Washington Office, "This information will be crucial for the U.S. Congress when they begin debate on amending and/or expanding the PATRIOT Act. . . . We also hope to segue into a more long-term, broad understanding of the impact of weakened privacy protections on the attitudes and actions of people who use libraries and the services that libraries provide."[51] Care will be taken in the survey not to ask library staff to violate the USA PATRIOT Act's gag rule.

Response of Libraries to the USA PATRIOT Act

The University of Illinois's 2002 survey indicated that there is some disagreement in the profession between those who believe in holding firm to the principle of protecting patron privacy and confidentiality of library records while "others believe that it may be necessary to compromise some of those principles to deter terrorism or abide by the law."[52] Judith Krug, director of the ALA's Office for Intellectual Freedom, counsels, "People are scared and they think that by giving up their rights, especially their right to privacy, they will be safe. But it wasn't the right to privacy that let terrorists into our nation. It had nothing to do with libraries or library records."[53]

Libraries across the country have responded to the USA PATRIOT Act in a variety of ways. According to the University of Illinois 2002 survey, 69.1 percent of libraries have informed staff or library boards about library policies relating to patron privacy.[54] Among one of the first library systems to post warnings about the USA PATRIOT Act, the Santa Cruz Public Library System now shreds discarded library documents containing patron identification once a week instead of once a month.[55] Like other libraries, staff have informed patrons the library is considering what records need to be kept. Mark Corallo, spokesperson for the Justice Department, noted that it is legal for libraries to destroy records; however, it is illegal to destroy records that have been subpoenaed.[56]

The Skokie, Illinois, public library posts this sign throughout the facility:

> The Skokie Public Library makes every effort to guard your privacy in use of library materials and computers. However, due to the terms of the USA PATRIOT Act (Public Law 107-56), federal officials may require the library to provide information about your use of library resources without informing you that we have done so. The USA PATRIOT Act was initiated by Attorney General John Ashcroft.[57]

On the other hand, Maurice J. Freedman, former ALA president and director of the Westminster (New York) library system, stated, "Many other libraries including those in Westchester, decided that warnings might unnecessarily alarm patrons. There are people, especially older people who lived through the McCarthy era, who might be intimidated by this."[58]

On June 12, 2003, the Greenfield (Wisconsin) Public Library Board passed a resolution supporting HR1157, the Freedom to Read Protection Act, which would exempt libraries and bookstores from Section 215 of the USA PATRIOT Act. The board's president also sent a letter to Wisconsin Senators Russ Feingold and Herbert H. Kohl regarding the board's action.[59] This resolution joins those of 358 communities in 43 states to oppose the intrusive provisions of the USA PATRIOT Act.[60]

Whatever the philosophy of the library's director and governing body, the ALA has provided written guidance to staff who receive visits from city, county, state, and federal law enforcement agencies. The guide "Confidentiality and Coping with Law Enforcement Inquiries: Guidelines for the Library and Its Staff" is available on the ALA Office for Intellectual Freedom web pages (http://www.ala.org/oif).

Attorney General John Ashcroft's Defense of the USA PATRIOT Act

During 2003, U.S. Attorney General John Ashcroft aggressively defended the USA PATRIOT Act in a series of eighteen speaking engagements across the United States. The tone of the attorney general's speeches changed as he found increasing media references to breaches in library patron privacy under the USA PATRIOT Act. On September 15, speaking to the National Restaurant Association in Washington, DC, the attorney general ridiculed librarians' concerns, stating, "The Justice Department has no interest in your reading habits. Tracking reading habits would betray our high regard for the First Amendment."[61] He "accused the ALA and other administration critics of fueling 'baseless hysteria' about the government's use of the PATRIOT Act to pry into the public's reading habits."[62]

ALA President Carla Hayden responded quickly to Ashcroft's attacks for the association. "We are deeply concerned that the attorney general should be so openly contemptuous of those who seek to defend our Constitution. Rather than ask the nations' librarians and Americans nationwide to just trust him, Ashcroft could allay concerns by releasing aggregate information about the number of libraries visited using the expanded powers created by the USA PATRIOT Act."[63]

On September 17, 2003, in a telephone call to ALA President Carla Hayden, John Ashcroft pleaded misunderstanding of his commitment to civil liberties and said he would declassify the Justice Department's report on the use of Section 215. Following the call, Dr. Hayden noted, "I am glad the Attorney General finally agreed to declassify this report after almost two years of seeking an open and full accounting of activity by federal agents in libraries."[64]

Previously, Justice Department officials had indicated that the law had been used; however, they declined to give specifics citing national security concerns. Therefore, on September 18, 2003, Ashcroft surprised his critics with an announcement while speaking to law enforcement officials in Memphis. He read from a newly declassified memo to FBI Director Robert Mueller, "The number of times Section 215 [USA PATRIOT Act] has been used to date is zero."[65] He further responded to those who opposed the USA PATRIOT Act on the basis of violation of Constitutional rights by saying, "Not a single court in America has validated any of the charges of violations of constitutional rights in connection with the Patriot. And so the charges of the hysterics are revealed for what they are: castles in the air, built on misrepresentation, supported by the unfounded fear, held aloft by hysteria."[66] Ridiculing librarians' concerns over FBI visits to libraries, Ashcroft went on to say, "The fact is, with just 11,000 FBI agents and over a billion visitors to America's libraries each year, the Department of Justice has neither the staffing, the time nor the inclination to monitor the reading habits of Americans. No offense to the American Library Association, but we just don't care."[67]

Emily Sheketoff, executive director of the ALA Washington Office, acknowledged Ashcroft's comments by saying, "If this number [zero] is accurate, then they have demonstrated that there is no need to change the tradition of protecting library patrons' reading records."[68] Ironically, FBI records, obtained in June 2004 under a Freedom of Information Act (FOIA) request filed in October 2003 by the American Civil Liberties Union and others, indicate that less than a month after Ashcroft claimed no libraries were visited under Section 215, the FBI sought to use Section 215.[69]

Where does the truth lie? Some respondents to the University of Illinois surveys in 2001 and 2002 say they have been visited under Section 215, and there was also some information gained from records released from the ACLU et al. FOIA request described earlier. In an attempt to gain a current understanding of the situation, in January 2005 the American Library Association launched a set of web-based surveys to better assess the impact of the USA PATRIOT Act on public and academic libraries and their patrons. In conjunction with academic researchers, ALA will attempt to "quantify and examine contacts by federal law enforcement agencies."[70] The web-based surveys will ask 1,536 public and 4,221 academic library directors[71] about contacts with law enforcement agents in libraries, policy changes made since the USA PATRIOT Act was passed, and changes observed in patron behavior in libraries. The results are expected by June 2005 and may be used to create a resource for dealing with federal law enforcement agents. Even more importantly, results will provided to Congress to inform their debate about the sunsetting portions of the USA PATRIOT Act.[72] A full and far-reaching debate is expected over Section 215 and other sections of the PATRIOT Act that will sunset in December 2005.

Attempts to Amend the USA PATRIOT Act

In July 2004, House lawmakers attempted to rectify library concerns about Section 215 with the Freedom to Read amendment to the Commerce, Justice, and State Appropriations bill. It would have prohibited use of "section 501 of the Foreign Intelligence Surveillance Act of 1978 for an order requiring the production of library circulation records, library patron lists, library Internet records, book sales records, or book customer lists."[73]

When this change was first considered as an Amendment to a large appropriations bill, members of Congress had fifteen minutes to vote on it. At the end of the fifteen minutes, the bill appeared on the way to passage.[74] Rather than ending debate, the Republican leadership held open the voting for an additional twenty-three minutes, using that time to persuade ten Republican members to change their votes.[75] Unlike the many times Attorney General Ashcroft has claimed that the FBI is not interested in library records, the Department of Justice lobbied against passage of this amendment. "Representative Frank Wolf (R-VA) read a letter from the Justice Department stating that 'as recently as this past winter and spring, a member of a terrorist group closely affiliated with al-Qaida' had used Internet services at a public library."[76]

Ultimately, the amendment failed to pass, with the vote of record being 210 in favor, 210 against, and one member voting "present."[77] Support for Bernie Sanders' Freedom to Read Protection Act (H.S. 1157) continued to grow after the House defeat in July 2004. Since no action was taken, this bill and other bills in both Houses of Congress adding protections for libraries and booksellers died at the end of the 108th Congress's term in December 2004.[78] Some of the legislation, however, was reintroduced by pro-privacy legislators in the 109th Congress which began in 2005.

Given the 2004 reelection of George W. Bush, the further erosion of Democratic power in Congress, and the replacement of Attorney General John Ashcroft with former White House Counsel Alberto Gozales, it is impossible to foresee the outcome of the national security versus privacy and civil liberties debate. These have been only the opening skirmishes in what promises to be an epic battle over the sunsetting of portions of the USA PATRIOT Act on December 31, 2005. Yet as the library community and others interested in preserving civil liberties gear up for the upcoming debate, the words of the "ALA Privacy: An Interpretation of the Library Bill of Rights" remains as a reminder: "Lack of privacy and confidentiality has a chilling effect on users' choices. All users have a right to be free from any unreasonable intrusion into or surveillance of their lawful library use."[79]

Two Small Victories

In late September 2004, a federal judge in New York struck down as unconstitutional Section 505 of the USA PATRIOT Act, stating that "democracy abhors undue secrecy."[80] The lesser known Section 505 had given the government authority to issue "National Security Letters" to obtain customer records from Internet Service Providers and other businesses without judicial oversight. The court also found a gag provision in the law to be an "'unconstitutional prior restraint' on free speech."[81] The judge in *Doe and ACLU v. Ashcroft et al.* stayed his ruling for ninety days to give the government time to appeal.[82] The ruling is the second to strike down any part of the surveillance powers authorized by the USA PATRIOT Act. The first case involved five groups and two U.S. citizens who wished to provide support for nonviolent activities for Kurdish refugees in Turkey. In a 2003 decision, a U.S. District Judge said "the ban on providing 'expert advice or assistance' is impermissibly vague, in violation of the First and Fifth Amendments."[83]

The Campaign for Reader Privacy

In his January 2004 State of the Union address, President Bush asked Congress to reauthorize the USA PATRIOT Act to ensure that law enforcement agents have the tools they need to fight terrorism. "Booksellers are deeply concerned about the chilling effect of Section 215 and President Bush's stated intent to seek blanket reauthorization of the PATRIOT Act," said American Booksellers Association Chief Operating Officer Oren Teicher.[84]

In February 2004, the Campaign for Reader Privacy was introduced by the American Booksellers Association, the American Library Association, and the PEN American Center. The campaign aimed to gather one million signatures on petitions opposing Section 215 and asked Congress to amend Section 215 to restore the privacy of library and bookstore records to pre–USA PATRIOT Act standing. Signatures were gathered at libraries, at bookstores, and at the web site http://www.readerprivacy.com/. In September, the American Library Association, the Association of American Publishers, and the PEN American Center presented Congress with more than 185,000 signatures on Reader Privacy petitions.[85] "This isn't about stripping law enforcement of the power to investigate terrorism. It's about restoring confidence that our reading choices aren't being monitored by the government," said Larry Siems, director of PEN's Freedom to Write Program.[86] The drive continues as the three partnering organizations work to obtain their goal of one million signatures.

Conclusion

Libraries are part of a changing and seemingly more dangerous post-September 11 world. When the privacy and confidentiality of their patrons were threatened, librarians and their national organization stood firm. They re-evaluated their core values, created new policy statements and tools for ensuring patron privacy, notified their patrons of threats to privacy, and campaigned for changes in the USA PATRIOT Act. Although accused of being "hysterics," they understood what was at stake and chose to act upon their Code of Ethics.

The right of privacy in the use of a library's services and resources will remain of paramount importance to the library profession. This right rests on statutory protections, strong support and advocacy from professional associations, like the ALA, and local library policies upheld by committed staff and the full support of library governing authorities. Threats to library privacy did not start with the Library Awareness Program, and they will not end with the USA PATRIOT Act. As Thomas Jefferson stated, "The price of freedom is eternal vigilance,"[87] and the price to ensure library privacy requires the same vigilance.

Notes

1. "Libraries in the United States," World Book Online, http://www.world bookonline.com (accessed July 30, 2004).

2. Tomas A. Lipinski and Mary Minow, *The Library's Legal Answer Book* (Chicago, London: American Library Association, 2003), 166.

3. "State Privacy Laws Regarding Library Records," American Library Association, http://www.ala.org/alaorg/oif/stateprivacylaws.html (accessed April 7, 2004).

4. "Position Statement on the Confidentiality of Library Records," American Library Association, May 11, 2004, http://www.ala.org/ala/aasl/aaslproftools/positionstatements/aaslpositionstatementconfidentiality.htm (accessed April 7, 2004).

5. General Statutes of Connecticut, Title 11, Libraries Chapter 190 Public Libraries, http://www.cga.state.ct.us/2003/pub/Chap190.htm (accessed June 1, 2004).

6. New York State Consolidated Laws, Civil Practice Law & Rules, Article 45, Library records, section 4509, http://caselaw.lp.findlaw.com/nycodes/c16/a36.html (accessed June 2, 2004).

7. "Release of Library Record or Patron Information," Ohio Revised Code Title I, CHAPTER 149.432 (B)(1), http://onlinedocs.andersonpublishing.com/oh/lpExt.dll?f=templates&fn=main-h.htm&cp=PORC (accessed April 10, 2004).

8. Lipinski and Minow, *The Library's Legal Answer Book*, 200–210.

9. Mary Minow, "The USA PATRIOT Act and Patron Privacy on Library Internet Terminals," February 15, 2002, http://www.llrx.com/features/usapatriotact.htm (accessed April 13, 2004).

10. Robert Paul, interview by Robert Bocher, March 19, 2004.

11. Kansas Statutes, Chapter 45, Public Records, Documents And Information, Article 2, Records Open to Public, http://www.kslegislature.org/cgi-bin/statutes/index.cgi/45-221.html (accessed June 1, 2004).

12. Michael Cross, interview by Robert Bocher, Madison, WI, May 15, 2004.

13. "Public Library Records," Wisconsin State Statutes, Chapter 43.30, http://folio.legis.state.wi.us/cgi-bin/om_isapi.dll?clientID=31674222&infobase=stats.nfo&j1=43&jump=43&softpage=Browse_Frame_Pg (accessed June 1, 2004).

14. Lipinski and Minow, *The Library's Legal Answer Book*, p. 177.

15. "St. Louis PL Redefines Internet Sign-Up Sheets as Private," *American Libraries Online*, March 10, 2003, http://www.ala.org/ala/alonline/currentnews/newsarchive/2003/march2003/stlouisplredefines.htm (accessed April 14, 2004).

16. "Code of Ethics of the American Library Association," American Library Association, June 28, 1995, http://www.ala.org/ala/oif/statementspols/codeofethics/codeethics.htm (accessed April 12, 2004).

17. "Policy on Confidentiality of Library Records," American Library Association, July 2, 1986, http://www.ala.org/Template.cfm?Section=otherpolicies&Template=/ContentManagement/ContentDisplay.cfm&ContentID=13084 (accessed April 13, 2004).

18. "Policy Concerning Confidentiality of Personally Identifiable Information about Library Users," American Library Association, July 2, 1991, http://www.ala.

org/Template.cfm?Section=otherpolicies&Template=/ContentManagement/Con
tentDisplay.cfm&ContentID=13087 (accessed April 14, 2004).

19. "Policy Concerning Confidentiality of Personally Identifiable Information about Library Users," American Library Association, June 30, 2004, http://www.ala.org/Template.cfm?Section=Other_Policies_and_Guidelines&Template=/Con
tentManagement/ContentDisplay.cfm&ContentID=13087 (accessed April 14, 2004).

20. "Privacy: An Interpretation of the Library Bill of Rights," American Library Association, June 19, 2002, http://www.ala.org/ala/oif/statementspols/statement
sif/interpretations/privacyinterpretation.pdf (accessed April 14, 2004).

21. "Principles for the Networked World," American Library Association, February 2003, http://www.ala.org/ala/washoff/washpubs/principles.pdf (accessed April 14, 2004).

22. Herbert N. Foerstel, *Refuge of a Scoundrel: The Patriot Act in Libraries* (Westport, CT: Libraries Unlimited, 2004), 1.

23. Ibid., 2.

24. Herbert Foerstel, "Secrecy in Science: Exploring University, Industry, and Government Relationships" (Remarks, Panel II, Massachusetts Institute of Technology, Cambridge, Massachusetts, March 29, 1999).

25. Foerstel, *Scoundrel*, 3.

26. Ibid., 4.

27. Ibid., 9.

28. Ibid.

29. American Library Association Government Documents Round Table, "Resolution in Opposition to FBI Library Awareness Program," GODORT, 1988, http://sunsite.berkeley.edu/GODORT/resolutions/880713774.html (accessed July 4, 2004).

30. Ralph G. Neas, "After a Fifteen Year Absence, the FBI Returned to Your Library: The Patriot Act's Attack on the Freedom to Read," People for the American Way, http://www.pfaw.org/pfaw/general/default.aspx?oid=10341 (accessed July 4, 2004).

31. Foerstel, *Scoundrel*, 11.

32. "The Patriot," *Isthmus*, Vol. 28, No. 27 (July 4, 2003): 13.

33. "Protecting Civil Liberties in a Time of Crisis," http://www.cfr.org/pub4131/morton_h_halperin/protecting_civil_liberties_at_a_time_of_crisis.php (accessed July 12, 2004).

34. Poll: Security Trumps Civil Liberties, November 30, 2001, http://www.npr.org/news/specials/civillibertiespoll/011130.poll.html (accessed July 11, 2004).

35. Ibid.

36. NPR/Kaiser/Kennedy School Civil Liberties Update, September 9, 2002, http://www.npr.org/news/specials/civillibertiespoll2/index.html (accessed July 11, 2004).

37. Ibid.

38. "The USA Patriot Act: A Sketch," by Charles Doyle, Senior Specialist in American Law at the Congressional Research Service, http://fpc.state.gov/documents/organization/10091.pdf (accessed July 17, 2004). This source is an extremely readable summary of the changes the PATRIOT Act made to existing law. A more detailed legal analysis was published by the same author, at http://fpc.state.gov/documents/organization/10092.pdf.

39. Analysis by various legal scholars, http://www.abanet.org/irr/hr/winter02.html, particularly the article by former chief of staff to President Clinton, John

Podesta, http://www.abanet.org/irr/hr/winter02/podesta.html (both accessed April 25, 2004).

40. 50 U.S.C. 1861 §501 (Amended by §215 of the PATRIOT Act). The full text reads:

SEC. 215. ACCESS TO RECORDS AND OTHER ITEMS UNDER THE FOREIGN INTELLIGENCE SURVEILLANCE ACT.

Title V of the Foreign Intelligence Surveillance Act of 1978 (50 U.S.C. 1861 et seq.) is amended by striking sections 501 through 503 and inserting the following:

"SEC. 501. ACCESS TO CERTAIN BUSINESS RECORDS FOR FOREIGN INTELLIGENCE AND INTERNATIONAL TERRORISM INVESTIGATIONS.

"(a)(1) The Director of the Federal Bureau of Investigation or a designee of the Director (whose rank shall be no lower than Assistant Special Agent in Charge) may make an application for an order requiring the production of any tangible things (including books, records, papers, documents, and other items) for an investigation to protect against international terrorism or clandestine intelligence activities, provided that such investigation of a United States person is not conducted solely upon the basis of activities protected by the first amendment to the Constitution.

"(2) An investigation conducted under this section shall—

"(A) be conducted under guidelines approved by the Attorney General under Executive Order 12333 (or a successor order); and

"(B) not be conducted of a United States person solely upon the basis of activities protected by the first amendment to the Constitution of the United States.

"(b) Each application under this section—

"(1) shall be made to—

"(A) a judge of the court established by section 103(a); or

"(B) a United States Magistrate Judge under chapter 43 of title 28, United States Code, who is publicly designated by the Chief Justice of the United States to have the power to hear applications and grant orders for the production of tangible things under this section on behalf of a judge of that court; and

"(2) shall specify that the records concerned are sought for an authorized investigation conducted in accordance with subsection (a)(2) to obtain foreign intelligence information not concerning a United States person or to protect against international terrorism or clandestine intelligence activities.

"(c)(1) Upon an application made pursuant to this section, the judge shall enter an ex parte order as requested, or as modified, approving the release of records if the judge finds that the application meets the requirements of this section.

"(2) An order under this subsection shall not disclose that it is issued for purposes of an investigation described in subsection (a).

"(d) No person shall disclose to any other person (other than those persons necessary to produce the tangible things under this section) that the Federal Bureau of Investigation has sought or obtained tangible things under this section.

"(e) A person who, in good faith, produces tangible things under an order pursuant to this section shall not be liable to any other person for such production. Such production shall not be deemed to constitute a waiver of any privilege in any other proceeding or context.

SEC. 502. CONGRESSIONAL OVERSIGHT.

"(a) On a semiannual basis, the Attorney General shall fully inform the Permanent Select Committee on Intelligence of the House of Representatives and the Select Committee on Intelligence of the Senate concerning all requests for the production of tangible things under section 402.

"(b) On a semiannual basis, the Attorney General shall provide to the Committees on the Judiciary of the House of Representatives and the Senate a report setting forth with respect to the preceding 6-month period—

"(1) the total number of applications made for orders approving requests for the production of tangible things under section 402; and
"(2) the total number of such orders either granted, modified, or denied."

41. 50 U.S.C. §1861 et seq.
42. Deborah Caldwell-Stone, email message to author Helen Adams, August 9, 2004.
43. American Civil Liberties Union, Section 215 FAQ, October 24, 2002, http://www.aclu.org/Privacy/Privacy.cfm?ID=11054&c=130 (accessed July 18, 2004).
44. 50 U.S.C. §1861(a) (Amended by §215 of the Patriot Act).
45. American Library Association Council, "Resolution Reaffirming the Principles of Intellectual Freedom in the Aftermath of Terrorist Attacks," adopted January 23, 2002, http://www.ala.org/Template.cfm?Section=IF_Resolutions&Template=/ContentManagement/ContentDisplay.cfm&ContentID=32463 (accessed July 5, 2004).
46. American Library Association Council, "Privacy: An Interpretation of the Library Bill of Rights," adopted June 19, 2002, http://www.ala.org/Template.cfm?Section=interpretations&Template=/ContentManagement/ContentDisplay.cfm&ContentID=34182 (accessed July 5, 2004).
47. American Library Association Council, "Resolution on the USA Patriot Act and Related Measures that Infringe on the Rights of Library Users," January 29, 2003, http://www.ala.org/Template.cfm?Section=ifresolutions&Template=/ContentManagement/ContentDisplay.cfm&ContentID=11891 (accessed July 6, 2004).
48. Foerstel, *Scoundrel*, 89.
49. Leigh S. Estabrook, "Public Libraries and Civil Liberties: A Profession Divided," The Library Research Center, University of Illinois at Urbana-Champaign, http://alexia.lis.uiuc.edu/gslis/research/civil_liberties.html (accessed July 7, 2004).
50. "FBI Visited 16 California Libraries Since 9/11," *American Libraries* 34, no. 10 (November 2003), http://web5.epnet.com (accessed July 5, 2004).
51. American Library Association Public Information Office, "ALA to Launch USA PATRIOT Study," June 28, 2004, http://www.ala.org/la/press2004/PATRIOTSTUDY.htm (accessed July 9, 2004).
52. Estabrook, "Public Libraries and Civil Liberties."
53. "FBI Checks Out Library Records of Terrorists," *USA Today*, June 25, 2002, http://www.usatoday/com/news/sept11/2002/06/fbi-libraries.htm (accessed June 7, 2004).
54. Estabrook, "Public Libraries and Civil Liberties."
55. Dean E. Murphy, "Some Librarians Use Shredder to Show Opposition to New FBI Powers," *New York Times*, April 7, 2003, A12.
56. Ibid.
57. Gail Gibson, "Librarians Set Aside 'shhh' to Speak Out for Privacy; Patriot Act: Government Access to Data on Library Users Criticized by the Normally Quiet Types," *The Sun* (Baltimore, MD), June 24, 2004, http://proquest.umi.com (accessed July 6, 2004).
58. Murphy, "Some Librarians Use Shredder."
59. "Libraries Make Statements About USA Patriot Act," *WLA E-Newsletter*, Vol. 2, Issue 5, July 3, 2003.
60. Noah Leavitt, "Flipping Off Bush on Civil Liberties," Alternet, October 27, 2004, http://www.alternet.org/story/20300 (accessed November 11, 2004).

61. Eric Lightblau, "Ashcroft Mocks Librarians and Others Who Oppose Parts of Counterterrorism Law," *New York Times,* September 16, 2003, http://www.ny times.com/2003/09/16/politics/16LIBR.html?ex=10891 (accessed July 5, 2004).

62. "Ashcroft Mocks Librarians in Patriot Act Defense," *American Libraries,* November 2003, vol. 34, issue 10, p. 10, http://web5.epnet.com (accessed July 5, 2004).

63. Norman Oder, "Ashcroft Agrees to Release Report on FBI Library Visits," *Library Journal,* vol. 128, issue 17 (October 15, 2003):16.

64. Ibid.

65. Eric Mink, "A Culture of Mis/Disinformation: The Administration Works Harder to Obscure the Truth Than to Clarify It," Knight Ridder Tribune News Service, October 2, 2003, http://proquest.umi.com (accessed July 5, 2004).

66. Michelle Mittelstadt, "Justice Department Aggressively Defending the Patriot Act," Knight Ridder Tribune News Service, September 26, 2003, http:// proquest.umi.com (accessed July 5, 2004).

67. Ibid.

68. Knight Ridder, "Memo Shows US Has Not Used Patriot Act to Seek Library Data," September 18, 2003, Globe Newspaper Company, http://www.boston.com /news//nation/washington/articles/2003/0918/memo_shows_us_has_not_used_ patriot_act_toseek_library_data/ (accessed July 5, 2004).

69. American Library Association Public Information Office, "Just-Released FBI Documents Confirm ALA USA Patriot Act Concerns," June 22, 2004, http:// www.ala.org/pr2004/june2004/FOIA.htm (accessed July 9, 2004).

70. "ALA Begins PATRIOT Study to Measure Law Enforcement Activity in Libraries," Press Release, American Library Association, January 5, 2005; http:// www.ala.org/ala/pressreleases2005/january2005a/PATRIOTStudy.htm   (accessed January 21, 2005).

71. Brad Martin, "Anti-Terrorism Legislation and Libraries," *Cognotes,* Issue 4, January 17, 2005, 7.

72. "ALA Begins PATRIOT Study to Measure."

73. H.AMDT.652 to HR 4754, http://thomas.loc.gov (accessed July 17, 2004).

74. Comments of Normal Singleton, Legislative Director to Rep. Ron Paul (R-Texas), http://www.politechbot.com/2004/07/13/patriot-act-vote/ (accessed July 17, 2004).

75. AP Wire Service, "Bush Wins; House Leaves Patriot Act As Is," *New York Times,* July 9, 2004, http://www.nytimes.com/aponline/national/AP-Congress-Pa triot-Act.html?hp (accessed July 17, 2004).

76. Ibid.

77. Voting "present" was Rep. Zoe Lofgren. For a complete list of this roll-call vote, see http://clerk.house.gov/evs/2004/roll339.xml (accessed July 18, 2004).

78. "Freedom to Read Protection Act Co-Sponsors Now at 151," *Bookselling This Week,* July 28, 2004, http://news.bookweb.org/freeexpression/ (accessed August 6, 2004).

79. "Privacy: An Interpretation of the Library Bill of Rights."

80. "Censorship and Secrecy May Potentially Be Turned on Ourselves as a Weapon of Self-Destruction, Court Says," ACLU Press Release, September 29, 2004, http://www.aclu.org/SafeandFree/SafeandFree.cfm?ID=16603&c=282   (accessed November 16, 2004).

81. Ibid.

82. Ibid.

83. "Federal Judge Rules Part of Patriot Act Unconstitutional," January 26, 2003, Law Center, CNN.com, http://www.cnn.com/2004/LAW/01/26/patriot.act.ap/ (accessed November 16, 2004).

84. "Book, Library Groups Launch Petition Drive to Restore Privacy Safeguards to USA PATRIOT Act," Press Release, Campaign for Reader Privacy, February 17, 2004, http://www.readerprivacy.com/?mod[type]=press (accessed July 5, 2004).

85. "CRP Sponsors Vow to Continue Battle to Amend Section 215," *Bookselling This Week*, November 11, 2004, http://news.bookweb.org/3022.html (accessed November 11, 2004).

86. "Book, Library Groups Launch Petition Drive."

87. Thomas Jefferson, "Sayings," *Word iQ Encyclopedia*, http://www.wordiq.com/definition/Thomas_Jefferson#Sayings (accessed August 13, 2004).

CHAPTER 4

Privacy Issues for Public Libraries

Introduction

Public librarians have long concerned themselves with protecting the privacy of their patrons and their patrons' use of library resources and services. While some public libraries have restrictions on use (e.g., a patron residency requirement), they do not restrict by age, sex, employment, enrollment, or any other factors that narrow the focus and mission of other types of libraries. This core mission of public libraries—the commitment to serve any and all—has a parallel commitment in privacy protection. That is, public libraries have an ethical and often a legal obligation to protect the privacy of any and all patrons who use the library. Patrons of public libraries should feel that they enjoy the same right of privacy when reading a book in the library as they would when reading that book in the privacy of their own residence.

Privacy and Patron Use of a Library's Resources and Services

Privacy and the Circulation of Library Materials

Historically the protection of patron privacy in public libraries has centered on record keeping processes related to the circulation of materials. This is evident in the many state library privacy statutes that assert the need to protect in these or comparable terms, the "data that link a library patron's name with materials requested or borrowed."[1] In the past two decades, the increasing use of technology to access information services available through the library has significantly increased concerns related to patron privacy beyond just the items a patron has checked out.

While the dramatic increase of information in electronic form has greatly expanded library services, the circulation of print and nonprint materials remains an essential mission. Public libraries have a higher circulation rate than other types of libraries, and circulation is used as a key measure of library use. Many patrons still visit the library to check out popular materials, and for reading, print is still their medium of choice. (Of course print is usually the only choice for popular monographs.) A person's reading habits can tell much about that person and for this reason the circulation records held by libraries have sometimes been referred to as "social surveillance" systems.[2] Thus, the protection of circulation information, whether for print or nonprint titles, is still of paramount importance.

The typical circulation transaction involves several steps and points of interaction related to the item being checked out, the patron, and staff. Many of these transactions have privacy implications, for example,

- What titles a patron is checking out or has currently checked out
- What titles a patron has on hold or reserve
- What titles a patron has that have outstanding fines
- Items damaged or reported lost by the patron

Circulation: From Manual to Integrated Systems

Before the advent of automated circulation systems, most circulation information was maintained in paper files, or in some instances on microform. It was not unusual to find libraries with manual systems that had checkout cards in books which clearly identified patrons who had previously checked out the title. Manual systems of this type are still used in some smaller public libraries.

The decade from the mid-1980s to the mid-1990s saw the proliferation of Integrated Library Systems (ILS) in much of the library world, including public libraries. Early adaptors started with automating circulation, one of the most labor-intensive functions in public libraries. Later it became common for libraries to implement more complete integrated systems that included other modules for acquisitions, serials, cataloging, and an OPAC (Online Public Access Catalog). The implementation of an integrated system may not have in itself required a change in the library's privacy policy. However, such systems certainly required that substantial procedural changes be implemented to uphold that policy. For example, integrated systems require the security of current and archival data in formats that are obviously very different from older paper-based systems. Also, in older systems there was often a single physical location for protected patron circulation information, and anyone wanting to access the information had to be in that same location, which was almost always the library itself. With integrated systems there are multiple physical locations for circulation data and there can be an almost unlimited number of access points located far from where the protected circulation information is stored, and far beyond the physical boundaries of the library. This factor in itself—the decentralized location of information and the decentralized access to it—requires considerable changes in library procedures to ensure the security and protection of patrons' personally identifiable information (PII).

In an automated circulation system the process of checking out an item creates a circulation transaction record that is stored on a server. This record links the patron's ID (i.e., barcode) to the item's barcode. This link persists until the item is discharged. The discharge, or check-in function, while breaking the link between the patron's barcode and a specific item, does not mean that such a link cannot be reconstructed. As a matter of prudent system administration, all transactions from an integrated system are routinely backed up or archived. With the information from backup files it may be possible to reconstruct what a patron has checked out long after such a link has been severed during the real-time process of checking the item in. Library privacy policies, like the one at the Spokane, Washington, public library, should alert patrons to this possibility. Spokane's policy states that computer system backup files "are maintained for up to three months [and] could be used to reconstruct customer activity that occurred during that time period."[3] Besides data from regular checkout transactions, other circulation-related information, such as overdue items, outstanding fines, and items reported lost, is also retained by the ILS. In many public libraries, active files on fines and lost items may be kept for many months or even years, far longer than the maximum checkout period for the item. All these data, from current "live" transactions to archival records, which can link a patron's personally identifiable information to particular titles, are then readily available to anyone with access to the administrative or report functions of the integrated system. These data are also available to any law enforcement agency acting within proper legal channels to request them.

There are circumstances in which some data from the integrated system will be retained for very long periods. This is most often done for statistical purposes. Data such as circulation by month, by collection, by patron type, and so on are often kept long term as a valuable tool to help determine collection use patterns. When this occurs it is necessary to disaggregate a patron's PII from the use of any specific item. For example, it is useful to know that a given title has been checked out five times by adults at the north side branch in the past two years, but is it necessary to know which adults checked the item out? Like live data, any historical data that are retained linking use of a particular title to a particular patron are generally protected under state library privacy statutes.

Procedures must be in effect to ensure not just that active and archival files are secure but that no files related to patron PII are kept any longer than absolutely necessary. The American Library Association recommends retaining only the data necessary to conduct library business and only for the time needed to complete the transaction or business.[4] Some states have statutes that cover how long library records must be retained, and this may include records with patron information. A thorough review of your state statutes in this area is recommended. It is important to note that when complying with any legitimate request from law enforcement authorities for a specific patron's library use data, if the data do not exist, they cannot be provided. Furthermore, in the absence of state legislation defining the types of patron library use data that a public library must collect, this important responsibility is totally within the library's control.

By necessity, an automated circulation system has a patron database with information on each person that is registered. The types and amount of information stored in the patron database can be substantial. Much of the information is used for routine circulation functions and to formulate statistical reports to help the library better target its collection and services. Library management should thoroughly review the types and amount of information being collected as part of patron registration to determine whether there is a need for every data element. It is also critically important to determine whether confidentiality of the patron database is covered under state library privacy statutes. Statutory language typically refers to the protection of items or services a patron accesses or uses, but the law may not be clear as to whether the patron database itself is protected.

Radio Frequency Identification (RFID)

Some of the broader privacy aspects of RFID were covered in Chapter 2. Privacy issues related to RFID technology are of concern in the library environment too.

The vast majority of libraries with automated circulation systems still use standard barcodes to identify both items in the collection and patrons. However, in the past several years more than three hundred libraries, most of them public libraries, have replaced barcodes with RFID tags.[5] For libraries this is a fairly new technology, but it has been used in industry for many years. RFID offers several advantages compared to standard barcodes. For example, there is no need to precisely position the item as must be done when using a standard barcode scanner. This in turn has made it easier for patrons to use self-checkout stations enhancing their privacy. The Santa Clara, California, public library uses RFID, and its rate of patron self-checkout is between 35 and 40 percent.[6]

The use of RFID tags has raised privacy issues centered on concerns that the technology will make it easy to detect what patrons have checked out. In a more Orwellian scenario, Big Brother could be driving by your house with an RFID transponder and determine what items you have checked out from the library. Fortunately, the manner in which libraries are currently using RFID technology does not make this a realistic scenario.

> The use of RFID is a good example of technology outpacing policy, and while it may be too late to get ahead of the curve on this important issue, the library community needs at least to catch up with it. As Karen Schneider, well-known advocate for sensible library technology, has stated, "Many libraries are moving forward in implementing RFID technology without giving enough attention to its privacy implications."[7]

Library RFID tags are passive devices that usually cannot be read from more than a few feet away and they only store (or *should* only store) barcode numbers.

It behooves the library profession to make certain that all ramifications of the technology are fully addressed. This includes assurances that any changes, such as a move to "smart" tags that contain bibliographic or patron data, will employ encryption or other measures as needed to ensure patron privacy. In May 2004 the San Francisco Public Library Board passed a motion to move forward with one of the largest public library implementations of RFID yet undertaken even though several organizations spoke against approval partly because of concerns related to privacy.[8] Concerns about RFID and privacy led the American Library Association Council to pass a "Resolution on Radio Frequency Identification (RFID) Technology and Privacy Principles" (http://www.ala.org/ala/oif/stateme ntspols/ifresolutions/rfidresolution.htm) at its January 2005 mid-winter conference.

Interlibrary Loan

An ancillary function to circulation is interlibrary loan. Public libraries have a higher percentage of their circulation in interloans than any other type of library. In library cooperatives, where several libraries are part of a shared integrated system, patrons can often place their own holds directly on items held in the different libraries. In some shared systems, more than 20 percent of the circulation is really interloaning of items between libraries. In addition to the interloan function in shared integrated systems, separate automated interloan systems are becoming more common. In these systems patron data, or data that can be linked to a particular patron, may be held on a remote server at a library or vendor's facility a thousand miles away from where the interloan request originated. Many systems assign a separate ID number to track the activity on the request, but the ID may still be traced back to a particular patron. This is especially of concern where communication between interloan systems might take place over public (non-secure) Internet connections. Encryption or Virtual Private Network (VPN) tunneling strategies may be appropriate if there is potential for tracing requests back to individual users. Libraries using interloan systems where data are held at the vendor's remote facility should have privacy provisions written into any contract.[9] In addition the library should inquire if the vendor adheres to the *Privacy Guidelines for Electronic Resources Vendors* developed by the International Coalition of Library Consortia (ICOLC).[10]

The Checkout Process

Privacy concerns related to circulation extend beyond just maintaining the privacy and security of circulation data in the integrated system. Privacy is an issue even in the straightforward process of checking items out from the collection. Staff at the circulation desk should be circumspect about engaging patrons in casual conversations concerning what they are checking out. A staff comment about a patron checking out a popular cook book may not be much of an issue, but there are obviously other titles in the collection for which any comments by staff would be an invasion of privacy and inappropriate. Staff should also review the physical layout of the circulation area to make certain that the titles being checked out and returned by patrons are not needlessly displayed for wide public viewing. This includes taking sensible measures to make sure items on hold for patron pick-up are not prominently displayed in a public setting with the patron's name plainly visible. An increasing number of public libraries are installing patron self-checkout stations. As previously noted, these are most often installed to save on labor costs, but they also help safeguard patron privacy by giving patrons autonomy and control over their own circulation.

Other ILS Modules

Most privacy issues related to integrated systems focus on circulation, but other modules also must be considered. For example, online catalogs typically record searches and retain them for some period of time in transaction logs.[11] In most instances these logs do not identify an individual user, but there may be situations in which it is possible to link online catalog searches to a particular patron, for example, by correlating the timestamp on an OPAC search log with the same timestamp logged by workstation access management system software. In these systems patrons typically enter their library card number before they can use a workstation for either searching the library's catalog or surfing the web. (See the following section on workstation security.)

Privacy and Patron Use of the Internet in Public Libraries

If the decade from the mid-1980s to the mid-1990s saw the proliferation of integrated library systems, the decade from the mid-1990s to the mid-2000s saw public libraries embracing and providing patron access to the Internet. Survey data show the dramatic increase over the last decade in the number of public libraries offering public Internet access. In the first comprehensive nationwide survey of public library Internet use in 1994, only 12.7 percent had Internet workstations available to their patrons.[12] A similar survey conducted in 2002 showed that this figure had risen dramatically to 95.3 percent.[13] By now, no doubt, close to 100 percent of the just over 16,000 public libraries and branches in the country provide their patrons with access to the Internet.

Internet access is an ongoing issue in all libraries. Some considerations are rather mundane, but nevertheless very real, such as the messy task of dealing with printers attached to Internet workstations.

Other issues are much more substantive but difficult to address, such as patrons' accessing sexually explicit content. In relation to patron privacy, the use of a library's Internet workstations poses particular problems not found in more traditional services such as circulation. Public libraries offering Internet access confront additional concerns related to patron privacy that are not always pertinent to other types of libraries. The defining difference between public library Internet access and access in other types of libraries is the library's mission to address the information needs of any and all patrons, with the fewest restrictions and intrusions on their privacy. This mission is considerably different from that of K–12 schools in their provision of Internet access. Schools can have Internet use policies that are narrowly tailored to allow students Internet access only for a particular class assignment, or only under supervision of school staff. Legally, school staff act *in loco parentis* and thus can discipline students for inappropriate Internet use. Such restrictions and controls are exactly what public library staff do *not* want to impose on their patrons.

In addition to privacy concerns, legitimate restrictions on Internet use in K–12 schools raise very real First Amendment issues in public libraries. These concerns were noted in the Supreme Court's Children's Internet Protection Act (CIPA) decision when in his concurring opinion Justice Kennedy noted that "[i]f it is shown that an adult user's election to view constitutionally protected Internet material is burdened in some other substantial way," this could be the subject of future litigation.[14]

State privacy statutes should be closely reviewed to determine whether there is clear language covering Internet use and related issues such as Internet workstation sign-up sheets. A random review of fifteen state library privacy statutes found that only one of the fifteen, Ohio, specifically cited the need to protect patron Internet use.[15] Most privacy statutes were written before the Internet became a popular library service, and so it is not

---

Printers attached to public workstations are like public restrooms. They are messy and high-maintenance, and you never know what is happening inside them.

too surprising that there are few references to the Internet in state statutes. When no specific reference is found in the law, it then becomes necessary to determine whether other statutory language can be construed to ensure the privacy of Internet use. For example, Maryland refers to privacy as covering a patron's use of a "library's materials, services, or facilities."[16] One could reasonably argue that providing Internet access is a library "service" and thus covered under the law. Whether or not state law protects a patron's privacy when using the Internet, nothing prevents a library from having policies and procedures to ensure that only minimal electronic or paper recordkeeping is done regarding patron Internet use. Policies and procedures can also ensure that temporary Internet files stored on workstations are purged on a frequent basis. (See Chapter 3 where Internet issues in relation to state library privacy law are discussed in more detail.)

The issue of patron privacy when using Internet workstations in public libraries has taken on added significance since the terrorist attacks of September 11, 2001. After the FBI released the names of the hijackers, a staff member from a Florida public library notified authorities that one of the hijackers had visited the library and had used the Internet just a few weeks before the hijacking.[17] In subsequent actions, FBI agents seized Internet workstations from the library and reviewed Internet sign-up sheets from several other Florida public libraries. The federal agents complied with the provisions of Florida's library privacy statute.[18]

The librarian's action in notifying authorities that one of the suspected hijackers visited the library engendered considerable discussion in the library community on issues of patron privacy versus suspected criminal activity. Some of the discussion centered on such broad issues as, Is there a point at which the public welfare supersedes an individual's privacy rights? Some discussion was more narrowly focused, asking, for example, Is the mere fact of a patron's visit to the library protected under state privacy statutes or ALA statements on privacy? Or, What actions should staff take if they have reason to suspect a patron is using a library's Internet workstation or other services (e.g., a copy machine) to engage in illegal activity? Most questions of this type do not have clear, absolute answers. However, it must be noted that privacy provisions in library policy or state statutes do not extend to protecting any patrons engaged in illegal activities. But unless staff are peering over the shoulder of patrons, any use of the Internet to conduct illegal activity or any use of the Internet that violates the library's Acceptable Use Policy (AUP) can be very difficult to determine in a real-time environment. (The exception to this is a patron viewing possibly obscene images that may be visible from several feet away.)

From a privacy perspective, staff seldom want to be—nor should they be—placed in a proactive position of cyber police trying to determine what patrons will be doing at an Internet workstation. This issue has assumed considerable importance in light of the Supreme Court's decision in the CIPA case. The act allows staff to disable the Internet filter "during use by an adult, to enable access for bona fide research or other lawful purpose."[19] The ALA used the issue of patron privacy as part of its legal challenge to CIPA, noting in one of its trial briefs that "[p]eople will be reluctant to pursue the Act's disabling provisions [*sic*] if it requires them to reveal controversial, embarrassing or sensitive facts."[20] CIPA itself does not address the circumstances under which a patron can request unfiltered access, but the Supreme Court did in its decision. The court's opinion stated that adult patrons who want the filter disabled need only ask staff for unfiltered Internet access and need not explain why.[21] In light of the filter-disabling language in CIPA and the Supreme Court's ruling, public libraries should have a filter-disabling provision incorporated into their Internet AUP that both preserves a patron's privacy and protects basic First Amendment rights.

Helping to ensure patron privacy when using the Internet requires staff to be aware of several issues, including

- Internet workstation sign-up sheets
- Use of Internet management programs, including filtering software
- Web history, temporary Internet files, and cookies
- The physical location and provisioning of Internet workstations
- The possible introduction of spyware onto shared public computers, either deliberately or accidentally

Public libraries seldom have sufficient Internet workstations to meet patron demand. To address this issue, many libraries either use sign-up sheets or implement Internet time-management systems. To help retain some degree of patron privacy, libraries that use sign-up sheets may ask only for the patron's first name or some other innocuous non-PII identifier. This is especially important when the sheets are placed next to the Internet workstation or in clear public view in some other public service area. Sign-up sheets should be destroyed when they are no longer needed. Recent concerns about federal law enforcement authorities' enhanced powers under the USA PATRIOT Act have prompted many libraries to review their policies in this area. Libraries that had a rather lax policy on destroying sign-up sheets, or no policy at all, are now destroying the sheets on a more regular basis.[22]

Internet sign-up sheets can meet their demise by the timely use of a shredder, but many libraries are making the transition from paper sign-up sheets to computerized Internet time-management systems. Libraries are moving in this direction for a variety of reasons, including to make better use of staff time, to allow for more equitable use of the limited number of Internet workstations, and to address the differences (adult vs. minor) in Internet filtering defined in the Children's Internet Protection Act. With these programs patrons typically enter their card number at the workstation and they are then given a scheduled block of time online. In addition to recording the patron's identity, many of these systems can also be configured to track the web sites a patron visits. For privacy reasons, some libraries do not implement this tracking feature.[23] Regardless of how the system is implemented, staff should make certain that any files linking patron use to any particular workstation at a particular time and any files tracking the sites a patron has visited are purged on a regular basis. For example, the Seattle Public Library's Internet policy states: "When your [Internet] session ends and you log off, the system automatically deletes information about web sites you visited. The Library purges all patron booking information daily."[24]

Whether libraries have any manual or automated system for allocating scarce Internet workstations, patrons using the web leave a clear trail of where they have been. Web browsers keep track of every site that is visited by storing the data in a "history" or other temporary files. (See Chapter 2 for more information on this issue, including cookies.) Home users can set parameters in their browser on how much data to store temporarily, when to purge these files, and how to manage cookies. However, public libraries almost always have security software installed that locks down the desktop and prevents patrons from changing the browser's settings. If an Internet management system is used, it should be configured to purge all temporary Internet files when a patron's Internet use time has expired. There are also programs that will purge not just temporary Internet files but also changes made to any file whenever the workstation is rebooted. For example, all the computers offered to public libraries nationwide as part of the Bill and Melinda Gates Foundation's library program included a hardware safeguard that prevents patrons from storing files on the hard drive or making any permanent changes to the operating system or other programs. Whenever the workstation is rebooted, all programs, files, and operating system settings are restored to a virgin state. Whatever method a library employs to address the issue of temporary Internet use files, the library's Internet AUP should clearly state the policy followed and an explanation of actions the library takes in this area to help preserve patron privacy.

Patrons using the Internet are often engaged in interactive dialogs with web sites located outside the library. The privacy and security of any personal information entered on a web-based form will be dependent on the security measures implemented on the remote web site's server. Once patrons hit the "submit" button, the information sent as a result of the transaction is not under the protection of state privacy statutes and the library's privacy policy cannot be expected to cover such activity either. The same scenario applies to email. Most patrons have their own email account with one of the free email services, but the email messages are usually stored on the remote server, not on the library's server. While privacy breaches related to web forms or email may not be the fault or responsibility of the library, its privacy policy or Internet AUP should clearly inform patrons about the risks of entering personal information on web-based forms and the privacy risks of using email. Besides a simple warning, the AUP may be more proactive by outlining ways in which patrons can minimize threats to their privacy, such as looking for security icons on the screen and actually reading the privacy policy, which most commercial web sites do have.[25] Email is a notoriously open form of communication, and warnings of this fact should be in every library Internet AUP or privacy policy as a public service to patrons.

Privacy and the Use of Library Workstations

To further help protect a patron's privacy, many public libraries use privacy screens on monitors. Privacy screens fit over the monitor and limit viewing to only the person sitting directly in front of the monitor. Anyone viewing the monitor from another angle, including patrons or staff just passing by, see nothing but the opaque image of the privacy screen, or at most a very blurred image. While privacy screens are often thought of as a way to protect patrons' use of the web, they can also help protect privacy for other purposes too, as when a patron uses a word processor to write a job resignation letter. But privacy screens do have their limitations. To the annoyance of users, the screens often decrease the brightness of the image and the dimming may make the image appear slightly out of focus. Because of the need to sit directly in front of the monitor to view the image, privacy screens make it difficult for library staff to help patrons or for several patrons to view the screen at the same time. Along with these issues are concerns with initial costs and ongoing maintenance. Another option is to have the monitors recessed into the desk top. In addition to helping protect privacy, recessed monitors are more physically secure. With this option there is no need for privacy screens, and thus the image is clearer. But recessed monitors require the purchase of custom furniture or major modifications to existing workstation areas.

The physical placement of workstations in the library can enhance or detract from patron privacy. Some libraries purposely place monitors in locations that limit how much other patrons or staff can see. For example, the monitor may face a wall with only a few feet of clearance between it and the wall. Other libraries take an opposite perspective and, regardless of privacy issues, place the workstations in clear view of staff and other patrons. This is often done both for security reasons and to serve as a deterrent to viewing objectionable (e.g., sexually explicit) images. In this situation the placement of the monitors serves as a not-so-subtle enforcement mechanism for the library's AUP.

Privacy and the Library's Internet Acceptable Use Policy (AUP)

In 2000 almost 95 percent of public libraries with Internet access had formal policies on how this information resource was to be used.[26] These policies often cover a range of issues such as Internet time limits, printing, and engaging in activities or accessing sites that may be deemed inappropriate or even illegal. It is often the latter issue that elicits the most concerns about Internet use and the rights of patrons and patron privacy issues. Most often library Internet Acceptable Use Policies do not really address what is acceptable use; rather they address what is not acceptable use. Public library AUPs routinely prohibit such activities as viewing images that could be regarded as obscene, sending threatening emails, or engaging in disruptive or inappropriate behavior. A library's commitment to the First Amendment and patron privacy do not extend to such uses. The ALA's *Guidelines and Considerations for Developing a Public Library Internet Use Policy*[27] can be consulted for more information on issues related to Internet policies in public libraries. Regardless of whether the library has a brief or more lengthy AUP, there should be a section that addresses issues of patron privacy and confidentiality.

Libraries use a combination of methods to enforce compliance with their AUP. For example, to enforce the prohibition against accessing possible obscenity, 42 percent of public libraries nationwide use Internet filters.[28] This percentage will certainly increase following the Supreme Court's 2003 ruling that the filtering mandate in the Children's Internet Protection Act (CIPA) is constitutional.

Another enforcement method familiar to librarians is the well-known "tap-on-the-shoulder" technique. This popular enforcement tool has obvious privacy implications, because it requires staff to look directly at what the patron is viewing or to take action as a result of receiving a complaint from a patron who saw what another patron was viewing. Imagine a comparable intrusion where patrons are reading books in the public reading area of the library. Do staff routinely approach them and ask what they are reading? But, of course, public libraries do not collect sexually explicit titles with the types of graphical images available from thousands of "adult" Internet sites. Therein lies the conundrum. It is ironic that filtering software is a less intrusive enforcement mechanism than the tap-on-the-shoulder technique. Even the Supreme Court's decision in the CIPA case recognized this when the Court stated, "Monitoring of computer users would be far more intrusive than the use of filtering software."[29]

The library's commitment to maintain patron privacy while using the Internet and the need for staff to make judgments on what is acceptable use place staff in difficult and at times contradictory positions. The American Library Association's position exposes this difficulty. The ALA states that the library's Internet Acceptable Use Policy should "expressly prohibit any use of library equipment to access material that is obscene, child pornography, or 'harmful to minors'" and should also "provide for the privacy of users with respect to public terminals."[30] But this same ALA document states that when deciding what is obscene, and by implication intruding directly upon a patron's privacy, "Libraries and librarians are not in a position to make those decisions for library users." Only courts can make such determinations.[31] Yet such judgments are made in hundreds of public libraries every day in enforcing the library's Internet AUP. (It makes no sense to have policies on any library service, including Internet use, if such policies are not enforced.) Thus, from one perspective, staff are not in a position to determine the legality of what patrons view on the web; but from another perspective, they must still enforce the library's Internet AUP which requires them to make such judgments.[32] Regardless of privacy and First Amendment concerns, the tap-on-the-shoulder enforcement of a library's AUP often works because of the simple, if subtle, intimidation of patrons. Few patrons receiving the tap will publicly protest that their privacy rights are being violated and that they have a constitutional right to view whatever they are looking at.

The Internet and Library Network Issues

Libraries that offer high-speed, broadband access to the Internet almost always do so in a networked environment. There is a direct relationship between a library's network security and a patron's privacy. The more secure the library network, the more security is afforded to patron privacy. Security issues in today's complex network environments cannot be overestimated. Appropriate security measures, coupled with constant vigilance, must be an integral part of daily library operations.

Libraries with integrated systems need to be particularly careful that their network is designed in such a fashion that patrons cannot compromise the library's internal administrative network, the integrated system or the web server from inside or outside the library. Shared Integrated Library Systems (ILS) have additional network security issues. Some shared systems have more than fifty participating libraries and over a half-million registered borrowers. The consequences of a security breach in such large systems and the compromising of patron PII can be considerable. Shared system networks usually connect member libraries over private wide-area network links that are quite secure. However, some systems allow connectivity between member libraries using a public Internet backbone connection, usually because it is the only cost-effective means available. Without additional measures to encrypt communications or to use Virtual Private Network (VPN) tunneling technologies (neither of which are generally part of an ILS vendor's services or area of expertise), patron PII can be put at serious risk.[33]

Another networking issue that public libraries increasingly must address is the desire of patrons to bring their own laptop PCs to the library and get Internet access by connecting to the library's wireline or wireless network. A segmented network with a properly configured firewall between the patron network and the library's internal network can allow patron laptops to access the Internet in the library yet minimize the risk of compromising the library's network. Another privacy issue is to make certain that the access jacks for patron use are connected to an Ethernet switch, not an Ethernet hub; otherwise, one patron's computer will be able to view all the network communications of every other patron's computer.

An option growing in popularity is to configure a wireless network for patron laptop access that is totally separate from the library's wireline network. Unfortunately, using current technologies, no public access wireless network can offer any real guarantee of patron privacy. Knowledgeable persons within range of the wireless "hot spot" can configure their own laptops to eavesdrop on other wireless network traffic around them. Encryption, such as wired equivalent privacy (WEP), is often used with wireless networks to help prevent such eavesdropping. But to allow for easy access, most public wireless networks are not encrypted, and when they are, any information about the encryption configuration must be shared with each patron to enable network connectivity. (This is analogous to the situation in which a house is locked but everyone knows the key is under the "welcome" mat.) Libraries offering wireless access have an obligation to make certain staff are knowledgeable about wireless networks and privacy issues. Furthermore, staff should provide patrons with information on privacy issues in relation to the library's wireless network and address this in the library's AUP.[34]

Libraries can take small steps that, taken together, contribute to network security and ultimately to patron privacy. For example,

- Force the changing of workstation and server or network administrative passwords on a regular basis, and require the use of nontrivial passwords.
- Keep passwords secure. (No passwords and logins on sticky notes placed on the monitor.)
- Restrict staff access to network administrative services or sensitive data on a "need to know" basis.
- Use encryption on potentially sensitive communications, particularly on network connections used to administer servers and services.
- Make certain that any archival files with sensitive data are stored in a secure location. (An empty shelf in a staff work area is not a secure location.)
- Invest in a suite of network monitoring tools.

Larger libraries will have their servers and related network hardware housed in separate, secure rooms and locked wiring closets to which access can be controlled. Unfortunately, many smaller public libraries lack the physical space to do this. Their server (if they have one) is often located in a corner of an already crowded staff work area. In these circumstances, extra care must be taken to protect the security of the network, since every staff member has physical access to the server. It is important to address potential internal security threats as much as external ones. A surprising number of security breaches are caused by staff, whether by mistake or with malicious intent.[35]

If staff do not have strong networking skills and knowledge of network security, they should contract with a reputable networking firm to design the library's networks, incorporating security measures and, if needed, monitor network use on a 24/7 basis.

Personalized Library Portals

One of the newer services offered by public libraries is the creation of customized, personal web-based portals. The software for this is often available as part of the library's Integrated Library System (ILS), but it is available from other sources too. Personalized library portals can be viewed as library-centric versions of popular services such as MyYahoo that are offered to the general Internet community. Personal library portals are accessed by use of a library card or other patron ID, and often augmented by a patron-assigned password. Examples of the types of information a personalized library portal offers patrons are lists of what they have checked out or have on hold and lists of their favorite electronic periodicals and web sites. One can view this type of personalization as a "traveling set of bookmarks."[36] Patrons usually do not need to be in the library to access their portals. The service is available anywhere patrons have access to an Internet workstation. All the personalized data entered or selected by a patron are stored on a server in the library or at some outsourced location. Just as with the need to maintain the security and privacy of circulation records, staff must make certain that a patron's portal information remains secure.

Privacy and Outsourcing Library Services

As has been noted several times in this chapter, the outsourcing of library services is becoming more common in many types of libraries, including public libraries. This trend has been made possible by a combination of technology and budgetary expediency. From the technology viewpoint, the ubiquitous nature of the Internet and the web has made outsourcing a viable option for some services. From the budget viewpoint, it simply is less expensive to access some services and information resources remotely than to build the needed networking and computing resources to host these services locally in the library. Librarians have been accessing some services on an outsourced or contractual basis (e.g., CD-ROM periodical subscriptions) for many years, but this issue has taken on added concerns when the outsourcing involves accessing the service over the Internet. Whether the library is outsourcing access to periodicals, virtual reference, personalized portals, e-books, or other services, all of these services require some type of user authentication to restrict access to the customer base covered by the library's license. In instances where the library's license allows remote patron access from other locations (e.g., home, office), the authentication process may bypass the library entirely. Authentication of users often requires entry of their barcode or some PII, which raises concerns about privacy. To take an example, periodical databases may allow patrons to build personalized portals listing their favorite periodicals or individual articles of interest. As stated earlier in this chapter, regardless of what service is outsourced, libraries should make certain that privacy provisions are incorporated into any contract and that the vendor follows the International Coalition of Library Consortia privacy guidelines for vendors of electronic resources.[37]

Privacy and Reference Services

Whether information linking a patron to a particular reference request is protected by law will be dependent on how comprehensive the state privacy law is. For example, the law in New York refers to the need to protect records related to patron information collected as a result of "reference queries."[38] In this regard, any paper document or electronic file that can link a reference request to a specific patron must be protected. Language that extends protection to use of a library's "resources and services" can be reasonably argued also to cover reference interviews.

Technology continues to change the delivery of many library services. Reference is no exception with more libraries now offering virtual reference services via the web. It is common for staff serving on a virtual reference desk to ask for a patron's email address or library card number, and some libraries require the patron to be a registered library user. Personally identifiable information may then be electronically linked to a particular reference request. Furthermore, email is commonly used to send patrons information pertinent to their requests. When responding via email, patrons should be informed beforehand of the insecure nature of email. As with backup or archival files kept in an integrated system, procedures must be in place to purge these files on a regular basis, or at a minimum, to disaggregate any patron PII from the information provided in answer to a reference question.

Privacy and Children

Public libraries traditionally have emphasized services to children and young adults. For many public libraries, circulation of children's materials can be 30–40 percent of all circulation. The mix of library services, children, and privacy is a combination that often elicits very strong opinions from the library community. Add the First Amendment to this mix and it becomes even more volatile. Because library staff do not legally act in place of the parents (*in loco parentis*), they are never expected to intrude between parent and child. Yet, to preserve the privacy of minors under some conditions this may be necessary. This somewhat contradictory position can be clearly seen in the contrast of provision of Internet access compared with the more traditional circulation function. Many Internet use policies state that parents are responsible for what web sites their child visits while using the library's Internet workstations. This is supposedly a private matter between parent and child. Yet, when parents want to find out what materials their child has checked out, in most states librarians cannot legally divulge this information. In such cases, staff are placed directly between parent and child.

The degree to which the privacy afforded to adults also applies to minors varies. There are situations in which, by law or policy, minors are not afforded the same protections as adults. In the traditional area of circulation, whether a child's privacy is protected is dependent on the state's library privacy statute. An informal survey of the forty-eight states with library privacy statutes shows that fourteen of them allow the parents or guardian of a child to request information on what the child has checked out of the library. The statutes differ from one another in wording, but many are similar in language to the Wyoming law that allows access "by a custodial parent or guardian to inspect the records of his minor child."[39] Even in that majority of states where there are no age-based exceptions to privacy of library records, it is not unusual for libraries to follow a liberal statutory interpretation that allows parents to access their child's records under certain circumstances. Typically, the library will allow access if the parent is physically with the child or has the child's library card in hand. Some libraries may use the parent's signature on a child's library card as indication of the child's implied consent. Defenders of such policies note that it is the parent, not the child, who is responsible for the child's fines and lost or damaged items.

Another common issue relates to the age of minors. Should the level of privacy for a six-year-old differ from that of a sixteen-year-old? Children's privacy becomes much more of an issue when, for example, an adolescent checks out books on potentially controversial subjects such as divorce or sexuality. To partially address this issue, some states set the cutoff age for liability to parental review lower than age eighteen. A parental access law passed in Wisconsin in 2004 sets the child's age for parental access to library records at fifteen or younger. Attempts by the state's library association to reduce this to age fourteen were not successful.[40]

An area of library service generally not addressed in statute is restrictions on what children may check out. In providing background information on the Library Bill of Rights, the ALA has stated, "Library policies and procedures which effectively deny minors equal access to all library resources available to other users violate the Library Bill of Rights. The American Library Association opposes all attempts to restrict access to library services, materials, and facilities based on the age of library users."[41] ALA's position on this issue, which is supported by many in the library community, is that parents, not librarians, are responsible for what their children check out of the library.[42] ALA policy not withstanding, there are public libraries that have established circulation policies based on the types of materials and the age of patrons. Most common are limitations on minors' checking out R-rated videos.

Issues involving children's access to the Internet often elicit strong arguments from a variety of perspectives. As stated earlier, most public library Internet Acceptable Use Policies clearly state that parents, not library staff, are responsible for their children's use of the Internet. Some libraries also require a parental signature before a minor can use the Internet. Library staff cannot legally act in place of the parents (*in loco parentis*) and this should be emphasized in the library AUP.

Privacy and Surveillance Cameras

The use of surveillance cameras as part of an overall security system is becoming more common in both the private and the public sector. In public libraries, as in the private sector, cameras are used for a variety of purposes—for example, to deter or detect theft and vandalism. Cameras can be placed both outside and inside the library in inconspicuous locations, although in some libraries the cameras are purposely placed where they will be noticed. Most security systems are programmed to recycle the tape or digital image at a set interval, which can be from an hour to several days or more. It might be assumed that surveillance cameras do not link a patron with a particular book or a specific web site, since most cameras do not have this degree of resolution. Yet, because cameras track imaging by time, it could be fairly easy to tell exactly when a particular patron entered and exited the library and when and whether that patron checked out an item or accessed the web. For example, a camera focused on a bank of Internet workstations can determine who is using which workstation at what time, even if the library does not manage Internet use via such methods as sign-up sheets. As with questions on whether state library privacy laws cover Internet use, it will be necessary for staff and legal counsel to review closely their state library privacy statute to determine whether images from surveillance cameras are protected under the law. The library should have explicit policy language on who can see the images and for what purposes and should inform patrons that surveillance cameras are being used.

The use of inexpensive web cams in the library, making the live image available to anyone with Internet access, greatly increases privacy concerns.

This issue was discussed in an email thread on the national PUBLIB list, and most of the members who posted stated their objections to library web cams, primarily because of privacy concerns.[43]

Privacy and the Use of Library Meeting Rooms and Facilities

One of the missions of most public libraries is to serve as a center of community activities. For years libraries have sponsored or helped promote reading clubs or similar groups. Over the past decade workshops and other programs related to technology and the Internet have become very popular. In many instances programs and workshops require patrons to register in advance. Whether such registration lists are covered under the library's state privacy law can be open to interpretation. Even if sign-up sheets are not protected by state law, the library should have a policy on what it will do with such sheets after the course or workshop is over.

With public libraries being a "limited public forum,"[44] the use of library meeting rooms by nonlibrary groups is common in many public libraries. The privacy of who uses such meeting rooms and the further extension of privacy to who comes to whatever meeting or program is being held are again highly dependent on the interpretation of the state statutes. The library's privacy policy should clearly inform these groups on what they can expect in relation to the privacy of those attending.

Actions Public Libraries Should Take to Preserve Privacy

Public Library Privacy Policies

As has been shown throughout this chapter, public libraries not only have an ethical commitment to maintain their patrons' privacy; they also have a legal mandate to do so in at least forty-eight states.[45] State statutory protections serve as the foundation upon which the public library's privacy policy is based. Considering this, one of the first actions by staff is to review thoroughly their state's library privacy law. As discussed in more detail in Chapter 3, library privacy laws vary considerably from state to state. It is especially crucial to review statutory language to see whether more recent library services, such as public Internet access and virtual reference service, are covered. In addition to language in state privacy laws, the ALA recommends that staff incorporate the Federal Trade Commission's Fair Information Practice Principles (referenced in Chapter 1 as part of the Privacy Act of 1974) into their library's privacy policy.[46]

In a broad sense, a public library privacy policy will do the following. (An example of a public library privacy policy for staff is in Appendix III.)

- Use state library privacy statutes as a foundation and cite them as appropriate
- Reference ALA privacy and intellectual freedom policies

- Inform patrons which types of patron PII are protected, which may be protected, and which are not protected
- State the circumstances under which protected patron PII can be released and to whom
- Show the relationship of privacy to other library policies, such as the Internet AUP
- Educate patrons on their privacy rights in the library and provide other appropriate references to aid patrons on issues related to privacy outside the library

Privacy protection needs to be incorporated into the library's policies and procedures for all services and resources that have any relationship to a patron's PII. Whether the library has a wholly separate privacy policy or simply incorporates relevant privacy issues into such policies as the Internet AUP is a local decision. Keep in mind that some parts of a library's privacy policy are really targeted at staff and are internal policies, while others are targeted at patrons. For example, the day-to-day processes to manage and maintain the security of circulation data are part of the system manager's policies. Placing such details in a public privacy policy is not just inappropriate; it may create a needless security risk. To accommodate these variables, a library should have internal, staff-oriented policies as well as a more public-oriented privacy policy directed to patrons. The public policy can be rather brief. Any public policy more than a page or two (or longer than two or three screens) will not likely be read by many patrons.[47]

Privacy policies, both staff and patron, must be reviewed and updated on a regular basis. With library services in a constant state of change—often driven by technology—a policy review should be done at least once annually, and certainly whenever there are major changes in library services that affect privacy. If the library is planning a major revision of its policy, or is developing one for the first time, it is highly advisable that this be done with citizen input and with direct participation of the library board. For major revisions of the public privacy policy, holding a public hearing as part of a regular board meeting is good public policy. Any new or revised policy should always be reviewed by legal counsel before final board approval.

The finished patron privacy policy should be readily available in several formats. Printed copies should be placed in public service areas, and the policy should be prominently linked on the library's web site.

Conduct a Privacy Audit

One process that can be used to develop an initial policy or revise an existing one is a privacy audit. A privacy audit is simply a systematic review of the kinds of personally identifiable information collected by the library, determining why it is collected and what is done with it, and reviewing the relationship of PII to the library's functions and services. This assessment serves as a tool to help identify areas of the library's services that impact privacy and helps to highlight areas of the library's privacy policy that must be revised or at least reviewed.

Here are basic questions that have to be asked as part of a privacy audit. (A more complete audit checklist can be found in Appendix II.) Among the key questions that must be asked, and answered, by an audit are

- What personally identifiable and other information is collected?
  - Is the same information collected from all patrons?
- For what reasons or purposes is it collected?
  - What library services or applications are using the data?
  - Exactly what data are they using?
  - How are data shared between services and applications?
- In what format is PII collected?
- Who has access to the PII for each library service and application?
- How long is the PII retained, both in active use and in archives?
- What security measures are in place to protect PII and networked systems?
- What PII is transmitted to or accessed by other libraries or third parties?
- Under what circumstances can what types of PII be released and to whom?

For many of the preceding questions the overriding question is, why? For example, why is the PII being collected, and why are some data retained for weeks and other data retained for months? This assessment should be conducted regularly to ensure that there is a current, accurate understanding of the library's data flow and information management practices in relation to patron PII.

Educate and Inform

An important aspect of any library privacy policy is to educate and inform all parties on patron privacy rights. No library needs the negative publicity or misunderstandings that can result when a staff member, a board member, or local law enforcement officials are not knowledgeable about patron privacy rights and they make some misguided or factually inaccurate statement, whether to the press or to some other organization or individual.

Library Board

In almost all public libraries the library board is the legal, statutorily authorized authority which has governing control over library policies and administration. Because of its authority, the board has a responsibility to be knowledgeable on key issues, and privacy is most certainly one of these issues. Library administrative staff must educate and inform the board about state statutory privacy protections, and the policies the library has developed based on these protections must be endorsed by the board. The protection of privacy and the library's privacy policy should be an important part of any orientation the library director conducts for new board members. Ultimately, the library's privacy policy is *the board's policy* and as such it must be supported by the board. Library staff need to review with their board how its members should respond when they are contacted by the press, law enforcement, other municipal authorities, or patrons on issues related to privacy. It is important that board members not just understand and support their library's privacy but that they speak with a common voice when confronted by any person or group that questions the policy.

Library Staff

Staff are the first line of defense in the protection of patron privacy. It is therefore essential that all staff be knowledgeable about both the law and the library's privacy policy. This is particularly important for staff working in the information technology area and staff who are in public service positions. Because the circulation area is a key focal point of patron-staff interaction, it is especially critical that staff in this area, including paraprofessionals and part-time students, have a solid grasp of privacy issues, privacy protections, and their responsibilities in this area. Any staff who are approached by patrons or law enforcement personnel with questions or requests that involve privacy issues should know exactly what procedures they are to follow, even if it is as simple as "contact the supervisor on duty immediately." Staff must know that while they need to cooperate expeditiously with law enforcement authorities, this must be done within the framework of their state library privacy statute.[48] See the "Sample Public Library Policy: Privacy of Library Records and Library Use" in Appendix III which offers more detailed discussion on law enforcement requests for library records.

Library Patrons

As it applies to patrons, a library's privacy policy has two basic goals: to protect and to inform. Staff should be proactive in informing patrons of their privacy rights and protections afforded under statute and the library's policies. This informational role also includes the need to make certain that patrons are equally aware of the limitations on the library's responsibility and ability to protect their privacy. (It is important that patrons realize that the library will take reasonable measures to protect their privacy but, for example, the library is not responsible for protecting information a patron enters on a remote web site.) As noted earlier, informing patrons can be done in any number of ways, from the traditional print information available at public service locations in the library to posting information on the library's web site.

Local Law Enforcement

Library staff should be proactive in making certain that local law enforcement officials and such other parties as the municipality's legal counsel and the district attorney are fully knowledgeable about the legal protections of privacy afforded to patrons under state law. Furthermore, libraries should have in place procedures for working with law enforcement officers when a subpoena, warrant, or other legal order is made for library records that contain patron PII. While law enforcement officials may pressure staff to turn over records on patron use of a library's resources, it is in the best interests of law enforcement not to do so.

Conclusion

Public libraries are in a unique position to serve all residents of their communities in a public and open manner, yet at the same time public libraries must preserve the privacy of those patrons who use the library's resources and services. Library staff and the library board have an ethical commitment, if not also a legal mandate, to uphold the library's privacy policy and ensure that patrons are free to use the library without fear that their freedom will be compromised.

Notes

1. Minnesota Statutes, Chapter 13.40, "Library and Historical Data," http://www.revisor.leg.state.mn.us/stats/13/40.html (accessed April 23, 2004).

2. Rhoda Garoogian, "Librarian/Patron Confidentiality: An Ethical Challenge," *Library Trends*, vol. 40, no. 2, Fall 1991, p. 218.

3. "Privacy Statement," Spokane County Library District, December 13, 2002, http://www.scld.org/privacy.htm (accessed May 22, 2004).

4. "Guidelines for Developing a Library Privacy Policy," American Library Association, Intellectual Freedom Committee, August 2003, http://www.ala.org/PrinterTemplate.cfm?Section=toolkitsprivacy&Template=/ContentManagement/ContentDisplay.cfm&ContentID=43556 (accessed May 10, 2004).

5. Scott Carlson, "Talking Tags: New High-Tech Labels Help Libraries Track Books, But Worry Privacy Advocates," *Chronicle of Higher Education*, Information Technology, August 6, 2004, http://chronicle.com/free/v50/i48/48a02901.htm (accessed August 6, 2004).

6. "Implementation—The Circulation Process, Easy Self-check for Our Patrons," Santa Clara City Library, http://www.library.ci.santa-clara.ca.us/rfid/11_self-check.html (accessed May 16, 2004).

7. Karen Schneider, Interview by Robert Bocher, Madison, WI, May 23, 2004.

8. "Minutes of Library Commission Meeting," San Francisco Public Library Commission, May 6, 2004, http://sfpl.lib.ca.us/librarylocations/libcomm/minutes050604.htm (accessed May 14, 2004).

9. "Final Report," American Library Association's Task Force on Privacy and Confidentiality in the Electronic Environment, July 7, 2000, http://www.ala.org/ala/lita/litaresources/taskforceonpriv/alataskforce.htm (accessed August 2, 2004).

10. "Privacy Guidelines for Electronic Resources Vendors," International Coalition of Library Consortia, July 2002, http://www.library.yale.edu/consortia/2002 privacyguidelines.html (accessed May 15, 2004).

11. "Privacy Audit and Guidelines," SOPAG Privacy Task Force, Draft 8/13/01, http://libraries.universityofcalifornia.edu/sopag/privacytf/privacy_audit.html (accessed August 2, 2004).

12. Charles R. McClure, John Carlo Bertot, and Douglas L. Zweizig, "Public Libraries and the Internet: Study Results, Policy Issues, and Recommendations," U.S. National Commission on Libraries and Information Science, p. 29, 1994.

13. John Carlo Bertot and Charles R. McClure, "Public Libraries and the Internet 2002: Internet Connectivity and Networked Services," School of Information Studies, Florida State University Information Institute, December 2002, http://www.ii.fsu.edu/Projects/2002pli/2002.plinternet.study.pdf (accessed May 3, 2004).

14. United States et al. v. American Library Association, Inc., et al., No. 02-361. Argued March 5, 2003; Decided June 23, 2003, http://a257.g.akamaitech.net/7/257/2422/23jun20030800/www.supremecourtus.gov/opinions/02pdf/02-361.pdf (accessed August 1, 2004).

15. "Release of Library Record or Patron Information," Ohio Revised Code Title I [1] State Government, §149.432, http://onlinedocs.andersonpublishing.com/oh/lpExt.dll?f=templates&fn=main-h.htm&cp=PORC (accessed May 17, 2004).

16. Code of Maryland, Title 10, Governmental Procedures, Subtitle 6, Part III, Access to Public Records Md. State Government Code Ann. §10-616, http://www.ala.org/ala/oif/ifgroups/stateifcchairs/stateifcinaction/marylandprivacy.rtf (accessed May 23, 2004).

17. Sue Anne Pressley and Justin Blum, "Hijackers May Have Accessed Computers at Public Libraries," *Washington Post*, September 17, 2001, page A04, http://www.washingtonpost.com/ac2/wp-dyn/A41034-2001Sep16? (accessed May 2, 2004).

18. "FBI Targets Library Computers in Terrorism Investigation," *American Libraries News Briefs*, September 24, 2001 (http://archive.ala.org/alonline/news/2001/010924.html (accessed August 2, 2004).

19. 47 USC Section 254 (h)(5)(D) (accessed May 24, 2004).

20. *American Library Association, et al. v. United States of America, et al.*, Civil Action No. 01-CV-13203 Plaintiff's Joint Post-Trial Brief, U.S. District Court for the Eastern District of Pennsylvania, p. 20.

21. *United States et al. v. American Library Association, Inc., et al.*, p. 12, http://www.supremecourtus.gov/opinions/02pdf/02-361.pdf (accessed May 7, 2004).

22. Deane E. Murphy, "Some Librarians Use Shredder to Show Opposition to New F.B.I. Powers," *New York Times*, Sec. A, p. 12, Col. 1, April 7, 2003, http://gateway.proquest.com/openurl?url_ver=Z39.88-2004&res_dat=xri:pqd&rft_val_fmt=info:ofi/fmt:kev:mtx:journal&genre=article&rft_dat=xri:pqd:did=000000321797961&svc_dat=xri:pqil:fmt=text&req_dat=xri:pqil:pq_clntid=48175 (accessed May 12, 2004).

23. John DeBacher, Interview by Robert Bocher, Madison, WI, May 1, 2004.

24. "What You Need to Know About Reserving a Computer," Seattle Public Library, http://www.spl.org/default.asp?pageID=info_equipment_reservecomputer (accessed May 15, 2004).

25. Georgetown Internet Privacy Policy Survey: Report to the Federal Trade Commission, Study Director: Mary J. Culnan, 1999, http://www.msb.edu/faculty/culnanm/gippshome.html (accessed May 15, 2004).

26. "Survey of Internet Access Management in Public Libraries," survey prepared for the American Library Association by the Library Research Center Graduate School of Library and Information Science, University of Illinois, June 2000, http://www.lis.uiuc.edu/gslis/research/internet.pdf (accessed May 1, 2005).

27. "Guidelines and Considerations for Developing a Public Library Internet Use Policy," American Library Association, November 2000, http://www.ala.org/ ala/oif/statementspols/otherpolicies/guidelinesinternetuse.pdf (accessed August 2, 2004).

28. Bertot and McClure, "Public Libraries and the Internet 2002."

29. *United States et al. v. American Library Association, Inc., et al.*, p. 10.

30. "Guidelines and Considerations for Developing a Public Library Internet Use Policy," American Library Association, June 1998; revised November 2000, http://www.ala.org/Template.cfm?Section=otherpolicies&Template=/ContentMa nagement/ContentDisplay.cfm&ContentID=13098 (accessed May 1, 2004).

31. Ibid.

32. Gregory K. Laughlin, "Sex, Lies, and Library Cards: The First Amendment Implications of the Use of Software Filters to Control Access to Internet Pornography in Public Libraries," 51 *Drake Law Review* 215, 2003.

33. Greg Barnikis, Interview by Robert Bocher, Madison, WI, June 8, 2004.

34. Ibid.

35. David L. Margulius, "Tackling Security Threats from Within," *InfoWorld*, April 25, 2003, http://www.infoworld.com/article/03/04/25/17FEinjob_1.html (accessed May 7, 2004); Thomas J. Harvey, "Battling Employee Sabotage in the Wired Workplace," http://www.centeronline.org/knowledge/whitepaper.cfm?ID=833&Content ProfileID=122431&Action=searching (accessed June 4, 2004).

36. "MyLibrary Personalized Electronic Services in the Cornell University Library," *D-Lib Magazine*, April 2000, Vol. 6, No. 4, http://www.dlib.org/dlib/ april00/mistlebauer/04mistlebauer.html (accessed May 15, 2004).

37. "Privacy Guidelines for Electronic Resources Vendors," International Coalition of Library Consortia, July 2002, http://www.library.yale.edu/consortia/2002 privacyguidelines.html (accessed May 15, 2004).

38. New York Consolidated Laws Civil Practice Law and Rules Article 45, Evidence, NY CLS CPLR § 4509, Library records.

39. Wyoming Title 16-4-203 City, County, State and Local Powers, Right of Inspection; Grounds for Denial; Access of News Media; Order Permitting or Restricting Disclosure; Exceptions, http://legisweb.state.wy.us/statutes/titles/title16. htm (accessed May 20, 2004).

40. 2003 Wisconsin Act 207, http://www.legis.state.wi.us/2003/data/acts/03 Act207.pdf (accessed May 22, 2004), "WLA's State Legislative Agenda for the 2003-05 Biennium," Wisconsin Library Association, November 12, 2003, http:// www.wla.lib.wi.us/legis/2004agenda.htm (accessed May 22, 2004).

41. "Interpretations of the Library Bill of Rights," American Library Association, http://www.ala.org/ala/oif/statementspols/statementsif/interpretations/ Default675.htm (accessed May 19, 2005).

42. "Free Access to Libraries for Minors: An Interpretation of the Library Bill of Rights," American Library Association, http://www.ala.org/Template.cfm?Section= interpretations&Template=/ContentManagement/ContentDisplay.cfm&Con tentID=8639 (accessed May 20, 2004).

43. Email, Subject: Live Web cams, posted by Kate Wolicki to PUBLIB Sep-

tember 6, 2001, http://sunsite.berkeley.edu/PubLib/archive/0109/0073.html (accessed August 11, 2004).

44. *Brown v. Louisiana*, 383 U.S. 131 (1966).

45. "State Privacy Laws Regarding Library Records," American Library Association, http://www.ala.org/alaorg/oif/stateprivacylaws.html (accessed April 7, 2004).

46. "Guidelines for Developing a Library Privacy Policy," American Library Association, August 2003, http://www.ala.org/Template.cfm?Section=toolkitsprivacy&Template=/ContentManagement/ContentDisplay.cfm&ContentID=43556 (accessed May 15, 2004).

47. Karen Coyle, "Protecting Privacy," published in Library Journal's NetConnect, Winter 2001, http://www.kcoyle.net/privacy_lj.html (accessed May 15, 2004).

48. "Q&A on the Confidentiality and Privacy of Library Records," American Library Association, http://www.ala.org/ala/pio/qandaconfidentiality.htm (accessed August 2, 2004).

CHAPTER 5

Privacy Issues in K–12 School Library Media Centers

Introduction

> We need to allow students to preserve whatever private spaces within themselves they hold sacred.
> —Kay E. Vandergrift, Associate Professor, School of Communication,
> Information and Library Studies, Rutgers University,
> *School Library Journal,* January 1991

There are many privacy issues facing school library media specialists and other educators today, and it is important for them to be knowledgeable about student and staff privacy in schools. Privacy and confidentiality are a bit different in K–12 school libraries in that, with the exception of faculty and other staff, the majority of patrons are minors. In public libraries, patrons fall into the "cradle to grave" age groups, and in academic libraries, staff are working with mainly adults. In order for free and open inquiry to take place, students must feel confident their privacy will be respected in the library media center, and the staff will hold confidential any knowledge about library transactions and information seeking.

In this chapter, seven topics, each with a connection to school library media programs, will be discussed in depth. These include: (1) confidentiality of library records, (2) the USA PATRIOT Act in school libraries, (3) privacy in the district's acceptable use policy, (4) students providing personal information about themselves on the Internet, (5) conducting market research on students, (6) Internet use logs as public records, and (7) the impact of technology on school library privacy. Of the seven issues, the most important is confidentiality of library records; the other issues flow from it or are tangential to it.

Confidentiality of Library Records

Confidentiality of library use records is fundamental to free and open inquiry for young children, preteens, and teenagers in school library media programs. This key concept of intellectual freedom is supported by the "Position Statement on the Confidentiality of Library Records," adopted by the American Association of School Librarians which states, "The library community recognizes that children and youth have the same rights to privacy as adults."[1] It should be noted, however, this freedom is *not* always recognized in state law.

ALA Policy 52.4, "Confidentiality of Library Records," defines the parameters under which confidentiality is extended for all library users, including minors, by stating in part:

> The ethical responsibilities of librarians, as well as statutes in most states and the District of Columbia, protect the privacy of library users. Confidentiality extends to "information sought or received, and materials consulted, borrowed, acquired," and includes database search records, reference interviews, circulation records, interlibrary loan records, and other personally identifiable uses of library materials, facilities, or services.[2]

In January 2005, the American Library Association's Intellectual Freedom Committee updated its "Questions on Privacy and Confidentiality" to further clarify the privacy rights of minors in relation to those of adults.

> The rights of minors vary from state to state. Libraries may wish to consult the legal counsel of their governing authorities to ensure that policy and practice are in accord with applicable law. . . . In all instances, best practice is to extend to minor patrons the maximum allowable confidentiality and privacy protections. . . . [School] librarians should not breach a child's confidentiality by giving out information readily available to the parent from the child directly. Libraries should take great care to limit the extenuating circumstances in which they will release such information. . . . The rights of minors to privacy regarding their choice of library materials should be respected and protected."[3]

FERPA and School Library Records

Circulation records are maintained by school library media center staff to manage use of the collection, not to track what *student or adult* patrons are reading, listening to, or viewing. Is the confidentiality of *student* school library media center circulation records protected under federal law? There is no federal law protecting the confidentiality of library records for any library—school, public, or academic. However, the Family Educational Rights and Privacy Act of 1974 (FERPA) protects the confidentiality of "education records" of students in *any* school receiving federal funds and gives parents the right to inspect and review the minor student's education records and the right to request the correction of records they believe to be incorrect or misleading. This right to access a student's education record transfers to the student at the age of eighteen. Schools must obtain written permission from the parents, guardians, or the adult student to release the student's education records.

The definition of "education records" is very broad and does not specifically mention school library circulation records or Internet logs or histories that contain personally identifiable information about a student. The definition, within the law, is:

20 U.S.C. § 1232g (FERPA)

(4) (A) For the purposes of this section, the term "education records" means, except as may be provided otherwise in subparagraph (B), those records, files, documents, and other materials which—

(i) contain information directly related to a student; and

(ii) are maintained by an educational agency or institution or by a person acting for such agency or institution.

(B) The term "education records" does not include—records of instructional, supervisory, and administrative personnel and educational personnel ancillary thereto which are in the sole possession of the maker thereof and which are not accessible or revealed to any other person except a substitute;[4]

Although library circulation records and Internet history logs with student personally identifiable information are not mentioned specifically under the definition of education records in FERPA, can student library records be construed to be "education records" as defined under the law? The answer to this question is unclear at this time because no court has determined whether school library records are "education records" and thus protected. There appear to be differing interpretations, but there is no definitive answer.

Anne Levinson Penway, former assistant director of the Office for Intellectual Freedom until 1995, notes, "The language of the law [FERPA], and the Department of Education's interpretation of it, are broad and inclusive, *suggesting* that *all* records containing personally identifiable information about a student are covered.[5]

In 2001, however, the U.S. Supreme Court determined some limitations on the definition of "education records." In its first ruling interpreting FERPA, the Court determined that when students graded peer's assignments, the scores were not protected as "education records" because they were not "maintained" within the meaning of § 1232g(a)(4)(A). The student graders only handled the assignments for a few moments as the teacher called out the answers. The Court interpreted the word "maintained" in relationship to education records in the following way, "the word 'maintained' suggested that FERPA records would be kept in a filing cabinet, in a records room at a school, or on a permanent secure database, perhaps even after a student was no longer enrolled."[6]

According to the American Library Association's Office for Intellectual Freedom's executive director, Deborah Caldwell-Stone, the Court "discussed the nature of educational records and suggested the kinds of records subject to FERPA disclosure are records that are retained in a student's permanent file as a matter of course—items such as grades, test scores, attendance records, and disciplinary records."[7]

To determine whether circulation records are "maintained" as a permanent record, consider your district's library circulation system. Are circulation records retained as part of a student's permanent record, possibly even after they have graduated, or erased when an item is returned? Deborah Caldwell-Stone further commented "If the school does not maintain circulation records as part of the student's permanent record jacket, FERPA may not apply. Librarians should consult with legal counsel on this issue, as no court has ruled on it."[8]

It should be noted that soon after its first FERPA case, the Supreme Court considered a second FERPA case, and ruled that there is no private right of action under the Act.[9] This means that a parent cannot bring a lawsuit to enforce FERPA's federally mandated student privacy restrictions.

To strengthen the justification for FERPA not applying to school library records, Penway makes the argument that children and young adults will not search out information or use resources freely if their reading or information seeking is monitored or can be divulged to a parent, guardian, or school personnel. She opposes the application of FERPA to school library records on two additional points. First, FERPA's purpose is to protect student privacy; and some state laws already protect the confidentiality of school library records, allowing their disclosure only under certain conditions. Some state laws explicitly allow disclosure to parents and guardians; others do not. Depending on the state, a parent may be required to get a subpoena or court order to access those records. To explain more fully Penway's point about state library records laws, there has been a recent trend to amend state library confidentiality laws to allow parents and/or guardians to access a minor child's library record. For example, the law was changed in Wisconsin effective April 30, 2004 so that "Upon the request of a custodial parent or guardian of a child who is under the age of 16, a library supported in whole or part by public funds shall disclose to the custodial parent or guardian all library records relating to the use of the library's documents or other materials, resources, or services by that child."[10] This would include records of items currently checked out, due dates for those items, overdue items, and any fines owed, as well as any records of the use of library computers, such as computer sign-up records.[11]

Penway's second objection to the application of FERPA to school library records is that library records exist solely for management purposes, and the link between an item and the borrower's name is broken in automation systems when the item is returned. However, some circulation systems can be configured to hold information on borrowers after the item is returned. Other library records such as Internet sign-up sheets and paper or electronic records on interlibrary loans are not likely to be kept as permanent records. According to Penway, library records are not maintained as a record of scholastic development of a student and thus should not fall under FERPA's purview.[12]

While school librarians *may prefer to interpret* school library records as outside the purview of FERPA, in order to safeguard privacy, academic librarians may prefer to interpret library records as "education records," protected by FERPA.[13] As an example, Macalester College in St. Paul, Minnesota, states the following in its "Policy on the Privacy of Library Records, U.S.A. PATRIOT Act":

> The DeWitt Wallace Library of Macalester College observes state and federal laws, including the Family Educational Rights and Privacy Act (FERPA), regarding the disclosure of personal information in library records.[14]

Although the interpretations of the ambiguous legal definition of "education records" in FERPA differs dramatically, the privacy principle grounding both types of libraries is consistent. The user, regardless of age, is entitled to privacy with regard to his or her reading interests.

There is no definitive answer at this time whether school library circulation records and Internet history logs with personally identifiable information about students are considered education records under FERPA and thus accessible to parents and/or guardians until the child is eighteen. At the moment, the answer appears to lie with seeking an interpretation from the school or district's legal counsel. The best advice for school library media specialists, who are concerned with student privacy, is to create as few records as possible and to destroy those records as quickly as possible following the school or district's retention policy. School library media center retention policies will be discussed later in this chapter and a sample may be found in Appendix III. This advice will certainly be unpopular with parents who desire to know what their minor children have borrowed and the items on which they owe library fines. For example in Wisconsin, a parent's inability to learn the title of the book on which her child had an outstanding fine created a controversy which led to the change in the library records law. As a result, custodial parents and guardians have access to their minor children's library records.

The uncertainty over whether school library records are "education records" as defined under FERPA leaves minors using school libraries in a

vulnerable position and school library media specialists with a legal and
ethical dilemma. It would be beneficial to all involved if the status of library records in K–12 schools was clarified with respect to FERPA. This
could be done by amending FERPA and its regulations, specifying that
K–12 school and/or university records can only be given to the individual,
not to parents or guardians, subject to the exceptions already outlined in
the law (for example, compliance with judicial orders and subpoenas).
Leaving the confidentiality of K–12 library records for our youngest library
users in an indeterminate state between protection and disclosure is un-
tenable. Student library users will not freely and confidently use libraries
to seek information if they know items borrowed, sites visited on the Internet, or reference questions asked may be readily given to their parents.

State Library Records Confidentiality Laws

Is the confidentiality of student school library center circulation records
protected under state law? As noted in Chapter 3, forty-eight states and the
District of Columbia have laws relating to the confidentiality of library patron and use records. The laws vary from state to state, and it takes careful
reading to determine whether school libraries are included. An analysis of
the laws shows eighteen state statutes refer only to "a library" or to "any library," fourteen specifically include school libraries by name, eight include
libraries that are "wholly or in part supported by public funds," and seven
have language referring to "public libraries." Although it depends on the
definition of "public libraries," the use of the term in this instance means
that in some states school library records are not protected unless they are
shielded in another way, such as under district policy.

As also reviewed in Chapter 3, two states, Kentucky and Hawaii, have no
legislation shielding the confidentiality of library records; however, in both
cases their state attorneys general have written opinions respecting the individual's privacy rights regarding library records. In Kentucky, the opinion
is the law extends to public, school, and university libraries.[15] According
to Lucretia Leong, school library services specialist at the Hawaii Department of Education, school library patron data are to be kept confidential.[16]
Texts of all state confidentiality laws and the documents relating to Kentucky and Hawaii are posted on the American Library Association's Office
for Intellectual Freedom web site: http://www.ala.org/alaorg/oif/state
privacylaws.html/ and a web site maintained by Paul Neuhaus of Carnegie
Mellon University at http://www.library.cmu.edu/People/neuhaus/state_
laws.html.

Most states also have liberal open records laws allowing access to almost all information created and retained by any public sector agency, including public schools. However, such laws generally have a caveat that is
applied unless other sections of the statutes, like the library privacy sec-

tion, provide an exemption. Obviously, without this exemption state library confidentiality laws would be of no value.

Whether school library media center circulation records are protected under state law depends on whether school libraries are covered under the state's library confidentiality law. Therefore, school library media specialists are directed in their actions to protect school library patron records by state library confidentiality laws *if applicable* in the state in which they work. In some states, including New York, the state library confidentiality law defines records to be covered broadly "including but not limited to records related to the circulation of library materials, computer database searches, interlibrary loan transactions, reference queries, requests for photocopies of library materials, title reserve requests, or the use of audio-visual materials, films or records."[17] In others, the law has a more narrow scope. For example, Pennsylvania covers only circulation records.[18]

It is important for school library media specialists to read the state confidentiality law carefully to determine whether school libraries are covered, which records must remain confidential, and to whom the records may be released legally. Many states allow records to be released only to the individual, by court order or subpoena, or to staff in pursuit of their duties. Some states, including Alaska, Alabama, Colorado, Florida, Georgia, Louisiana, Ohio, New Mexico, South Dakota, Utah, Virginia, West Virginia, Wisconsin, and Wyoming, make library records of minors available to parents and guardians.[19] The type of library records accessible may vary, and library staff should review their state's statute.

There may be other instances in which requests are made to reveal a student's circulation records. A teacher may ask the library media specialist or other library personnel to check a student's circulation records to learn whether the student has read from a required reading list. The principal may casually request that a school librarian divulge what a particular student has checked out or is reading. This is not legal under state library confidentiality laws where school library records are protected, nor is it ethical. Students will not feel comfortable in reading or checking out materials in the school library if they feel their choices of titles or topics may be examined by an adult or a peer, although this information is always subject to disclosure through court order or subpoena.

There is one last aspect to consider in relationship to FERPA and state confidentiality laws. If FERPA applies to school library records, yet a state's confidentiality law protects a minor's school library records from disclosure to parents or guardians, which law takes precedence? As a rule, federal laws take precedence over state laws. However, in this case, that principle for resolving conflicting laws is in tension with another principle of legal interpretation—that specific laws take precedence over general laws. In this case, the state law is more specific than the federal law, so there may be a basis for arguing the state law ought to apply. But the outcome is unclear. According to Deborah Caldwell-Stone, executive director of the ALA Office for Intellectual Freedom, "This is a legal question that must be answered by a court. To date, no court has ruled on this issue. As always, librarians should consult with legal counsel."[20]

Preserving Student Confidentiality in the Media Center

Library media specialists have a responsibility to protect the privacy and confidentiality of their patrons, no matter what age. Carrie Gardner, former coordinator for library services at Milton Hershey School in Hershey, Pennsylvania, and currently an Assistant Professor of Library and Information Science at Catholic University of America, describes how she feels about this obligation.

> Youth librarians in all settings, especially school settings, must protect the privacy of our patrons. If we don't, we are guilty of malpractice. Many times, youth do not have the means to get to another library or information source. For example, no one under the age of 16 can drive in my state [Pennsylvania] and many others. Because of this, a school library is often the only library a student can access. If protection of privacy is not at the core of the mission of that school library, scores of patrons can be negatively affected.[21]

The school library media specialist can take a number of actions to preserve the privacy and confidentiality of students' use of materials and services. First, learn about general privacy issues for adults and youth. Protecting one's personal privacy allows the media professional to help students maintain theirs. Second, satisfy legal responsibilities relating to student privacy by becoming versed in and following federal and state laws relating to student education records, confidentiality of library records, and online privacy protections.

Fulfill ethical responsibilities by upholding the policies and statements of the American Library Association (ALA) such as the "Confidentiality of Library Records" and the "Confidentiality of Personally Identifiable Information about Library Users." The ALA "Code of Ethics," reprinted in Appendix I, speaks directly to the personal responsibility of all librarians, stating, "We protect each library user's right to privacy and confidentiality with respect to information sought or received and resources consulted, borrowed, acquired, or transmitted."[22] It is important for school librarians and other library staff to confront the issue that they may inadvertently violate a student's privacy by speaking about their library use to a faculty member, administrator, or parent.

For many library media specialists, the term "intellectual freedom" has meant ensuring access to all library materials and services for patrons and protecting the rights of students to read, view, and listen to resources of their choices. Within the context of free choice of materials is the often unvoiced idea that use of such materials on any topic be free from scrutiny. The twin concepts of privacy and confidentiality have now attained the recognition they deserve as intellectual freedoms. When school library media specialists assist students in finding information on sensitive topics or notice the choice of materials in the course of daily media center activities, their lips are sealed. If students are to feel safe in their search for information, media specialists must be silent in their knowledge of individual student research. However, if student privacy is threatened, library media specialists will be advocates and strong protectors, standing for student patrons' rights.

Privacy and Library Services

School librarians are in a unique position to observe students at work and also in a more relaxed condition reading and researching for personal enjoyment and edification. It is the responsibility of the media specialist to create an atmosphere where students may seek and use information without fear someone will question their reason or right to the information. It is equally important that other adults not be able to "check on" what students or a particular student is reading or searching for on the Internet.

Since this is the case, privacy and confidentiality of students must also be protected while library services are being delivered. Library media center staff set the tone for interchanges during the circulation process. Comments on why materials on sensitive topics are being checked out may be acknowledged intellectually but not verbalized out of respect for the privacy of the student. The same is true for items placed on reserve. Paraprofessionals, secretaries, and parent and community volunteers working at the circulation desk should also be instructed in the tenets of confidentiality and not be allowed to examine records indiscriminately. Student assistants should not be allowed to view the records of fellow students. Care must also be taken to preserve student confidentiality in the matter of overdue items. Printing notices and giving them to a teacher to distribute compromise student confidentiality. Nor should lists of student names with titles of overdue items be posted on a bulletin board. If a library media center has automated circulation and still retains circulation cards in its materials, the cards should be removed. Lastly, it is important that the library media specialist, other library or support staff, and volunteers not inadvertently violate student privacy by indiscreetly speaking about patron library use to others.

When a library has automated, there are actions the library media specialist should take to ensure patron privacy. School library automation systems maintain a log of all patron transactions, and these records are retained until they are manually purged from the system. According to Tom Janiak, Rosholt School District technology coordinator, "Automation systems can have logs for 10 to 15 years, and library staff may not know it.

Many libraries have never purged these records, and therefore, can be required to supply this data if courts find cause."[23] Library staff need to consider what is a reasonable retention period of their electronic circulation records and conduct systematic purging of these data at least annually.

It is not only the circulation process that must be protected but also the interaction between a school library media specialist and a student when a reference question is asked. During the reference query, the verbal or email exchange, the electronic and paper resources consulted, and the records generated while helping a student obtain materials through interlibrary loan are all protected and remain confidential. It is also important for the media professional to ensure the reference interview does not focus on *why* the student needs the information sought. While it may be helpful to the librarian in determining exactly what is needed, it may also be an invasion of the student's privacy.[24]

The physical placement of equipment and furniture can also enhance or detract from student privacy. To protect students' privacy during the research process, placement of online public access catalog terminals and Internet-accessible computers equipped with privacy screens or recessed computer terminals should be considered. While the Children's Internet Protection Act (CIPA) requires schools to monitor student use of the Internet, there is a fine line between keeping students safe on the Internet and protecting their privacy. Keeping confidential the interests and intellectual pursuits of students with all their facets is a matter of keeping faith with student patrons and honoring professional ethical codes.

Former coordinator for library services at Milton Hershey School in Hershey, Pennsylvania, Carrie Gardner feels free inquiry is particularly important to teenagers.

> Our students have information needs that deal with very difficult topics. One in four girls will be sexually abused by the age of 18. One in 10 boys will be sexually abused by the age of 18. Sixteen million American children live in poverty. Often, if young people do not think their information requests and information-gathering activities are going to be kept private, they won't ask for the information. They would rather suffer the consequences of not knowing.[25]

Looking at privacy and confidentiality in school library media programs in another light, Pat Scales, director of library services for the South Carolina Governor's School for the Arts and Humanities, is concerned the protection not be carried too far.

> My primary concern regarding privacy issues as it related to children and young adults is that we cannot allow privacy to interfere with "best practice." This is especially true with reader guidance issues. For example, I feel that it is important that I know what a child likes to read in order to lead him/her to another

book they will like. I'm not going to reveal my knowledge to another person, but that child may need my guidance. I don't believe that we should force guidance on a child, but we cannot totally serve their needs if there is complete privacy.[26]

There are also times when a library media specialist may need to apply common sense to a situation involving intellectual freedom principles. For example, if a student has become withdrawn, is reading information about suicide, and is expressing feelings of hopelessness, the library media specialist may need to make a decision whether to violate the privacy of the student by speaking to the school's counselor. Just as educators are required to report cases of child abuse, there are times when concern for a student may move a library media specialist to seek assistance from another educator bound by confidentiality. Intervening may save a student's life. The intervention would be based on the historic doctrine of *in loco parentis*, or educators serving in place of the parent or guardian while the child is within the school. This concept has been in effect since the beginning of public education in the United States. In 1765, legal scholar Sir William Blackstone wrote that a father "may also delegate part of his parental authority, during his life to the tutor or schoolmaster of the child; who is then in loco parentis, and has such a portion of the power of the parents committed to his charge."[27] According to Dr. Anthony Conte, "Schools continue to be institutions to which parents look for help in their efforts to best serve their children. Schools are doing more because other elements of society (home, church, community) seem to be unable or unwilling to continue their historic roles."[28] In the end, school library media specialists must follow their moral compass and take any needed action they believe is in the best interest of the student.

Confidentiality, Privacy, and Retention Policies

School library media program materials selection policies and reconsideration procedures have been in place and used successfully across the country to retain challenged materials. Other policies can also *protect* and *promote* intellectual freedom in the school media center. A confidentiality of library records policy aimed at staff actions to protect records and a privacy policy to let student patrons know their privacy rights in a school media center are also needed. A records retention policy is also useful to ensure the safe collection, storage, transfer, and destruction of library records. Those policies will be invaluable to school media professionals as they protect student privacy and confidentiality and to expand the strong tradition of intellectual freedom in the school media center.

As an advocate for library records privacy and confidentiality, the media specialist should urge district administrative personnel to develop and

adopt policies and procedures that will protect library use records of patrons. To protect the privacy and confidentiality of student patrons, a
school library media specialist must bridge district policies and educational
practice and the ethics and core values of librarianship. Achieving the appropriate balance can be tricky given the uncertainties of whether districts
view library records as coming under FERPA and the lack of coverage of
school library records under some state library record confidentiality laws.

The ALA urges libraries to develop two policies—a confidentiality policy and a privacy policy. The confidentiality policy is aimed at library staff
and focuses on their responsibility to keep patron personally identifiable
information (PII) about materials checked out and services used confidential. Information on developing a confidentiality policy may be found
on pages 347–355 of the *Intellectual Freedom Manual*, sixth edition, developed by the Office for Intellectual Freedom, American Library Association
in 2002. A sample "Confidentiality of School Library Media Program
Records Policy" is located in Appendix III.

According to Nancy Kranich, editor of the ALA "Privacy Tool Kit" and
chairperson of the ALA Intellectual Freedom Committee from 2002 to
2004, "a privacy policy is aimed at users, covers a broader array of information services, and communicates the library's commitment to protecting users' PII."[29] "Privacy: An Interpretation of the Library Bill of Rights"
states, "Users have the right to be informed what policies and procedures
govern the amount and retention of personally identifiable information,
why that information is necessary for the library, and what the user can do
to maintain his or her privacy."[30] To assist librarians from all types of libraries in developing a privacy policy, the ALA Intellectual Freedom Committee developed "Guidelines for Developing a Privacy Policy." Located on
the Office for Intellectual Freedom's web pages, it encompasses what
should be included in the policy, notes some policy considerations for
school library media programs, and provides a checklist of basic questions
to help guide the policy drafting process. A sample "School Library Media
Program Privacy Policy," based on the ALA's guidelines, is located in
Appendix III. Privacy policies should be displayed prominently within the
school library media center and posted on the library's web pages.

A third policy—a school library media program records retention policy—would also be useful to protect privacy and confidentiality of school
library media center patrons. The most important thing to remember is
that records should be kept as long as they are needed and no longer. A
school library media program records retention policy reinforces the concept of retaining minimal library records. One cannot produce records
that are not retained. Necessary statistical information should be gleaned
from library records such as circulation or interlibrary loan, and then the
raw data that connects a particular patron's name with an item should be
purged. According to Deborah Caldwell-Stone, executive director of the
American Library Association's Office for Intellectual Freedom, "Record

retention policies assure that records due to be erased or shredded actually are erased and shredded, and they also provide evidence of the library's everyday practices, should anyone question why a record has not been retained."[31] It is important for school librarians to develop a retention policy, specify how long they will retain the designated records, and implement the schedule. The shortest possible retention of records will help ensure patron privacy. A sample "School Library Media Program Records Retention Policy" with more detailed information is located in Appendix III. As with all library policies, they should be reviewed by legal counsel and adopted by the governing board of the public or private school.

Privacy Audit

How will you know if you are protecting the privacy and confidentiality of school library media center patrons? Conduct a privacy audit. Many school library media specialists may not be familiar with this term, but it is becoming more common in post–September 11, 2001, library literature. In the broad sense, "The privacy audit is a process used by an organization to ensure that the organization's goals and promises of privacy and confidentiality to its various constituencies are supported by its practices, thereby protecting confidential information from abuse and the organization from liability."[32] In the more narrow definition as applied to libraries, a privacy audit is a process during which library staff evaluate how and what types of library patron data are "collected, stored, shared, used, and destroyed."[33] The goal of the audit is to ensure the privacy of patrons. Their personally identifiable information and their library activities are kept confidential, viewed only by library staff in the pursuit of their management duties or by those persons designated under state library confidentiality laws, if applicable to school libraries.

In K–12 schools, audits are frequently conducted by outside agencies to ensure that educational requirements, for example, for special education or equity, are being met. While a school library records privacy audit will most likely be conducted internally, it is important to obtain administration and school board's support before embarking on this undertaking. Without this support the necessary policy or procedural changes are unlikely to occur.

Most school audits are done every few years or when a concern is noted; however, in the school library media center, privacy auditing is a process, not a one-time evaluation. With the swift changes in technology, auditing privacy practices in school libraries on a regular schedule, possibly every three years, is important. A library privacy audit may be done informally in a single media center by the media specialist and support staff. It can also be performed more formally district-wide, led by the administrator in charge of the library media program, and supported by a subcommittee created for that purpose. It is crucial that the district's instructional technology staff be a part of the audit, because many library records are in an electronic format, the institution's network is involved, accessing remote subscription databases may require authentication, and security of records is involved. IT staff will also be able to advise library personnel on risk management and security issues. Utilizing an outside library or technical consultant also brings a set of "fresh eyes" to look at data collection and handling processes. Consideration should also be given to including parents in the process, because parents will have another perspective on protecting student personally identifiable information.

During the audit, there are several data collection and usage principles to be aware of, especially since the enactment of the USA PATRIOT Act in 2001: (1) create and retain the minimal records necessary to effectively manage the school media center, (2) restrict access to patron personally identifiable information and disclose it only as allowed by law, (3) train staff to follow data collection, usage, retention, and removal procedures, and (4) establish procedures on handling law enforcement requests and train all staff to forward requests to the designated staff member.[34]

In performing a privacy audit in a school media center or district-wide library media program, there are a number of areas to cover. Begin by evaluating the library's policies in the context of the larger body of school district policies, especially those relating to confidentiality of student records. This step should be followed by a systems and procedures review in which staff evaluate the types of data and how those data are collected, where they are stored, who has access to them, how long data are retained, and how disposal of data occurs. Levels of security should also be assessed.[35] Additionally, it is important to determine the *entire* library staff's knowledge about privacy as it relates to patron information and library operation. Equally valuable is to consider the knowledge or lack of knowledge about library privacy on the part of patrons.[36] "Privacy Audit Guidelines for School Library Media Programs" are found in Appendix II and will provide an outline of steps for conducting a privacy audit.

When an audit has been completed, the results should be used to modify current library media center records practice. All data should be examined in various contexts. In what areas are privacy and confidentiality practices adequate? In what areas is personally identifiable information at risk to exposure from unauthorized persons? What policies and procedures need to be developed or revised? Who will undertake the needed changes? Implementation of audit findings will involve library and IT staff and administrators and possibly require school board action.

Conducting a privacy audit and developing and adopting confidentiality, privacy, and retention policies are not enough. It is important that *all library staff*—the library media professional, paraprofessionals, student assistants, volunteers, and district or school technical staff—be knowledgeable about library privacy, state and federal legislation, and the library's policy and procedures to ensure patron privacy. Additionally, *all school staff* should have some understanding of library policies as they relate to intellectual freedom. Providing staff development in this area will enable teachers and administrators to have a better understanding of basic intellectual freedom principles including privacy and confidentiality. It is also important that patrons be made aware of the privacy policy and the school's efforts to protect their personally identifiable information. A library's privacy policy should be posted in the media center and accessible to all students. It is also useful to publicize the policies through parent and community programs, newspaper or district newsletter articles, and notices on the library media program section of the district or school's web site.

The USA PATRIOT Act in School Libraries

As discussed in Chapter 3, the USA PATRIOT Act amended over one hundred sections of fifteen federal statutes including the Foreign Intelligence Surveillance Act (FISA), making it easier for FBI agents to view library and bookstore records. While most media and library literature refer to concern over the USA PATRIOT Act in public libraries, the records of patrons in school libraries are also vulnerable. Although a visit from the FBI may seem unlikely in a school library media center, it is important to be prepared. The ALA has created "Confidentiality and Coping with Law Enforcement Inquiries: Guidelines for the Library and Its Staff." These guidelines include steps to take before, while, and after law enforcement agents visit. The guidelines also give specific instructions on how to proceed if the court order is in the form of a subpoena, a search warrant, or a search warrant issued under FISA. The guidelines may be found within the ALA Office for Intellectual Freedom web pages (http://www.ala.org/oif).

There are two critical points to remember in dealing with law enforcement visits. First, *all* library staff, including student assistants and volunteers, should be trained on the first step to take when approached by an FBI or other law enforcement agent. This includes knowing the person designated to respond to requests and answer questions. Second, law enforcement agents must follow a legal process of producing a FISA warrant, subpoena, and so on; and these legal processes existed prior to passage of the USA PATRIOT Act. According to noted privacy authority Mary Minow, "The USA PATRIOT Act merely lowered the hurdles that law enforcement must surmount to get the orders."[37] It is important to know gag orders apply only to court ordered search warrants issued by a FISA court, not to informal questions or subpoenas.

In the previous section on preserving privacy and confidentiality in the library media center, the privacy audit was introduced and reference made to "Privacy Audit Guidelines for School Library Media Programs" located in Appendix II. It cannot be stressed enough that preserving the privacy of patrons and the confidentiality of their personally identifiable information is directly related to the amount of information gathered and retained. Less is better. School library media specialists cannot divulge information they have not collected and retained. While the FBI may never visit a school media center under Section 215 of the Foreign Intelligence Surveillance Act (FISA), the steps taken in a privacy audit will also safeguard student and staff privacy in the day-to-day educational setting. In a perverse way, librarians can thank the USA PATRIOT Act for creating the sense of urgency that has prompted libraries to audit their information gathering processes and to develop or revise their privacy policies.

Student Privacy in the District's Acceptable Use Policy

With the arrival of the Internet in schools, districts began writing and adopting a new type of policy—the acceptable use policy, or AUP. The Virginia Department of Education's "Acceptable Use Policies: A Handbook" defines an AUP as "a written agreement in the form of guidelines, signed by students, their parents and their teachers, outlining the terms and conditions of Internet use—rules of online behavior and access privileges."[38] The National Education Association recommends that an effective AUP contain the following six key elements:

- preamble,
- definition section,
- policy statement,
- acceptable uses section,
- unacceptable uses section, and
- violations/sanctions section.[39]

The Children's Internet Protection Act (CIPA) and the Neighborhood Children's Internet Protection Act (NCIPA) require a school district receiving funds for certain services under the Library Services and Technology Act (LSTA), Title III of the Elementary and Secondary Education Act (ESEA), or the E-rate program must comply with provisions relating to Internet safety policies and technology protection measures that block or filter access to visual depictions that are obscene, child pornography, or harmful to minors. The Neighborhood Children's Internet Protection Act (NCIPA) specifically requires libraries and schools receiving Universal Service [E-rate] discounts to:

Adopt Internet safety policies that address [the following] . . .

- Safety and security of minors when using email, chat rooms, and other forms of direct electronic communication; . . .

- unauthorized disclosure, use, and dissemination of personal identification information on minors.[40]

Under CIPA in addition to filtering, districts taking the federal funding listed above must also address privacy in their AUPs. What type of privacy issues should be included in the AUP? Project Interconnect, a K–12 education and public library confederation for interactive video based in Brooklyn Park, Minnesota, is specific in the types of privacy issues it considers should be included in an AUP. These include (1) not guaranteeing the privacy of student and staff email accounts or user files stored on school servers and accessed via a school's server, (2) not including confidential student information in staff email, (3) students not disclosing personal contact information about themselves or others without school or parental permission, (4) developing safety rules relating to others "met" online, and (5) password use and protection.[41]

NCIPA requires district Internet safety policies to protect student privacy in forms of electronic communication such as email and chat. To guide districts, Nancy Willard, author of *Computer Ethics, Etiquette, and Safety for the 21st Century Student,* recommends districts consider the following principle when developing AUP privacy language: "Student [email] accounts should not be established unless there is a clear educational purpose, no advertising is directed at students, and parents have been fully informed about such accounts, and parents have approved those accounts."[42]

A second requirement under CIPA and NCIPA is that districts make no unauthorized disclosure, use, and dissemination of personal identification information on minors. It should be noted CIPA defines a minor as any person less than seventeen years of age.[43] Personally identifiable information (PII) was once defined as that information which would allow recognition of a specific individual such as full name, home address, email address, and telephone number. In the past few years, the coverage of what is included in PII has broadened significantly to include financial profiles, Social Security number, and credit card information.[44] Another definition of PII is "any information that links a user's choices of taste, interest, or research to that user's identity."[45] It does *not* include information that is collected anonymously or without a name or other identifier being attached.

The Wisconsin Rapids School District (Wisconsin) "Network and Acceptable Use Guidelines" cautions students not to provide personally identifiable information about themselves while using the Internet and also addresses vendor collection of user personally identifiable information for marketing or market research purposes.

- Students may not provide (Personally Identifiable Information) PII while on a district computer unless permission is given by the teacher (e.g., Wisconsin Career Information System, online curricular projects such as Cyber Surfari).

- Before granting permission, the teacher must review the site's privacy policy for compliance with Children's Online Privacy Protection Act (COPPA) and seek parental permission if necessary.
- No third-party disclosure of PII is acceptable. If the company either shares PII or reserves the right to share PII with third parties, then the web site is not acceptable for use by WRPS students.
- Sites that do not purge collected information should be avoided.[46]

Jeff Gibson, technology coordinator for the Wisconsin Rapids School District, explains the district's rationale for its policy language related to privacy.

> When developing its policy language, the Wisconsin Rapids School District Information Technology Committee was most concerned about identifiable student information floating about the Internet or worse being sold to advertisers. We were concerned with our students becoming the targets of marketers or other predatory behavior. When researching web site privacy policies, we discovered that many sites reserved the right to disseminate this information at their convenience. We felt that allowing the use of those sites put our students at risk and thus forbid their use. Since the policy was written, most sites serving students in an educational setting have adopted privacy protections that make it easier for our teachers to find acceptable sites.[47]

The AUP should also address concerns about any personally identifiable information collected by vendors of subscription databases or other electronic educational products a school media center purchases or may use under a state contract. More detailed information on privacy as it relates to electronic publishers and the collection of personally identifiable and commercialization can be found in Chapter 4 within the "Privacy and Outsourcing Library Services" section and in Chapter 6 in the "Electronic Publisher Policy" section.

Many school districts and libraries already have acceptable use policies that include privacy issues as they relate to network and Internet use; however, addressing electronic library reference services from a privacy standpoint in the AUP also protects student privacy and confidentiality. Some school libraries are part of multi-type library systems or other consortia offering virtual reference services. It is important for the media professional to understand what type, if any, of personally identifiable information is required by the online reference service. For example, the AskAway 24X7 reference service, offered by the South Central Library System (Wisconsin) to all system residents, requires only that students or faculty accessing its services list their local public library, give a first name or pseudonym, and provide an email address to which the search transcript will be sent. Establishing individual student email accounts using a unique identifier rather than the student's name minimizes a student's vulnerability when using electronic reference services. If classroom, not individual student email accounts, are used, the risk to a student's privacy is also minimal. For more information on privacy and virtual reference services, see the "What Is the Nature of Information Collected about Patrons?" section in Chapter 6.

In addition to adhering to CIPA and NCIPA, districts have a moral obligation to address privacy for students and staff in their acceptable use policies. Specific policy language relating to protecting student and staff privacy in Internet and network use varies around the country, and a simple Internet search will yield many examples posted by districts. Additionally, technology consultant Nancy Willard has four model documents: a District Internet Use Policy, Internet Use Regulations, Student Internet Use Policy, and a Student Internet Account Agreement which can be found at the Center for Safe and Responsible Internet Use web site (http://re sponsiblenetizen.org). The documents are part of the online lengthy publication "Safe and Responsible Use of the Internet: A Guide for Educators." The student documents give guidelines on privacy and communications with others related to the age of the student. It is prudent for every district to review its AUP periodically. Language should be added where omissions are found.

Students Providing Personally Identifiable Information About Themselves or Others

With the advent of the Internet, millions of children and young adults have become adept at using web sites for school-related assignments and recreational purposes. The growing predatory nature of web sites collecting personally identifiable information from youth caused Congress to pass the Children's Online Privacy Protection Act (COPPA), the Children's Internet Protection Act (CIPA), and the Neighborhood Children's Internet Protection Act (NCIPA). While this federal legislation is helpful, it is not a cure-all, and privacy issues for children and young adults online continue.

While the Children's Online Privacy Protection Act (COPPA) established privacy protection regulations for younger children, the need to safeguard teenagers who are not covered by COPPA remains. "The Internet and the Family 2000," a study released May 16, 2000, by the Annenberg Public Policy Center at the University of Pennsylvania, found teenagers between thirteen and seventeen are more likely to give personal information about themselves, their parents, and their schools in exchange for a free gift than are those ages ten to twelve.[48] The study also found 96 percent of parents and 79 percent of children agree parental permission should also be required before teenagers give out personal information on the Internet.[49] The results of this study lead persons concerned with the privacy of youth to question why Congress did not also protect the privacy of teenagers online under COPPA and whether the increasing commercial online marketing to teens will lead to extending the privacy protection law to those above age twelve.

These statistics from the Annenberg study are no surprise to school librarians and other educators who observe young adults using the Internet. For example, fantasy sports and health information sites are very popular with teenagers and often require those registering to give personal information about themselves. This may include name, address, telephone number, and email address. However, few preteens or teenagers stop to consider the implications of giving this information or read any privacy statement that may be present. The issue of students providing personally identifiable information about themselves is closely related to the privacy issues in the "Student Privacy in the District's Acceptable Use Policy" section in this chapter.

Email is another area that poses potential threats to privacy through the actions of students themselves. Preteens and teens have grown up with the Internet, email, and instant messaging and do not think about how they may be revealing personal information about themselves or others. In an innocent message, a student may disclose privileged information about another student. Or, given the fickleness and emotional volatility of preteen and teen relationships, today's friend may be tomorrow's foe, and the secret shared one-on-one with a best friend may become the subject of an email message to a new "best" friend.

More dangerous than interpersonal student email, students may begin corresponding with someone they "met" on the Internet and be led into potentially dangerous situations. The FBI's statistics on the increase of cases involving pedophiles using the Internet to lure children into meeting them is reinforced by a recent study of cybersex advances toward children and young adults. According to a survey of 5,001 youth conducted by the University of New Hampshire's Crimes Against Children Research Center with assistance from the National Center for Missing and Exploited Children, 19 percent of those surveyed between the ages of ten and seventeen were propositioned for cybersex, with 65 percent of the advances occurring in chat rooms and 24 percent through an instant message system.[50] It is estimated that approximately 25 percent of the advances are made by young adults ages eighteen to twenty-five.[51]

Preserving Students' Online Privacy

"Wired Teens Aren't Naïve About Online Privacy," a study by Forrester Research released in July 2001, studied 10,000 online consumers ages thirteen to twenty-two. While 12 percent said they did not take any privacy precautions online, the majority reported they have used the following four strategies to hide their true identities: (1) erased bookmarks or site names from browser histories, (2) avoided sites asking for personal information, (3) entered bogus information, (4) erased cookies from their computers, or disabled the cookie function.[52] Although some American teenagers may be savvy about protecting their online privacy, it is doubtful whether the majority are really cognizant of the importance of not sharing personally identifiable information online. Library media specialists can take the lead in helping to educate students about protecting their personal privacy online as well as in the physical world.

If students are to feel they have the right of privacy in their school library media centers, it is worthwhile to articulate what responsible actions are expected of students while online and how the district or school will enforce its AUP either by supervision, monitoring technologically, or both. Equally critical is the need to delineate in the library's privacy policy what privacy students can reasonably expect while online in the library media center.

As previously noted, it is critical that the school or district acceptable use policy restrict the personally identifiable information students reveal about themselves. Schools should also enforce their AUPs in regard to students respecting the privacy of others in email and other forms of online communication. It is also important to reinforce the purpose of individual student and classroom email accounts. Additionally, districts can further protect the privacy of students' email accounts by setting them up with a "unique student identifier," rather than exposing the students' real names to the outside world.[53] Some districts may choose not to establish individual student email accounts but rather use classroom accounts under direct teacher supervision for obtaining information for school-based projects. Many schools do not allow students to access their individual personal home email accounts from school.

Supervision and monitoring of students' activities online is another way to protect students from providing personally identifiable information about themselves or others and to help them understand the importance of protecting their personally identifiable information. While students should have the right to engage in inquiry without being closely scrutinized, the Children's Internet Protection Act (CIPA) does require districts to enforce the Internet safety policy and monitor the online activities of minor students. Monitoring is not clearly defined, so it could consist of both library staff supervision of students while online and the use of technology to check if a student's Internet usage is violating the district's AUP.[54]

Supervision is defined by *Webster's New World Dictionary of the English Language* as "to oversee, direct, or manage."[55] According to Nancy Willard, author of *Safe and Responsible Use of the Internet: A Guide for Educators,* "Supervision requirements should be appropriate to the age and circumstances of the students."[56] Supervision in an elementary school library media center or lab may consist of assisting and guiding students online. At the middle and high school levels, supervision may be more a dual issue of enforcing the AUP and protecting students from potentially unsafe be-havior. Teens feel particularly invulnerable to any dangers, whether it be fast and reckless driving or providing personal information online. Older students should have more freedom to use the Internet; yet they must also demonstrate their sense of responsibility. Since students mature at differ-ent rates, supervision balanced with sensitivity to the need of preteens and teens to explore their questions freely is important. Supervision is not a black and white activity but rather a delicate balance between privacy and protection.

Monitoring using technology "real-time" involves school library media program staff or lab supervisors remotely viewing the screens of students as they search, checking for actions not allowed under the AUP. Filtering or blocking software will also technically monitor student use of the In-ternet to a certain degree, but it will not stop students from supplying per-sonally identifiable information about themselves or others. After-the-fact monitoring is accomplished by staff looking at student Internet usage records or by more advanced "packet sniffing technology" that filters and analyzes all web traffic and email communications. Administrators and other authorized staff can view the reports and easily determine if a stu-dent has violated the AUP by intentionally visiting an educationally unac-ceptable site for longer than the few seconds it takes to realize a site has been accidentally accessed.[57]

Using technology to monitor where students have been on the Inter-net may seem invasive of their privacy, but a National Research Council re-port, "Youth, Pornography, and the Internet," published in 2002, addressed the issue in terms of expectation of privacy by students in a school.

> The level of privacy that students can expect in school—using a computer as well as other aspects of school life—is different from what they can expect at home, and school computer systems are not private systems. The expectation of privacy when students use computers in schools is more limited, as is evi-denced by a variety of actions that have been supported in court decisions, in-cluding searching of student lockers, backpacks, and so on. Thus provided that students have been given notice that their use is subject to monitoring, the use of monitoring systems raises fewer privacy concerns.[58]

Although students are cautioned to protect their personal information, use of the school library's public access computers does require students to provide a user name and password supplied by the school. With that in-formation, the network "authenticates" that the individual logging in is a legitimate student user entitled to make use of network resources as well as access the Internet and email. It is important that students guard their passwords to protect against someone misusing network and Internet re-sources under another individual's user name and password. Authentica-tion is also needed to access the library's electronic resources such as an online encyclopedia and subscription databases. The authentication process assures vendors that only those patrons of libraries that have paid the required subscription fee are accessing the electronic resources. Both types of authentication require the student library patron to give up a bit of privacy by allowing their network and Internet activities to be tracked in Internet usage records. For more information on authentication, see "The Delicate Balance" in Chapter 6.

From an IT standpoint, it is important to remember all use of library computers to search the Internet creates temporary files from sites the computer has accessed. The temporary files are retained in the computer's cache, and unless set to automatically clear after each searching session, the files will remain until the amount of space allotted to them is used. Files will then be cleared to make room for new ones. Then there are cookies. Once a lovely sweet treat, the term now refers to a text file placed on a computer's hard drive by web sites visited while online and may hold such information as the name of the Internet service provider, type of computer and browser, passwords, and the last site visited. Browsers on public access library computers can be configured to delete temporary files as well as cookies. School library staff should ensure cookies, Internet searching history, cached files, and other temporary Internet use records are removed regularly.

The Children's Online Privacy Protection Act (COPPA) requires commercial web site operators to obtain verifiable parental consent before collecting any personal information from children under age thirteen. COPPA also allows teachers to act on behalf of a parent during school activities online, but the law does not *require* teachers to make decisions about the collection of their students' personal information.[59] School library media specialists should be involved in how COPPA is implemented in their schools. According to the ALA Office for Information Technology Policy, "School librarians must balance the mandate to provide access to information with the restrictions of COPPA. Ultimately, school librarians seek to make sure COPPA protects children's privacy rights without unduly restricting their access to information."[60] Districts may authorize school library media specialists to act *in loco parentis* (in place of the parent or parent's authority), may opt to obtain parental consent through an AUP signed by the parent and student, or may leave all decisions on consent of collection of personally identifiable information to parents. For more information, the Federal Trade Commission, which enforces COPPA, has provided "How to Protect Kids' Privacy Online: A Guide for Teachers" (http://www.ftc.gov/bcp/conline/pubs/online/teachers.htm).

Conducting Market Research on Students

Prior to January 2002 when President Bush signed the Elementary and Secondary Act (ESEA), there was no legal protection against companies conducting market research on students for commercial purposes in schools without the knowledge of parents. Because estimates of teenage personal spending "range from $24 billion to more than $140 billion annually in direct sales" and teens influence an estimated nearly $500 billion in sales of their parents' spending annually, companies were eager to research and reach teens.[61]

Until it found itself in financial trouble, the ZapMe! Corporation provided 1,800 schools in forty-five states with computer labs, software, and access to selected sites students had to use. The selected web sites had advertisements, and the company's contract with schools allowed it to gather and sell collective student data showing who searched where.[62] According to ZapMe!, it did not collect personally identifiable information, only students' login name, age, and location. The information was sold to advertisers in aggregate form.[63]

Other companies were offering revenue for placing ads, giving free email accounts, and supplying easy-to-use web pages and better content than those to which schools currently had access.[64] Providers such as Tripod.com, The Learning Network, and Highwired.com offered free web page hosting if a teacher or district would accept ads when the pages were accessed.[65]

According to "Public Education: Commercial Activities in Schools," a report published by the General Accounting Office (GAO) in September 2000, increasing fiscal pressures had forced school districts to find alternative revenue sources. The result was that schools allowed consumer research and marketing to students.[66] In response, Senators Christopher Dodd (D-Connecticut) and Richard Shelby (R-Alabama) and Representative George Miller (D-California) teamed together to write the Student Privacy Protection Act. Following release of the GAO report, Senator Dodd, one of the sponsors of the Student Privacy Protection Act, stated, "Many schools enter into commercial contracts with advertisers because, as the GAO found, they are strapped for cash. Schools are often faced with two poor choices—providing computers, books and other educational . . . equipment with commercial advertising, or not at all."[67]

Although the Student Privacy Protection Act guarding against market research on students in schools did not pass as a separate law, its language was inserted into an amendment to the Protection of Pupil Rights Amendment (PPRA) within the Elementary and Secondary Act of 2001 (ESEA). This means companies can no longer lure schools to accept free computer equipment, Internet access, or other benefits in exchange for information about students' web surfing and purchasing choices. The language prohibits schools that receive ESEA funding from "allowing third parties to monitor, receive, gather, or obtain information intended for commercial purposes without prior, written, informed consent from the student's parents."[68] Under the law's requirements, schools must develop and adopt policies that address "the collection, disclosure, or use of personal information collected from students for the purpose of marketing or selling or otherwise providing information to others for that purpose; and the right of parents to inspect, upon request any instrument used to collect such data."[69] However, this provision does not apply to the "collection, disclosure, or use of personal information collected for the exclusive purpose of developing, evaluating, or providing educational products or services for students or educational institutions including: . . . book clubs, magazines, and programs providing low-cost literacy products" to students.[70] According to Senator Dodd, "This . . . will return to parents the right to protect their children's privacy."[71]

Internet Use Logs as Public Records

Since 1998, there have been two legal battles as to whether Internet use or history logs of schools or educational networks are public records and subject to review. In the first case, Michael Sims, co-founder of the Censorware Project, filed a Freedom of Information request in April 1998 to obtain the history logs of the Utah Education Network (UEN), a statewide educational computer network for forty Utah school districts. His purpose was to determine what types of sites were blocked by SmartFilter, the filtering system used by the UEN. The UEN refused his request to see the records, asserting districts might not want the logs made public because they might identify students and staff who attempted to visit objectionable web sites. UEN executive director Stephen Hess stated, "As far as we are concerned, the superintendents [of the public schools] are the last word. . . . It's their data."[72] He also implied an agreement with the districts that UEN would not make the data public. Under the Utah Government Records Access and Management Act (GRAMA), the State Records Committee voted to order UEN to give Sims the logs after deleting personally identifiable information identifying any student or faculty member.[73] While Sims had a legal right to the logs, he shortly learned from UEN he would be unable to obtain them because they are overwritten every thirty days. According to Hess, this fact had been reported to the State Records Committee, but the committee had failed to order UEN to preserve the files it had ordered to be transferred to Sims. In exchange for the overwritten records, UEN officials offered Sims logs from the last six weeks even though this was not a good sample.[74] Sims was incensed, and the State Records Committee voted to ask the Salt Lake County district attorney to investigate the deletion of records. Despite the fact that Sims did not receive the specific logs he sought, the State Records Committee "voted to officially remind the UEN that all future computer logs are open to Sims— and anyone else."[75] Sims did eventually receive UEN SmartFilter logs and released a report on the over-blocking by the filtering software in 1999.

In the second case a parent in Exeter, New Hampshire, filed a lawsuit to require the Exeter Region Cooperative School District and the Exeter

School District to release their Internet logs after the districts had decided not to install filtering software. Instead, the decision was made to have faculty supervise student use of the Internet rather than rely on Internet filters. The parent wanted to use the logs to learn whether students were accessing objectionable sites despite staff supervision and spot checks. The school districts denied the request based on the federal Electronic Communications Act of 1986 and the New Hampshire Right-to-Know law, which prohibits an individual from going to a public library and learning who borrowed specific materials. A Rockingham County Superior Court Judge disagreed and ruled the Internet logs were public records.[76] The judge ordered the districts to turn over logs from January 1, 1998, to the present; however, the districts did not have records dating back that far. Originally, the Exeter Region Cooperative School District had retained logs based on a five-week rotational system and then overwrote them. Exeter School District superintendent Arthur Hanson said in an affidavit the district never stated it had Internet logs dating back to January 1, 1998.[77] He felt the case was tried on whether the logs were public records and therefore accessible, not the period for which they were archived. Following the filing of the suit, both districts installed new equipment and saved the files for longer periods. Hanson stated, "None of the defendants has adopted any records destruction policy or destroyed any records because of this case. To the contrary, [the Exeter Region Cooperative School District and the Exeter School District] commenced new practices of retaining [log files] for extended periods of time because of this case."[78] The judge ordered all personally identifiable information be removed before the log files are turned over to the parent, and the cost of "sanitizing" the records be borne by the complainant or anyone who requests the records.[79]

As a result of the New Hampshire case, school library personnel in that state have become more familiar with New Hampshire's Right to Know Law, which makes it a crime to deliberately destroy public records that are being sought by a member of the public. According to Susan Ballard, director of Library Media Technology Services for the Londonderry School District, "Most (if not all) NH school districts now have a written policy which provides for purging identified electronic records (for example, like Internet logs) after a designated time period, for practical reasons (like lack of data storage space) and therefore, not in violation of the Right to Know [Law]."[80] The Londonderry School District policy relating to purging electronic records may be found at http://schools.londonderry.org/documents.cfm/ within the staff and student acceptable use policies.

The New Hampshire case was a wakeup call for school districts across the country. While the ruling in the New Hampshire case is valid only in that jurisdiction, other jurisdictions faced with a similar situation will certainly consider the reasoning involved. According to Nancy Willard, executive director of the Center for Safe and Responsible Internet Use, "Districts should identify what records are required to be retained under state laws and ensure that Internet usage records are retained and destroyed in accord with the provisions of state law."[81] Willard provides a clear, concise explanation of public records and school district responsibilities in her online publication "Safe and Responsible Use of the Internet: A Guide for Educators," Part III, Legal Issues—Internet Use in School, Chapter 5, Public Records, located at http://responsiblenetizen.org/online docs/pdf/srui/sruilisting.html/.

School districts should review their state's public records law as it relates to schools, and think seriously about their policies related to archiving of Internet logs since such logs have been declared public records in the two cases described in the preceding paragraphs. As previously noted in the "Privacy Audit" section, it is important to consider what records are being maintained, why they are needed, their retention period, what staff have access to them for specified purposes, how requests from parents and others will be treated, and the process for ensuring overwriting or erasing. Districts should include these decisions in a records retention policy.

The Impact of Technology on Privacy in School Library Media Centers

The transition from traditional school libraries with large print collections held within the walls of the facility to school library media centers with print, nonprint, electronic subscription databases, and free Internet resources exemplifies the way in which technology has changed the library media program. Dynamic school library media programs integrate technology not only to access resources globally but also to assist students in producing educational "products" in a variety of formats including digital video, web pages, and electronic "slide" presentations. Students and faculty search the library's online public access catalog and its subscription databases both in the library and remotely from home. Students dialog via email with peers in distant locations and engage in cooperative learning projects. Virtual reference services are available to many students and concerns for privacy surrounding this service were addressed earlier. The impact of technology is felt not only in the delivery of services and use of information but also in the way in which library resources and patron data are managed. Technology is also being used to keep the school campus, including the library media center, a secure place for students and faculty.

Library Automation Systems and Privacy

Because of the widespread use of automated circulation systems, students and staff are rarely required to sign their names on checkout cards in school library media centers. Automated circulation systems automatically break the record linking the user with the material when the resource is checked in, although it should be noted that data on previous borrowers of an item can be obtained. For example the Follett Software Company's Circulation Plus program allows the media specialist to view who currently has an item checked out as well as the last user's name. The Follett program also has a setting configurable by staff within the library or school that defines the disposition of additional book checkout history. This setting either allows all historical information about the checkout history to be retained in the database or automatically deletes this checkout history. If the history is retained it can be accessed via a separate utility.[82] According to a spokesperson from Follett Software, Ray Ledinsky, senior product manager, "We developed our systems to empower the school or library staff to decide whether this data should be retained or not. It's not Follett's role to decide the policies on this topic for the libraries, but rather to provide the tools to allow implementation of local policies and processes."[83] Follett is not the only vendor with this "history" feature. The Sagebrush library circulation software allows the number of previous borrowers of an item to be designated by the media specialist. It is important to be cognizant of how local school automation systems operate and what types of confidential data may be retrievable. It is also important to remember server backups of these records may exist, further compromising student privacy.

RFID in School Libraries

Most public schools are facing shrinking financial resources. This means not only will there be fewer dollars to spend on library resources, but also there is the constant pressure to keep service levels high with fewer staff. Retiring school library media specialists are often not replaced, or library professionals are required to work in multiple buildings. Loss of materials due to theft is also a concern. At the same time, library journals and conference sessions tout the RFID technology. Could RFID be a solution for school library media programs? Are there privacy implications for school media center staff and patrons?

As described in Chapter 2, "Radio frequency identification, or RFID, is a generic term for technologies that use radio waves to automatically identify people or objects."[84] In appearance, the RFID tag is a small, paper-thin label that can be applied to a library book or other item. Some public and academic libraries are moving to RFID. Use of RFID technology is still rare in schools; however, a private school in Buffalo, New York, is using the technology for "access control, cafeteria purchases, library books, and laptops."[85] The Miami-Dade School System has purchased a radio frequency (RF) security system.[86]

RFID technology has the advantage of allowing libraries to combine a number of functions into a single adhesive label: security of library materials from theft, easier and faster check-in and checkout, and more efficient inventorying no longer requiring the physical tipping out or touching of each item. Vendors also claim the tags will last longer than barcodes with a minimum of 100,000 transactions before replacement is needed. On the other hand, there are disadvantages to RFID. The major disadvantage is higher cost of the necessary equipment and tags.[87] Another disadvantage is the tags are in the open and easily shielded or removable, not "covert" as are the strips of current library security systems.[88]

As libraries have implemented RFID technology, privacy groups have raised concerns; however, those developing the technology are quick to allay those fears. First, the data stored on the RFID tag have an item ID similar to barcode information, a security bit (on or off like a magnetic security strip), and possibly shelving location information if used in conjunction with sorting equipment. Second, reading the tag requires an RFID-based reader within a short distance—inches—of the tag. Lastly, to reduce privacy risk even further, it is possible to encrypt the item ID.[89]

While it would appear from library literature and vendor information that current RFID technology does not pose a threat to student privacy, this is a very dynamic situation, and future technological advances may create that possibility. Beth Givens, director of the Privacy Rights Clearinghouse, said at an FTC RFID workshop recently, "The FTC or other agencies could conduct an 'impartial' assessment of RFID and its potential effects on privacy."[90]

Thus far there is little experience in the use of RFID technology in school library media centers. When the cost of RFID drops or when new construction is being done, more schools may begin to switch from the traditional barcodes and electromagnet theft detection systems to RFID technology. After all, school media professionals would certainly welcome the increased productivity they would experience if they are able to check in multiple items simultaneously, have patrons use self-checkout, secure library materials from theft, and manage the inventory process more efficiently. More information about RFID may be found in Chapter 2 in the "Radio Frequency Identification (RFID)" section and Chapter 4 in the "Radio Frequency Identification (RFID)" section.

Surveillance Technology in Schools and the School Library Media Center

As we go about our daily lives, we encounter security cameras in many places—banks, convenience stores, highway toll booths, the mall, public transportation, sporting events, and now schools. Following the tragedy at Columbine High School in 1999 and other incidents of school violence, student safety, rather than privacy, is a greater concern for school boards, administrators, and parents. Although the privacy of students and staff was discussed before surveillance cameras were installed in the Rosholt School District (Wisconsin), according to middle school/high school principal Ken Camlek, "We feel the camera surveillance system . . . has fostered a sense of heightened safety amongst our students, staff, and parents."[91] More recently, child abductions and terrorism have been added to the list as reasons to employ technology to make schools more secure. Just as metal detectors and security guards have become familiar in some urban districts, surveillance cameras and other forms of security technology are increasingly being installed in both urban and rural schools. A security specialist at Sandia National Laboratories in Albuquerque, Mary Green, estimates 30 percent of high schools, 15 percent of middle schools, and 2 percent of elementary schools have surveillance cameras.[92] Joe Ziegler, marketing communications manager for Honeywell, also indicates an attitude shift. "One of the compelling things that has changed is that security has gone from being a negative sell to becoming a requirement, very much like lighting and heating."[93]

The U.S. Department of Justice's "Safe Schools Manual" allows school and law enforcement personnel to use "surveillance technology that enhances the ability to protect health, welfare, and safety of students and staff," and its use is limited to "places where students and staff lack reasonable expectation of privacy, such as hallways, classrooms, the cafeteria, library, and parking lot."[94]

Cameras have also been installed in school library media centers and computer labs across the country. A media specialist in Las Vegas, Nevada, reported each secondary school in her district has one video surveillance camera in the library. She noted "before [the] cameras, we were broken into three times in one year and lost $50,000 worth of equipment, not to mention the damage. Since then, no break-ins. The cameras are a deterrent."[95] A school media professional in Charlotte, North Carolina, declared her school had cameras since Columbine and it "seems to make our students feel more secure."[96] As to the issue of privacy, a school library media specialist in Maine replied, "The camera does not show anything that cannot be seen by looking through the library's main entrance . . . nor does the detail seem sufficient to, for example, determine what individual students are reading (Internet filters are far more intrusive)."[97] To protect the privacy of students, the media specialist in Redford, Michigan, requested the camera not be directed toward the circulation desk to take patron privacy into consideration.[98]

Schools that install surveillance cameras and other forms of technology to protect the general security of students and staff need to ensure privacy does not get breached in the process. Having a district policy covering the purpose of the surveillance ensures the administration and Board of Education have discussed the important issues of school safety as well as the equally important concerns for maintaining privacy. District guidelines should cover where the cameras will be placed, how they will be used, who may view the surveillance videos, record-keeping of those who view the tapes, and how long the tapes will be retained. Additionally, students, staff, and visitors to the school facilities should be apprised of the fact that surveillance technology is being employed through the use of signs, and the information should be communicated through letters to parents, articles in district newsletters, and notices at the entrances to the facilities.

The School District of Belleville (Wisconsin), which has a camera in the library computer lab and also in the main library, has a comprehensive "Use of Silent Video Surveillance Equipment" policy that delineates the purpose of the equipment, where surveillance may take place, who is authorized to view the resulting surveillance tapes, and areas where privacy may reasonably be expected and addresses the security of the data. According to Dan Huebsch, district librarian for Belleville, "We haven't seen them [the cameras] as an intrusion at all at this point. It has actually helped to deter vandalism in our computer lab."[99]

While the technology available to schools is becoming increasingly more sophisticated and expensive, it is worth remembering technology is not the only answer. No technology is fail-safe, and the value of the human factor must also be considered. Positive interactions among students, staff, and the community can help improve the school's climate for students and enrich their educational experiences. Dr. Kathleen Martinsen, district administrator in the Rosholt School District (Wisconsin), where forty-two surveillance cameras were installed around the perimeter and within the PK–12 facility, stated, "Security cameras have helped improve school climate because they are a deterrent to school vandalism and theft. In addition, students feel safer because there are fewer incidents of aggressive behaviors in the hallways. This allows students to focus on their educational program in an atmosphere that is positive and productive."[100]

Privacy and District or School IT Staff

The amount of technology in a library media center and its connection to the local area network as well as wide area networks mean actual management of the technology assets is in the hands of the IT (information technology) staff—a technology coordinator, technicians, and other specialized staff. The school library media program staff must rely on the district's technical staff to keep the computers and allied equipment operational, Internet access fast and reliable, and library data and access to library systems secure. For more information on library network concerns relating to privacy, see "The Internet and Library Network Issues" section in Chapter 4.

It is important the library media professional establish and maintain positive and frequent contact with IT staff to be aware of decisions being made which may impact library services and patrons. During a privacy audit, the library media specialist and IT staff may have an opportunity to discuss data security and the need for both privacy for student patrons and confidentiality of their circulation and other library records. Working together, the media professional and IT staff may find more effective practices to meet the needs of both departments. Once the privacy audit is completed and the confidentiality, privacy, and records retention policies are either written or reviewed, it is important for all technical staff to also receive training on the district or school policies and procedures. Keeping IT staff informed of privacy and confidentiality issues and working with them to resolve these issues are another way to ensure student patron privacy.

Conclusion

A wide range of privacy concerns exist in school libraries, and it is important for library media specialists to have a basic knowledge of these issues. The actions of school media professionals are directed by federal and state laws and the ALA "Code of Ethics." While the school library media specialist will obey laws and consider strongly professional ethics codes, they will also apply common sense in protecting the privacy and confidentiality of their patrons.

Notes

1. American Association of School Librarians, "Position Statement on the Confidentiality of Library Records," http://www.ala.org/ala/aasl/aaslproftools/positionstatements/aaslpositionstatementconfidentiality.htm (accessed July 13, 2004).

2. Ibid.

3. American Library Association, Office for Intellectual Freedom, "Questions on Privacy and Confidentiality" (revised January 4, 2005), http://www.ala.org/Template.cfm?Section=interpretations&Template=/ContentManagement/ContentDisplay.cfm&ContentID=83504 (accessed January 20, 2005).

4. Family Educational Rights and Privacy Act, (FERPA) 20 U.S.C. §1232g; http://www4.law.cornell.edu/uscode/20/1232g.html (accessed July 21, 2004), and 34 CFR Part 99, http://www.access.gpo.gov/nara/cfr/waisidx_03/34cfr99_03.html (accessed January 26, 2005).

5. Anne Levinson Penway, "The Buckley Amendment: Student Privacy versus Parents' Right to Know," Office for Intellectual Freedom, American Library Association, *Intellectual Freedom Manual*, 6th ed. (Chicago: American Library Association, 2002): 320.

6. *Owasso Independent School Dist. No. I—011 v. Falvo*, 534 U.S. 426, 433 (2002), http://supct.law.cornell.edu/supct/html/00-1073.ZO.html (accessed July 21, 2004).

7. Deborah Caldwell-Stone, email message to author Helen Adams, July 20, 2004.

8. Ibid.

9. *Gonzaga Univ. v. Doe*, 536 U.S. 273 (2002).

10. Wis. Stat. § 43.30 (2004).

11. "Wisconsin Department of Public Instruction, "Frequently Asked Questions About Compliance With the New Parental Access to Library Records Law" (April 23, 2004), http://www.dpi.state.wi.us/dltcl/pld/ab169faqs.html (accessed January 27, 2005).

12. American Library Association, *Intellectual Freedom Manual*, 6th ed., 319–321.

13. Lee Strickland, Mary Minow, and Tomas Lipinski, "Patriot in the Library: Management Approaches When Demands for Information are Received from Law Enforcement and Intelligence Agents," *Journal of College and University Law*, 30, no. 2: 401, http://www.librarylaw.com/ND.pdf (accessed January 27, 2005). Note: Universities acting on a request to divulge student library records with personally iden-

tifying information must make a reasonable effort to obtain written permission from the student before complying. If no reply is received in a given time frame, FERPA allows release of the records. Libraries should be alert, however, to check their state library confidentiality law, to see if the records requested are protected.

14. "Policy on the Privacy of Library Records, U.S.A. PATRIOT Act," Macalester College, http://www.macalester.edu/library/about/policies/patriotact-.html (accessed January 20, 2005).

15. "Kentucky and Hawaii State Confidentiality Laws," http://www.ala.org/ala/oif/ifgroups/stateifcchairs/stateifcinaction/stateprivacy.htm (accessed July 14, 2004).

16. Lucretia Leong, email message to author Helen Adams, August 19, 2003.

17. ARTICLE 45—EVIDENCE, S 4509. New York State Consolidated Laws Civil Practice Law & Rules, http://assembly.state.ny.us/leg/?cl=16&a=36 (accessed July 22, 2004).

18. Paul Neuhaus, "Privacy and Confidentiality in Digital Reference," *Reference & User Service Quarterly* 43, no. 1 (Fall 2003): 32.

19. "State Laws on the Confidentiality of Library Records," maintained by Paul Neuhaus, Carnegie Mellon University, updated December 31, 2004, http://www.library.cmu.edu/People/neuhaus/state_laws.html (accessed January 27, 2005).

20. Deborah Caldwell-Stone, email message to author Helen Adams, July 20, 2004.

21. Carrie Gardner, email message to author Helen Adams, August 9, 2002.

22. *Intellectual Freedom Manual*, 407.

23. Tom Janiak, interview by Helen Adams, November 22, 2004.

24. Kay E. Vandergrift, "Privacy, Schooling, and Minors," *School Library Journal* 37, no. 1 (January 1991): 26–31, http://web17.epnet.com (accessed August 14, 2004).

25. Helen R. Adams, "Privacy & Confidentiality: Ensuring the Rights of Minors," *American Libraries* 33, no. 10 (November 2002): 44.

26. Pat Scales, email message to author Helen Adams, August 13, 2002.

27. David Weigel, "Welcome to the Fun-Free University," *Reason*, 36, issue 5 (October 2004): 41–47, http://web17.epnet.com (accessed January 20, 2005).

28. Anthony E. Conte, "In Loco Parentis: Alive and Well," *Education* 121, issue 1 (Fall 2000): 195, http://web17epnet.com (accessed August 25, 2004).

29. Nancy Kranich, email message to author Helen Adams, August 11, 2003.

30. American Library Association, Office for Intellectual Freedom, "Privacy: An Interpretation of the Library Bill of Rights," http://www.ala.org/ala/oif/state mentspols/statementsif/interpretations/privacy.htm (accessed July 23, 2004).

31. Deborah Caldwell-Stone, email message to author Helen Adams, July 22, 2004.

32. Judith Krug and Dorothy Ragsdale, "Report of the [ALA] Audit Committee, Appendix I, Background of the ALA Privacy Audit, Defining the Privacy Audit," July 28, 2004, 13.

33. American Library Association Intellectual Freedom Committee, "Conducting a Privacy Audit, Appendix 2, Guidelines for Developing a Library Privacy Policy," http://www.ala.org/ala/oif/iftoolkits/toolkitsprivacy/libraryprivacy.htm#pri vacyaudit (accessed July 29, 2004).

34. Based on information obtained from the American Library Association, Office for Information Technology Policy, "Online Privacy Tutorial #27: Conducting a Privacy Audit," 2002, and Karen Coyle, "Make Sure You Are Privacy Literate,"

Library Journal 127, issue 16 (October 1, 2002): 55–57, http://web17.epnet.com (accessed July 14, 2004).

35. American Library Association Intellectual Freedom Committee, "Conducting a Privacy Audit."

36. Karen Coyle, "Make Sure You Are Privacy Literate."

37. Mary Minow, email message to author Helen Adams, January 17, 2005.

38. "Acceptable Use Policies: A Handbook," Virginia Department of Education, http://www.pen.k12.va.us/go/VDOE/Technology/AUP/home.shtml (accessed March 30, 2003).

39. Sharon Cromwell, "Getting Started on the Internet: Developing an Acceptable Use Policy (AUP)," *Education World*, 1998, http://www.education-world.com/a_curr/curr093.shtml (accessed March 30, 2003).

40. "Children's Internet Protection: A Summary," American Library Association, http://www.ala.org/cipa/Summary.PDF (accessed March 25, 2003).

41. "Acceptable Use Policy-Privacy Issues," Project Interconnect, http://projectinterconnect.org/filters/auppriv.htm (accessed July 11, 2004).

42. Nancy Willard, "Ensuring Student Privacy on the Internet: Technology in the Classroom," *Education World*, 2002, http://www.education-world.com/a_tech/tech120.shtml (accessed August 9, 2003).

43. Pennsylvania Department of Education, "Definition of Terms-CIPA," http://www.pde.state.pa.us/ed_tech/cwp/view.asp?a=169&q=87755 (accessed July 11, 2004).

44. "Personally Identifiable Information," P3P Writer, http://www.p3pwriter.com/LRN_000asp (accessed July 29, 2004).

45. American Library Association, Office for Information Technology Policy, "Online Privacy Tutorial #4, Privacy and the Library Professional," http://privacytut@ala.org (accessed March 18, 2003).

46. "Network and Acceptable Use Guidelines," Wisconsin Rapids School District, http://www.wrps.org/inservice/aup.htm#guidelines (accessed July 12, 2004).

47. Jeff Gibson, email message to author Helen Adams, July 13, 2004.

48. "Study: Teens More Likely to Divulge Personal Information on the Web," School Technology News ALERT, May 30, 2000, Vol. 3, No. 22, http://www.eschoolnews.org/technews2 (accessed June 15, 2000).

49. "Children and the Web," Edupage, May 19, 2000, News Abstracts from Information Inc. and Edupage, 2000.

50. "Kids Run a 20% Risk of 'Cybersex' Advances," Edupage, June 9, 2000, News Abstracts from Information Inc. and Edupage, 2000.

51. Ibid.

52. Robyn Weisman, "Study: Web-Wise Teens Savvy About Online Privacy," NewsFactor Network, http://www.newsfactor.com/perl/printer/12301/ (accessed August 10, 2003).

53. Nancy Willard, "Ensuring Student Privacy on the Internet."

54. Nancy Willard, "Safe and Responsible Use of the Internet: A Guide for Educators," Responsible Netizen Institute, 2002–2003, http://responsiblenetizen.org/onlinedocs/pdf/srui/sruilisting.html (accessed July 27, 2004).

55. *Webster's New World Dictionary of the American Language*, 2nd college ed. (New York: Simon & Schuster, 1986): 1430.

56. Nancy Willard, "Safe and Responsible Use of the Internet."

57. Ibid.

58. Ibid.

59. Federal Trade Commission, "How to Protect Kids' Privacy Online: A Guide for Teachers," http://www.ftc.gov/bcp/conline/pubs/online/teachers.htm (accessed July 18, 2004).

60. American Library Association, Office for Information Technology Policy, "Online Privacy Tutorial: Children and Privacy in School Libraries," http://www.fontanalib.org (accessed July 10, 2004).

61. Nora Carr, "School Web Sites for Sale: Breach of Trust or Smart Business?" eSchool News, July 31, 2000, http://www.eschoolnews.com/archive.html (accessed August 5, 2000).

62. "Market Research in the Classrooms," *Consumer Reports* (June 2000): 6.

63. Rebecca S. Weiner, "Lawmakers Push for Parental Consent on Commercialism in Schools," eSchool News online, August 1, 2000, http://www.eschoolsnews.com/news/showStory.cfm?ArticleID=1508 (accessed July 3, 2002).

64. Carr, "School Web Sites for Sale: Breach of Trust or Smart Business?"

65. Lynn Waddell, "Flap Erupts Over Ads on School Websites," *Christian Science Monitor,* http://www.scmonitor.com/durable/2001/05/02/p2s.1.htm (accessed July 1, 2002).

66. Cara Branigan, "Senate Bill Aims to Restrict Commercialism in Schools," eSchool News Online, April 1, 2001 (accessed July 3, 2002).

67. Ibid.

68. National PTA, "This Week in Washington—August 3, 2001: ESEA Highlight: Student Privacy Protection Act," www.pta.org/ptwashington/news/dcnews/010803.asp#2 (accessed July 19, 2004).

69. National School Boards Association, "Guidance for School Districts on Student Education Records, Directory Information, Health Information and Other Privacy Provisions," Resource Document #2, 9/30/2003, http://www.nsba.org/site/docs/32500/42420.pdf (accessed July 19, 2004).

70. Ibid.

71. Brannigan, "Senate Bill."

72. Glen Warchol, "Activist Wins Access to School Internet Records," *Salt Lake Tribune,* June 26, 1998, http://proquest.umi.com (accessed July 20, 2004).

73. Ibid.

74. Glen Warchol, "Computer Logs Released—Into Oblivion; Internet-Freedom Activist Gains Access to School Records After They Have Been Erased," *Salt Lake Tribune,* August 10, 1998, http://proquest.umi.com (accessed July 20, 2004).

75. Glen Warchol, "Utah Records Panel Approves Probe into Destruction of Files: Records Panel Orders Probe into Destruction of Files," *Salt Lake Tribune,* August 11, 1998, http://proquest.umi.com (accessed July 20, 2004).

76. Associated Press, "Court Tells School Give Dad Internet Log," November 7, 2000, http://www.eagletribune.com/news/stories/20001107/FP_008.htm (accessed September 28, 2002).

77. Jason Schreiber, "Exeter Officials Defend Selves in Internet Log Case," *Exeter News-Letter,* December 8, 2000, http://www.seacoastline.com/2000news/exeter/e12_8a.htm (accessed September 28, 2002).

78. Ibid.

79. "Court: Schools Must Let Parents View Internet-Use Logs," eSchool News Online, January 1, 2001, http:// www.uintah.k12.ut.us/tech/laws/filterlog.htm (accessed September 28, 2002).

80. Sylvia K. Norton, email message to author Helen Adams, January 10, 2005.

81. Nancy Willard, "Safe and Responsible Use of the Internet: A Guide for Educators, Part III. Legal Issues-Internet Use in School, Chapter 5, Public Records," p. 3, http://responsiblenetizen.org/onlinedocs/pdf/srui/sruilisting.html (acessed January 10, 2005).

82. Marty Johnson, email message to author Helen Adams, October 29, 2003.

83. Ibid.

84. "Frequently Asked Questions," *RFID Journal*, http://www.rfidjournal.com/article/articleview/207#Anchor-What-363 (accessed July 22, 2004).

85. Norman Oder, "RFID Use Raises Privacy Concerns," *Library Journal* 128, no. 19 (November 15, 2003), http://web11.epnet.com (accessed July 19, 2004).

86. David Dorman, "RFID on the Move," *American Libraries Online*, October 2003, http://www.ala.org/al_online (accessed July 22, 2004).

87. "An Overview of RFID," *Library Technology Reports* 39, no. 6 (November/December 2003), http://weblinks1.epnet.com (accessed July 19, 2004).

88. Rebekah Anderson, telephone interview by Helen Adams, July 27, 2004.

89. Vinod Chachra and Daniel McPherson, "Personal Privacy and Use of RFID Technology in Libraries," October 31, 2003, http://www.vtls.com/documents/privacy.pdf (accessed July 22, 2004).

90. Grant Gross, "Privacy Advocates Ask FTC for RFID Technical Review But RFID Backers Said It's Too Soon for Such an Assessment," *Computer World*, June 22, 2004, http://www.computerworld.com/mobiletopics/mobile/technology/story/o,10801.94019.00html (accessed July 19, 2004).

91. Ken Camlek, interview by Helen Adams, August 22, 2003.

92. Katie Hafner, "Where the Hall Monitor Is a Webcam," *New York Times*, February 27, 2003, http://web11.epnet.com (accessed March 3, 2003).

93. Rebecca Sausner, "Seeing is Believing," District Administration, July 2003, http://www.districtadministration.com/page.cfm?p=451 (accessed August 20, 2003).

94. Letenyei, Danielle. "Students Adapted Well to Use of Cameras: Both Officials and Students Say the Security Cameras Have Prevented Problems," *Wisconsin State Journal*, December 15, 2002, http://web11.epnet.com (accessed March 2, 2003).

95. Lee Gordon, "Surveillance Cameras in Libraries and Computer Labs," March 11, 2003. AASLFORUM:975 aaslforum@ala.org.

96. Gay Ann Loesch, "Surveillance Cameras in Libraries & Computer Labs," March 11, 2003. AASLFORUM :976 aaslforum@ala.org.

97. Gretchen Asam, email message to author Helen Adams, March 21, 2003.

98. Dee Gwaltney, "Surveillance Cameras in Libraries & Computer Labs," March 11, 2003. AASLFORUM:972:aaslforum@ala.org.

99. Daniel Huebsch, email message to author Helen Adams, March 11, 2003.

100. Dr. Kathleen Martinsen, interview by Helen Adams, September 16, 2003, Rosholt School District, Rosholt, Wisconsin.

CHAPTER 6

Privacy Issues for Academic Libraries

Introduction

An academic library nested in the cloistered world of ivy-covered towers is as anachronistic as the stereotypical librarian who zealously guards a print collection, aggressively maintaining silence. No longer self-contained, the academic library has embraced technologies that create complex new dimensions to its mission and its commitment to protecting patron privacy. Automated circulation and reserve services, web-based reference services, licensed and networked electronic information, email, interlibrary loan, and consortia agreements allow academic libraries to disregard boundaries that once defined the campus life of a university. This chapter describes the risk to privacy that accompanies accessing resources and services that have become the daily fare of academic libraries and examines policies and procedures that define the role of the academic library in protecting patron privacy.

Doing Business in an Academic Library

What are the privacy risks lurking within the walls of the academic library as well as within the pages of its web site? Upon entering and leaving a modern university library, patrons pass through security gates with the expectation that they will be asked to reveal the contents of their purses, briefcases, or duffel bags. They may be asked to show their university identification cards. As they roam the stacks they may not be aware that video surveillance is recording their movements. Privacy statements found on university web sites assure users that information that personally identifies them is not collected. The university and its departments, however, do not enjoy complete control over the digital environment of information access. When patrons check out library materials at the circulation desk or renew them online, personal information such as name, address, university identification number, email address, university status (e.g., faculty, student, staff), and PIN, or personal identification number, is linked to their transactions. The library management software retains circulation records while materials are in circulation and deletes them when materials are returned. Until that time, these records are subject to search and seizure by government agencies under the USA PATRIOT Act. When they sit down at a computer to browse a web site, read pages, or download, information about their sessions is collected and stored through client/server technology. This information usually includes the Internet domain visited, the type of browser and operating system used to access the site, the date and time of the visit, and the pages visited and may include personal information such as PIN numbers and email addresses.

When patrons access resources or services through the library web site, they identify, or authenticate, themselves to the network through smart identification cards or Radio Frequency Identification (RFID) as a requirement for using library resources and services. When they bring their laptops to the library, wireless networks allow them to access the secured academic library web site via the Virtual Personal Network (VPN) within the walls of student dormitories as well as academic libraries. No longer restricted to "library computers," patrons are using their personal computers as client machines in the university network to access information and the attendant collection of information about themselves and their sessions. "A clear problem is that in an electronic environment, it becomes hard to differentiate between a private and public place and therefore what should be protected and what should not."[1]

These trends place the conversation about privacy in academic libraries in a technological arena that is riddled with privacy risks. Additionally, libraries without walls remind the profession of its primary mission: "to create an awareness of 'knowledge space' where libraries become centers of active learning; where the development of the intellectual scaffold to connect with, interact with, and use information to construct deep knowledge and meaning become the highest priority."[2] To that end, it is not enough for Internet search engines and artificial intelligence to "googlize" academic research. The deep web, where peer-reviewed, scholarly information and research are embedded in subscription databases and are protected by firewalls and passwords, is not accessed by Google. Protected by copyright and licensing, scholarly information that resides in the deep web is not for sale, but it is for lease, and university libraries pay a heavy price for access. Their patrons pay the price in accepting privacy risk, including authentication, or identification upon logging in, and the collection of personal information.

Publishers of the electronic resources that license scholarly and copyrighted information to academic libraries collect cookies that distinguish among uses of a web site. Patron requests that involve email, web forms, and authentication, such as interlibrary loan made available through consortia, do require personal information that is needed to fill the information request. The use of "ask-a-librarian" online reference services, not always limited to a particular university's community, can now be contracted to outside providers who offer 24/7 (24 hours a day, 7 days a week) reference services on a national and international basis. These contractors are subject to confidentiality agreements that restrict use and disclosure of information about patrons such as IP addresses, name, email address, ZIP code, telephone number, and library card number. However, when patrons enter the world wide web (WWW), either directly through a browser or through links from a university web site, the university and the electronic publishers are not responsible for the content or privacy practices of those web sites and they issue disclaimers to that effect. Information collection practices of WWW sites may include use of personal information for commercial purposes such as selling that information to a third party. Academic libraries face the dilemma of balancing privacy protection while offering state-of-the-art services through electronic media that require patron identification and authentication. At the heart of this issue is a narrowing definition of what constitutes personally identifiable information.

The college classroom itself is becoming part of a networked environment. "A third of higher education institutions offered distance education courses in fall 1995, another quarter planned to offer such courses in the next 3 years."[3] Even the conventional classroom is donning electronic features as software such as CTWeb, Blackboard, and CourseInfo offer email, electronic syllabi, online grading, and access to a library of resources that may be customized to include academic library resources. As the line between classroom and "library" blurs, implications for electronic access to resources, with the attendant privacy concerns, raise new issues for academia. University instructors are subject to the same privacy risks as students. For example, faculty reserve records may contain names, email addresses, and sometimes mailing addresses. This information may be available to those who have the password to access electronic reserve records. In both classroom and library, issues of intellectual freedom are tied to confidentiality and privacy. "Lack of privacy and confidentiality has a chilling effect on users' choices. All users have a right to be free from any unreasonable intrusion into or surveillance of their lawful library use."[4] When patrons do business with their academic libraries, whether in person or through the library web site, no transaction is free from privacy risk.

The Delicate Balance

For academic libraries the concern for intellectual freedom, a cornerstone of university life, exacerbates the growing distance between ideals and practice. Balancing traditional values of intellectual freedom, unrestricted access, and protection of patrons' privacy is a challenge for academic libraries. "To sustain this balance academic librarians and their communities have come up with a pragmatic balance best characterized as 'mutually assured anonymity' (MAA)."[5] Prior to computers and global information networks, MAA was sustainable as librarians kept a watchful eye on reference desks and patron records. Authentication requires patrons to enter a user name and password when they log in to public access computers in the academic library or onto the library web site. This practice violates mutually assured anonymity as well as traditional values of librarianship that ensure unrestricted access to information. The rationale for authentication rests on the tension between access and security: authentication protects academic libraries from anonymous computer hacking and Internet crime. "We are walking a tightrope," says Mark McFarland, assistant director of digital-library services at the University of Texas at Austin. "We don't want to facilitate criminal behavior, but we don't want to close off access to information."[6] Authentication has a sobering consequence: law enforcement and government authorities can identify users and their network activity through authentication procedures that are automatically stored on web servers. Authentication has a practical function for electronic publishers: it assures that only authorized members of the licensed academic community are accessing their products and that the number of simultaneous users specified by the licensing agreement is not exceeded. A librarian noted that a local sandwich shop had open access to computers and asked, "If you can get it (anonymous and open web surfing) at Schlotsky's, shouldn't you be able to get it at the library?"[7] Just as the little red school house has given way to an industrialized and commercialized educational institution, the library has moved into the complex electronic age of information delivery. It now stands at the crossroads of legal, ethical, civic, and commercial interests as the agents of government, the information industry, and society invent the consequences. "To sustain its institutional purpose to gather and organize knowledge, academic libraries are withdrawing the easy anonymity of just a few short years ago"[8] as patrons authenticate themselves before they even use a library resource.

Privacy Protection Policy

Academic librarians juggle issues of access and security that evolve from heavy reliance on networked technologies for the delivery of services and resources. Since the 1980s, debate about library policy has changed: "shifts in the technical, economic, and policy domains have brought us to a new landscape that is more variegated, more dangerous, and more hopeful than before."[9] Specifically, technological developments such as data mining algorithms, market segmentation methods, computer networking, digital wireless communication, advanced sensors, and an intelligent transportation system[10] exist alongside the realities of operating an academic library as an entity and as part of the library system in real time and space. Policies and procedures of academic libraries are driven by these shifts as they affect the physical and virtual arenas of operation. A privacy policy statement is a prerequisite for evaluating how effectively an academic library is balancing the issues of intellectual freedom and privacy protection. Academic libraries must consider university policy, as well as the policies and practices of the Information Technology department and the electronic information publishers from whom licenses for electronic information are purchased.

University Policy

The intersection and divergence of individual and organizational rights are central to the underlying questions that drive formulation of policy. These questions focus on the specific areas of confidentiality that the university considers essential and on the laws and regulations that dictate procedure. For example, library policy that appears on the web site of a university should reference federal law, such as FERPA (the Family Education Rights and Privacy Act), which protects the privacy of student educational records and state confidentiality statutes. Risk management enters into the picture as the university, usually with the help of legal counsel, decides how much risk it is willing to take and how strict its security policy will be.

> Many academic libraries depend on the American Association of University Professors (AAUP) academic freedom principles as sufficient backup in case of a First Amendment problem. However, the consequences of intellectual freedom issues, including unrestricted access and protection of patron privacy, have become so complex that complementary statements, based on the American Library Association's intellectual freedom principles, need to be part of any campus' comprehensive policies on academic freedom.[11]

While this sets the tone for formulating library policy, university policy statements tend to be generic statements about privacy that support state statutes. In addition to the university policy statement, various departments such as Human Resources, Security, Internal Audit, and Information Technology have a role to play in the information-gathering phase of formulating a library privacy policy.

Information Technology Policy

While academic libraries are concerned with access and protecting patron privacy, they must also be concerned with managed networks and security. "For libraries, the issues of privacy and network security are

Figure 1
Privacy Warning

> You have requested an encrypted page. The web site has identified itself
> correctly and information you see or enter on this page can't easily be read
> by a third party.
>
> • Alert me whenever I am about to view an encrypted page

intimately intertwined, and managing computer networks to protect user
privacy is critical."[12] Information Technology departments share this concern, with emphasis on network security. Academic library departments include a library systems administrator and technicians who may be trained
librarians and who may report to the IT department. This staff is cognizant
of measures to protect the library network and knowledgeable of the technological infrastructure of the university as it is managed by the IT department.

Policy is more often evident through practice than in written policy
statements posted on Information Technology web sites. Typically, IT posts
"just-enough-just-in-time statements," like the example shown in Figure 1,
which places the onus on the individual user to decide what is acceptable.

A similar message is displayed when the patron is about to leave an encrypted page, warning that the information sent or received from now on
could be read by a third party. The onus is on the patron to evaluate the
risk, but the decision is a moot question. Access to electronic information,
including indices, citations, and full-text, is not really an option for the university student who must complete a literature review, especially if the academic library has dropped its print subscriptions in favor of electronic
indices and journals.

Digital access to information for library patrons requires a sophisticated
infrastructure for which IT departments are responsible and they are usually not bound to consult with other departments, including academic libraries, although a cooperative working relationship is the ideal. Often the
practices of IT departments are modeled on formal or informal library policy. A typical IT policy bans the sharing of log files collected on university
servers with one exception: IT allows each department in the university to
have access to its own logs for their business purposes so that they can gen-
erate usage statistics. Like academic libraries, IT departments are concerned about how electronic publishers who license their databases to
universities protect the privacy of university users.

IT protects the university network with firewalls or series of firewalls
that prevent outsiders from access to the web site. It is the configuration
of the firewall that is a critical factor in its effectiveness. In some universi-

ties a library system administrator constantly monitors security threats that can take advantage of flaws in firewalls or misconfigurations. Another kind of threat comes from within the network when individuals try to penetrate the security of internal systems and servers. "With the growing popularity of wireless network services in libraries, libraries can no longer simply monitor what is happening on the public access computers to ensure security; instead, library networks need to be actively secure, using encryption, internal firewalls, VPNs, and authentication to protect the most valuable assets a library has—the trust of patrons that their privacy is and will continue to be secure."[13]

Electronic Publisher Policy

The increasing reliance of academic libraries on electronic indices and full-text databases, and even full-text books licensed through the world wide web by means of browser-based interfaces, raises privacy concerns that are beyond the control of academia. This interface provides commercial companies that produce and distribute electronic information with a rich source of information about the interests, behavior, and habits of web users without the permission of the individual using the product.[14] The privacy concern is the potential sharing of personally identifiable information with third parties. For example, DoubleClick, Inc., the nation's largest advertising agency, has been tracking Internet users by name and street address as they move from one web site to another. "On March 2, 2000, the company announced that it will not move forward on its plans to tie personally identifiable information to Internet users' online surfing habits until government and industry have reached a consensus on privacy rules for the Internet."[15] It is this clash between the commercial interests of the information industry and the academic focus of their customers that marks the relationship between academic libraries and electronic publishers as rocky, at best. Issues of pricing, access, copyright, preservation, and patron privacy have clouded ongoing negotiation of licenses that require consistent monitoring by academic librarians who specialize in electronic resources.

The guidelines of the International Coalition of Library Consortia (ICOLC) for electronic information publishing companies alert ICOLC member libraries who purchase licenses for electronic information. These guidelines state that the publisher: (1) will not disclose information about any individual user of its products; (2) will not deny an authorized user access to its product on account of that user's election not to permit distribution of personal information to a third party; (3) will post a privacy statement on its online site; (4) will maintain full control over its site to prevent any violation of the privacy by a third party, such as an advertiser or ISP; (5) will review regularly the functioning of its web site to ensure that its privacy policy is enforced and effective. ICOLC assures that "Nothing in these guidelines is intended to interfere with a publisher's right to enforce license terms concerning which users are authorized to use its products. It is understood and accepted that owners of licensed web products may need to transmit information such as an IP address or user ID to a third party as part of the mechanism by which the owner limits use of its product to authorized users. These guidelines do not prohibit such transmission."[16]

The policies of electronic publishers regarding privacy protection are primarily found in the contractual agreements with academic libraries. This can vary among publishers and between publishers and their academic customers.

Library Policy

The library profession has a long-standing commitment to an ethic of facilitating, not monitoring, access to information. This commitment is implemented locally through development, adoption, and adherence to privacy policies that are consistent with applicable federal, state, and local law. Users have the right to be informed about policies and procedures that govern the collection of information about them and/or their information use. Through state laws many users have a right to have their personal information protected and kept private and confidential by those who have direct or indirect access to that information. When users recognize or fear that their privacy or confidentiality is compromised, true freedom of inquiry no longer exists.[17]

A comprehensive approach to privacy policy takes into account federal and state laws, as well as the policies of the university and its departments, and documents generated within the library community. The American Library Association "Code of Ethics" is the backbone of library policy. It states, "We protect each library user's right to privacy and confidentiality with respect to information sought or received and resources consulted, borrowed, acquired or transmitted."[18] The Library Bill of Rights affirms the ethical imperative to provide unrestricted access to information and to guard against impediments to open inquiry. Article IV states: "Libraries should cooperate with all persons and groups concerned with resisting abridgement of free expression and free access to ideas."[19] Article V states, "A person's right to use a library should not be denied or abridged because of origin, age, background, or views."[20] This article precludes the use of profiling as a basis for any breach of privacy rights. Users have the right to use a library without any abridgement of privacy that may result from equating the subject of their inquiry with behavior.

The ALA Council adopted the "Intellectual Freedom Principles for Academic Libraries, An Interpretation of the Library Bill of Rights" that meets the specific needs of academic libraries. It can be found at http://www.ala.org/Template.cfm?Section=Interpretations&Template=/ContentManagement/ContentDisplay.cfm&ContentID=8551. It states:

A strong intellectual freedom perspective is critical to the development of academic library collections and services that dispassionately meet the education and research needs of a college or university community. 2) The privacy of library users is and must be inviolable. . . . Policies should be in place that maintain confidentiality of library borrowing records and of other information relating to personal use of library information and services.[21]

In addition to these documents, academic libraries would also find "Guidelines for Federal and ACT Government Web Sites" a useful document for designing a privacy policy. Designed for use by government agencies, the intent of these guidelines is to assist in adopting best privacy practices and compliance with the Privacy Act of 1988 as follows:

- State what information is collected about individuals visiting the site, how it is used, and if it is disclosed.
- Prominently display privacy statement.
- Agencies that collect personal information must comply with Internet Privacy Principles under the Privacy Act of 1988.
- If personal information is collected it should be done by sufficiently secure means. Individuals should be provided with alternative means of providing personal information to the agency via the web site.
- When agencies are considering the publication of personal information regarding individuals on the web they should comply with Internet Privacy Principles 1–3.[22]

One college's web site privacy policy defines personal information as "any information concerning a natural person which, because of name, number, symbol, mark, or other identifies, can be used to identify that natural person."[23] This definition is widely accepted today, as evidenced by the privacy policies of academic libraries. For the most part, however, academic library privacy policies, notably those posted on university library sites prior to 2002, tended to be oriented to procedures. More recent postings are privacy statements, rather than policy statements, and are explained in briefer and clearer terms of intent. A content analysis of over thirty academic library policy statements and procedures revealed that privacy statements share some common elements:

- Commitment to protecting privacy of library users.
- Reference to documents of professional library organizations (e.g., the ALA "Code of Ethics," the "Library Bill of Rights," the "Intellectual Freedom Principles for Academic Libraries of the Association of College and Research Libraries") and relevant state law.
- Clear statements of information collection practices such as browser detection, cookies, use of Internet Protocol (IP) addresses, server logs (for example, "Un-

less you choose to provide that information to us, such as by submitting a question, requesting an item, or otherwise 'doing business' with the library. We do not collect personal information from such communications for any purpose other than to respond to you. The web site does not collect any personal information about you unless you provide that information by sending an email or completing a request or other type of form.").[24]

- Identification of types of information collected which fall into two categories: (1) personal, for example, name, email address, or credit card number; and (2) nonpersonal, for example, address of server, IP address, browser type, date and time of access, pages viewed, or files downloaded. Information is considered personal if the user can be personally identified.

- Statements about how the information in data logs is used (use of resources, summary statistics, determining technical design specifications, identifying system performance or problem areas).

- Procedures followed to protect patron's privacy, for example, retention of information for limited periods of time, restriction of access of information to authorized staff, or referral of an agent with a subpoena or search warrant to university counsel.

- Disclaimers that relieve the university of Internet use consequences.

Academic libraries should also have an acceptable use policy which explains computer use and makes patrons responsible for the material they access. These policies are meant to prevent overloading of computer networks while universities maintain services related to their educational missions.[25]

Privacy seal organizations presently certify an organization's compliance with their stated privacy policy in areas such as notice, choice, access, security, and redress with regard to personal information.[26] An example of such a company is TRUSTe, an independent nonprofit privacy initiative that uses software that formulates privacy policy. A similar product is available from the Direct Marketing Association. The content of such a policy addresses the kind of information sought by patrons and the benefits patrons will receive as a result of the library's use of this information.

Privacy Protection Procedures

As reported in Chapter 3, a grim reminder of the importance of procedures that are well communicated to library staff was the FBI's secret counterintelligence operation called the Library Awareness Program. Conducted between 1973 and the late 1980s to track the reading material of Soviet and Eastern European citizens in America's science libraries, the initiative had no legal foundation and was, in fact, a violation of patrons' privacy. Herbert Foerstel, a science librarian during that time, noted, "FBI agents would approach clerical staff at public and university libraries, flash a badge and appeal to their patriotism in preventing the spread of 'sensitive but unclassified' information."[27] The passage of the USA PATRIOT Act has revived concerns in American academic libraries where the patron population includes large numbers of international students, faculty, and researchers. Librarians should be aware that the rights of all patrons, regardless of citizenship, are protected by the First Amendment.

Best practice with regard to privacy protection offers patrons opportunities to make decisions about the selection of, access to, and use of information and the attendant privacy risks. Procedures that involve the collection of personally identifiable information are stated in the privacy statements posted on the library web site. Typical statements assure patrons that collection of such information becomes a matter of routine or policy when necessary for the fulfillment of the mission of the library. Implicit in these statements are procedures and practices that reflect the values of librarianship as stated in professional documents referenced in the privacy statement. "Everyone who collects or accesses personally identifiable information in any format has a legal and ethical obligation to protect confidentiality."[28] Typical privacy statements posted on academic library web sites indicate that libraries do not reveal personally identifiable information without the user's consent, except to the extent required by law. They do not retain the information longer than necessary and patrons may withhold personal information if they wish. This will, however, affect availability of some library resources and services. In order to define procedures that flow from a privacy protection policy it is important to understand the kind of information about a patron that is collected and who has access to that information.

What Is the Nature of Information Collected about Patrons?

Information is collected about patrons either internally within the academic library or externally by outside contractors who deliver resources or services through the library's web site. Internal patron information collection is discussed using circulation and interlibrary loan procedures as examples. Patron information collected by external contractors is discussed using electronic reference services and licensed electronic information as examples.

Personally identifiable information collected by the library to deliver circulation or interlibrary loan services is needed for administrative purposes, for example, collecting overdue materials, recalling a book, or delivering a document and includes name, address, phone number, university identification number, a designator that indicates patron status as student, faculty, or staff member, email address, and Personal Identification Number (PIN). It also contains the names of checked out materials and fines owed. There is no permanent record linking a user to library material after the library material has been returned if there are no outstanding charges. Academic libraries and their branches may provide information to third parties under contract to the university in order to obtain payment of fees or return of library materials.

Electronic reference services and electronic publishers collect personally identifiable information that may be needed for administrative purposes and for product improvement or marketing. These services may collect a patron's name, email, zip code, telephone number, library card number, and other information that may not be required for the reference service to function but may enhance the service. For example, the email addresses of patrons allow the service to send transcripts of the reference sessions to patrons. These transcripts may also be sent to the library to improve service. Electronic reference services also collect IP addresses to help libraries understand how patrons use the site for the purposes of evaluation and performance improvement. Electronic reference services may also collect cookies for the purposes of system administration and sometimes for authentication. Cookies are small pieces of information that are stored by the user's browser on the hard drive of the user's computer. They are simple text files used by the web browser to provide a means of distinguishing among users of a web site. Cookies can be used in two ways: (1) to access previously stored questions when the patron logs into the site, and (2) to maintain the connection. Patrons can configure their browsers to refuse cookies or to notify them when they have received one. If patrons reject cookies, though, they are not able to use certain features of the web site such as the ability to share web pages with the librarian who is answering the reference question. Even when patrons accept cookies, the reference service cannot use them to identify the patrons or collect any other personal information about them.

Policy statements of electronic publishers say they are committed to protecting personal information and are legally bound to do so when they enter into confidentiality agreements with their customers, that is, academic libraries. All information that patrons provide is stored on their secure servers. However, these services issue disclaimers on their sites that caution users that they cannot ensure or warrant the security of any information transmitted to them, and that the user does so at his or her risk.

Patron choice is a key element in collecting personally identifiable information. Electronic reference services offer some options. Patrons may opt to deactivate their accounts or edit collected information about them by contacting a site coordinator. These services caution patrons to log out when using computers to which others have access, such as in a computer lab, Internet café, or library. In an academic environment this is akin to cautioning motorists that driving on an expressway while commuting to work may be dangerous and that they do so at their own risk. It is a choice, but is the alternative a viable option?

Another type of information is collected about each library in the university library system. The nature of that information depends on the way resources are connected. The logs that are generated contain information necessary for analyzing the use of resources, troubleshooting problems, and improving services. Log data may be used to distribute resource costs among the libraries and faculties. These anonymous logs are retained for approximately one fiscal year. Academic libraries may use software to create customized web pages and maintain user profiles to collect information about new library resources. These services are optional and patrons are given the option of discontinuing these services at which time all records are deleted.

How this information about patrons and sessions is collected is significant in that the academic library may not have control over what is collected. Network traffic logs are generated by software programs to monitor network traffic, identify unauthorized access or access to nonpublic information, detect computer viruses and other software that might damage university computers or the network, and monitor and tune the performance of the university network. These programs may detect such information as email headers, addresses from network packets, and other information. Information from these activities is used only for the purpose of maintaining the security and performance of the university's networks and computer systems. Personally identifiable information from these activities is not released to external parties without the patron's consent unless required by law.

Information collected through server logs can help analyze use of the library web site, diagnose server problems, and administer the web site. Information may include: user/client hostname or IP address; http header, user agent information (browser, its version, and operating system); system date (date and time of the request); full request (exact request made); pages visited; status (status code returned in response to the request); content length (in bytes, of the file sent in response to the request); method (request method used); Universal Resource Identifier (URI location of a resource on the server); query string of the URI (anything after the question mark in a URI); protocol (transport protocol and version used); and the address from another web site, if a patron linked to it. Web server log information is used to create internal summary reports about web site use. Some reports may identify the host name of the computer used by the patron. The information is not collected for commercial marketing purposes and university libraries are not authorized to sell or otherwise disclose the information collected from this web site for commercial marketing purposes.

Universities may not use cookies, or may use temporary ones to track session characteristics on the web catalog. No personally identifiable information is received or kept and no persistent cookies are placed on users' computers. Electronic publishers do use cookies in their electronic information databases.

University web sites routinely collect and store information from online visitors using web site logs to help manage those sites and improve service. The information includes pages visited on the site, the date and time of the visit, the Internet address (URL or IP address) of the referring site, the domain name and IP address from which the access occurred, the version of browser used, the capabilities of the browser, and search terms used on our search engines. Usually no attempt to identify individual visitors from this information and any personally identifiable information is made and it is not released to external parties without the user's consent unless required by law.

Information collected automatically when patrons visit the library web site includes:

- Internet protocol address of the computer that accessed our web site;
- The type of browser, its version, and the operating system on which that browser is running;
- The web page from which the user accessed the current web page;
- The date and time of the user's request;
- The pages that were visited and the amount of time spent on each page.

None of the above information is deemed to constitute personal information by the Internet Privacy and Security Act. The information automatically collected is used to improve the web site's content and to help librarians understand how users are interacting with its web site. This information is collected for statistical analysis and to determine what information is of most and least interest to users.

What Can Librarians and Library Administrators Do?

The university limits employee access to personal information collected internally through its web site to those employees who need access to the information in the performance of their official duties. Employees who have access to this information should follow appropriate procedures to protect the personal information and safeguard the integrity of its IT assets, including, but not limited to, authentication, authorization, monitoring, auditing, and encryption.[29] These security procedures have been integrated into the design, implementation, and day-to-day operations of the web site as part of a commitment to the security of electronic content as well to the electronic transmission of information.

The collection of information through a library web site and the disclosure of that information are subject to the provisions of the Internet Security and Privacy Act. Librarians collect personal information through their web site or disclose personal information collected through the web site if the user has consented to the collection or disclosure of such personal information. The voluntary disclosure of personal information by the user constitutes consent to the collection and disclosure of the information for the purposes that the user disclosed the information. However, academic libraries may collect or disclose personal information without consent if the collection or disclosure is (1) necessary to perform the statutory duties of the university libraries or necessary for the university libraries to operate a program authorized by law or authorized by state or federal statute or regulation; (2) made pursuant to a court order or by law; (3) for the purpose of validating the identity of the user; (4) for the purpose of using the information for statistical purposes that is in a form that cannot be used to identify any particular person. The disclosure of information, including personal information, collected through this web site is subject to the provisions of the Freedom of Information Act and relevant state laws, such New York's Personal Privacy Protection Law.

Librarians need to guard the confidentiality of interlibrary loan requests, online surveys, and routing slips that can result in a loss of privacy for patrons and therefore violate their intellectual freedom. There is a need for discretion in the notes and emails they write to each other regarding the research needs of patrons. Only library staff should have access to circulation records of materials currently checked out. During a broadcasted satellite teleconference at the School of Library and Information Science, Indiana University, Tracy Mitrano stated, "Policies, protocols, and procedures are the best bulwark we have against abuse."[30] Gary Strong advised libraries to adopt state confidentiality legislation and policy and establish clear procedures for staff if they are approached by law enforcement, fellow staff members, or patrons.[31] Mitrano cautioned, "Unless the party requesting information has a warrant, the library staff does not need to respond to the request immediately. . . . If anyone approaches you alleging to be a law enforcement office requesting information, do not disclose any information without first contacting your supervisor and legal counsel."[32] Strong advised that when a librarian is presented with a subpoena, "It's the library being served, not the librarian. The librarian should immediately contact his or her supervisor and legal counsel, but does not have to disclose any information at that time."[33]

"Everyone (paid or unpaid) who provides governance, administration, or service in libraries has a responsibility to maintain an environment respectful and protective of the privacy of all users. Patrons as well have a responsibility to respect each others' privacy.[34] It is especially important to teach student workers how these laws apply when users request information that may be privileged. For example, a user can request a 'recall' of a circulating book, but can not be told who currently has the book. Reserve book circulation records cannot be shown to professors, who sometimes want to determine which student has consulted which book. Similarly, committees evaluating faculty for promotion and tenure cannot consult circulation records to see what books were consulted."[35]

Patron information collected by external sources require legal agreements. Electronic reference services sign agreements with academic libraries as part of the licensing process to ensure they will disclose personal information only to the extent necessary to fulfill the information request.

For example, they may need to refer your question to a librarian in our network who will have access to your information in order to get back to you with an answer to your questions. The service does not give, rent, lend, or sell individual information to any advertisers. It may disclose aggregate information (e.g., 5 million library users clicked on the site last month) in order to describe services to library partners and other third parties and for other lawful purposes. The service employs contractors to help with operations. Some or all of these contractors may access the databases to use this information. These contractors are subject to confidentiality agreements that restrict their use and disclosure of all information they obtain through their relationship with the reference service. The services do not disclose identifiable information about users, except as described in the Privacy Statement, or to comply with applicable laws or valid legal process, or to protect the rights or property of electronic reference services.

Academic library staff need to be aware of who they are serving. Patron constituency of academic libraries is diverse with regard to age, nationality, status, and need. This diversity raises a variety of questions with regard to privacy and confidentiality. Universities consider students adults, although some may be minors. Increasingly academic libraries are opening their doors to high school enrichment programs. It is not uncommon for high school students to use resources in their local community college or university libraries. While the ALA's "Free Access to Libraries for Minors" interpretation calls for unrestricted access, academic libraries could well begin to experience the kinds of book challenges so familiar to K–12 and public libraries that threaten unrestricted access and privacy policy.[36]

Librarians should review all clerical workflow to make sure that printouts of patron circulation or fines information are not reused, that all information is mailed in an envelope, not on a postcard.[37] It is questionable practice to keep sensitive materials behind a desk when other materials are on the open shelves. Some students might well be reticent to ask a librarian for such materials.[38] In the digital environment academic librarians can use the technology they have to move toward the concept of personalized service. Personally identifiable information retained on server logs or collected manually as the library conducts its everyday business through circulation, interlibrary loan, reference services, and electronic searching can be used to deliver one-to-one library services to patrons. This implies a shift in policy: academic libraries and Information Technology departments may want to revisit their policy statements and procedures with regard to collection and use of personally identifiable information to better serve the individual patron.

Many privacy-related situations relate to use of the campus computer network. Most campuses keep transaction logs far longer than libraries keep automated circulation records. Care should be taken to protect the privacy of students on campus networks, in regard to library records, reference questions, and other communications via the Internet. Librarians must not assume that campus network administrators are necessarily knowledgeable or sensitive to such potential invasions of privacy. If a network user violates campus policy, he or she should be granted due process.[39]

Libraries manage computer networks to protect user privacy by active management of software downloads, cookies, and other possible means of third-party online data collection through a library network. Librarians should regularly remove cookies and other software code that is placed on their networks in order to make sure that library networks are secure and are not being used illegally or in violation of library policies. They should purge web history, cached files, or other computer and Internet use records, which are considered business records and are subject to disclosure. To guard against unauthorized access, maintain data accuracy, and promote the correct use of information, libraries implement physical, electronic, and managerial procedures to safeguard and secure the information collected online. However, despite site security software, no assurances can be given that they will always and in all cases prevent or protect against invalid access or improper activity and any expectation or warranty of unassailable site security is expressly disclaimed.[40]

Privacy Ethics

Academic librarians are becoming increasingly involved in the ethical issues that are dramatized by the technology of information access and retrieval. Neil Postman, a well-known critic of digital technology, writes, "information appears indiscriminately, directed at no one in particular, in enormous volume and at high speeds, and disconnected from theory, meaning or purpose."[41] This significant change in the medium of written discourse results in questions of intellectual property rights, plagiarism, piracy, and privacy. Academic librarians grapple with the conflict between the benefits of information sharing and efforts to protect the integrity, confidentiality, and availability of information. Technology can be vulnerable to unethical practices because of the lack of means of authorization and authentication.[42] Questions of intellectual property also emerge in a digital environment that offers a range of formats from email to e-books. Do traditional values apply? Ambiguities and complexities of law, such as the Digital Copyright Act, make copyright guidelines vulnerable to interpretation. Do students recognize ethical behavior issues? Do they recognize an ethical dilemma and know what is right?[43] Do traditional values for intellectual property and privacy apply, or is there a need for new ones?[44] The scope of library instruction for academic librarians is widening as ethical questions about the authority and authenticity of students' term papers and scholars' published research arise. What is the content of this instruction? What are the boundaries? How can librarians effectively work with instructors to establish clear policy and fair procedures to help students use electronic information ethically? These issues have a place in the policies of academic libraries.

Privacy Personnel

Given the complexity of privacy concerns and the connection between privacy and the unrestricted access necessary for intellectual freedom, universities and academic libraries may want to consider staffing roles with regard to privacy. Best practice advises that the director of libraries is considered custodian of library records who receives requests for public records or inquiries from law enforcement officers. The director may delegate this authority to designated members of the library's management team. The director confers with the legal counsel before determining the proper response to any request for records, which should be accompanied by a subpoena, warrant, court order, or other investigatory document issued by a court of competent jurisdiction, showing good cause and in proper form. Staff is trained to refer law enforcement inquiries to the Office of the Director of Libraries.[45]

The position of a privacy compliance officer is a solution to requests for review of personal information collected by the university or library. State laws govern this process. For example, in Oregon patrons may submit a request to the privacy compliance officer who determines whether personal information pertaining to that user has been collected. Written requests are accompanied by reasonable proof of identity. The privacy compliance officer responds within five business days by: (1) providing access to the personal information; (2) denying access in writing, explaining the reasons; or (3) acknowledging receipt of the request in writing, stating the approximate date when the request will be granted or denied, which date shall not be more than thirty days from the date of acknowledgment. In the event that the university library has collected personal information through the web site and the information is to be provided to the user pursuant to his or her request, the privacy compliance officer informs the user of his or her right to request that the personal information be amended or corrected under the procedures set forth in Section 95 of the Public Officers Law.[46]

Other staff positions include an access services librarian and a director of public services and outreach. A privacy policy task force identifies existing policies to:

- Develop training program for faculty, staff, and students which will apprise them of such policies and alert them to the reporting structure and chain of custody established by the librarians;
- Establish dialogue in consultation and collaboration with assistant directors and directors on issues related to relevancy of information with campus units such as IT.

Privacy Audits

When academic libraries have their policy statements and procedures in place, they are ready to conduct privacy audits to ensure that they have the necessary guidelines and training in place in the event of an information inquiry.[47] Standards such as legality, consistency with regard to university culture and policies, and values of librarianship will align the library with institutional policies. Responsibility for generating, implementing, and enforcing the policy is a key question. The use, storage, distribution, and protection of the information within and outside of the organization are also important.[48] A privacy audit initially examines the organization's policies and procedures against standards such as legality and consistency. These standards may come from external or internal sources such as the Association of College and Research Libraries or university policies. James G. Neal, Dean of University Libraries at John Hopkins University, encouraged librarians to conduct privacy audits at a teleconference on the USA PATRIOT Act at the School of Library and Information Science, Indiana University. "Libraries need to be prepared to deal with the implications of this legislation. They need to make sure their staff receives the proper training and they retain legal counsel."[49]

The process of a privacy audit is a kind of "action research" that includes data collection and categorization. In addition to identifying privacy concerns, a privacy audit clearly identifies the sources of data that provide evidence. For example, a library may want to find out how their patrons feel about security measures in the library, or how they feel about the risks of online access. Instruments such as observation, surveys, and interviews may be used to collect data for analysis and evaluation of current practices. See Appendix II for privacy audit guidelines for academic libraries.

Privacy Enhancing Tools

It is common practice that the Information Technology (IT) department establishes policy and practice regarding transitioning from one level of risk to another throughout the university's web site. In fact, IT controls the digital environment and is ultimately responsible for protecting the technological infrastructure. In an ideal situation the library department would work collaboratively with IT to balance privacy and access concerns. In the complex technological environment of today's universities, the library department must go beyond its own boundaries to protect patron privacy. It is critical, therefore, for librarians, as well as technicians, to be aware of privacy enhancing tools such as anonymizers, cookie cutters, spam filtering software, and platforms for privacy preferences. On the other hand, it is critical for librarians to be aware of their limits in privacy protection. For example, libraries cannot control the process of information collection, patron access to that information, or a process for complaints and appeals in most university environments.

Privacy enhancing tools are valuable aids in building undetectable or unobtrusive protection protocols for patrons into the daily routines of doing business. The Platform for Privacy Preferences (P3P) Project, developed by the World Wide Web Consortium, provides a way for users to gain more control over the use of personal information on web sites they visit. It contains a standard set of multiple-choice questions covering all the major aspects of a web site's privacy policies. P3P-enabled web sites make this information available in a standard, machine-readable format. P3P-enabled browsers can read this snapshot automatically and compare it to the consumer's own set of privacy preferences. P3P makes privacy policies more readily accessible to users and enables them to interact with these policies.[50]

PGP (Pretty Good Privacy) was developed at MIT and distributed as freeware without cost for personal, noncommercial use in cooperation with Philip Zimmerman, the original author of PGP, Network Associates, and with RSA Security, which licenses patents and software for one of the public-key encryption technologies which PGP utilizes. PGP is distributed by MIT only to U.S. citizens in the United States or to Canadian citizens in Canada. PGP is a cryptographic, or coded, family of products that enables people to securely exchange messages and to secure files, disk volumes, and network connections with privacy and strong authentication. It provides users with the ability to encrypt messages. Authentication identifies the origin of the information, its authenticity, and that it is in its original state. PGP provides a tool in network security to verify the identity of an individual and provides secure data storage, enabling the user to encrypt files stored on his or her computer. PGPnet is a Virtual Private Network (VPN) client that enables secure peer-to-peer IP-based network connections. Self-Decrypting Archives allow users to exchange information securely with those who do not have PGP.[51]

Spychecker is freeware that can be downloaded from the web. These tools can detect keyloggers, activity monitoring software, web site loggers, and also common Adware, web bugs, tracking cookies, and many other items that are frequently encountered on the web. Many people consider them an invasion of their privacy, even though they are claimed to be mostly advertising related and usually limited to anonymous tracking.

Conclusion

Everyone involved with library services is experiencing the shifting boundaries between library and classroom, and between library and cyberspace. Rather than being marginalized by electronic delivery of resources and services, the academic library is becoming essential to the mission of its college or university. Privacy concerns are not restricted to those patrons who enter through library doors. The very nature of privacy concerns is broadening to embrace concerns for academic freedom and intellectual property rights. How will academic librarians reconcile their traditional professional values with their new world of information challenges?

Tim Lewontin, librarian at Boston University, observed, "Computer privacy is an oxymoron."[52] Technology has taken away our anonymity and, in many cases, our right to be left alone when seeking services and resources in an academic library. Academic librarians acknowledge the trade-off of patron privacy for improved information access. There is plenty of evidence that the price patrons pay is loss of privacy, and just as importantly, loss of control over one's privacy. Academic librarians, however, have a professional commitment to confidentiality, whether their libraries are located in a physical place or in cyberspace. Confidentiality is the underpinning principle of professional behavior because it serves the public good by ensuring that we can communicate our needs in an atmosphere of trust without sanctions. Doctors protect the privacy of their patients; lawyers protect their clients' privacy; educators protect their students' privacy; priests protect the privacy of their confessors; journalists protect the identities of their sources, even at the risk of serving jail sentences. Librarians have a long history of defending privacy, and its corollary, intellectual freedom. Whether the flow of information in a society is curtailed, for whatever reason, by a government, or facilitated by a technology, defense of patron privacy is critical to the essential services academic librarians provide that help patrons verify a fact, disprove an assumption, build new knowledge through research, gather a rationale for social reform, or question a political event. The academic library, in this sense, is the soul of an institution of higher education, and academic librarians are its conscience.

Notes

1. Fred H. Cate, *Privacy in the Information Age* (Washington, DC: Brookings Institution Press, 1997), 196.

2. Dr. Ross J. Todd, conversation with the author, August 5, 2004.

3. National Center for Education Statistics, "Distance Education at Degree-Granting Postsecondary Institutions, Executive Summary 2001–2002," http://nces.ed.gov/surveys/publications/2003017 (accessed July 29, 2004).

4. American Library Association, "Privacy: An Interpretation of the Library Bill of Rights," http://www.ala.org/Template.cfm?Section=Interpretations&Template=/ContentManagement/ContentDisplay.cfm&ContentID=31883 (accessed July 30, 2004).

5. John A. Shuler, "Privacy and Academic Libraries: Widening the Frame of Discussion," *Journal of Academic Librarianship* 30, no. 2 (March 2004): 157.

6. S. Carlson, "To Use That Library Computer, Please Identify Yourself," *Chronicle of Higher Education* 50, no. 2 (June 25, 2004): A39.

7. Ibid.

8. Shuler, "Privacy and Academic Libraries," 158.

9. Philip. A. Agre and Marc Rosenberg, eds., *Technology and Privacy: The New Landscape* (Cambridge, MA: The MIT Press, 1998), 1.

10. H. C. Releya, "Technology and Privacy," *Journal of Academic Librarianship* 24, no. 4 (July 1998).

11. B.M. Jones, "Academic Libraries and Intellectual Freedom," *Intellectual Freedom Manual*, 6th ed (Chicago: American Library Association, 2000), 41.

12. Kathy Mitchell, "The Online Privacy Tutorial, Message 22, Network Security," privacytut@ala.org (accessed June 5, 2003).

13. Ibid.

14. International Coalition of Library Consortia, "Privacy Guidelines for Electronic Resources Vendors, July 2002," http://www.library.yale.edu/consortia/2002privacyguidelines.html (accessed June 11, 2004).

15. DoubleClick, Inc., "The Center for Democracy and Technology," http://www.cdt.org/action/doubleclick.shtml (accessed July 20, 2004).

16. International Coalition of Library Consortia, "Privacy Guidelines for Electronic Resources Vendors."

17. New York Library Association, "Intellectual Freedom, Confidentiality and Privacy," http://www.nyla.org/index.php?page_id=449 (accessed July 29, 2004).

18. American Library Association, "Code of Ethics," http://www.ala.org/ala/oif/statementspols/codeofethics/codeethics.htm (accessed August 13, 2004).

19. American Library Association, "Library Bill of Rights," http://www.ala.org/oif/statementspols/statementsif/librarybillrights.htm (accessed July 29, 2004).

20. Ibid.

21. American Library Association, "Intellectual Freedom Principles for Academic Libraries: An Interpretation of the Library Bill of Rights," Adopted July 12, 2000, http://www.ala.org/alaorg/oif/ifprinciplesacademiclibraries.html (accessed July 29, 2004).

22. The Office of the Federal Privacy Commissioner, "Guidelines for Federal and ACT Government Websites," http://www.privacy.gov.au/internet/web (accessed February 6, 2005).

23. Schenectady County Community College, "Website Privacy Policy," http://www.sunysccc.edu/about/prvacypolicy2002.html (accessed February 6, 2005).

24. Washington University in St. Louis, University Libraries, "Washington University Libraries Policy Statement," http://library.wustl.edu/about/privacy.html (accessed July 29, 2004).

25. Charlene C. Cain, "Intellectual Freedom Manual: Intellectual Freedom Issues in Academic Libraries," http://www.llaonline.org/fp/files/pubs/if_manual/twelve.pdf (accessed July 30, 2004).

26. A. W. Hafner and J. J. Keating III, "Supporting Individual Library Patrons with Information Technologies: Emerging One-to-One Library Services on the College or University Campus," *Journal of Academic Librarianship* 28, no. 6 (November 2002): 427.

27. Herbert Foerstel, "Secrecy in Science: Exploring University, Industry, and Government Relationships," remarks delivered at MIT, Cambridge, MA, March 29, 1999, http://www.aaas.org/spp/secrecy/Presents/foerstel.htm (accessed July 30, 2004).

28. American Library Association, "Privacy: An Interpretation of the Library Bill of Rights," http://www.ala.org/ala/oif/statementspols/statementsif/interpretations/privacyinterpretation.rtf (accessed August 13, 2004).

29. The State University of New York: SUNY's Privacy Policy, "Confidentiality and Integrity of Personal Information Collected Through suny.edu," http://www.suny.edu/PrivacyPolicy/Privacy_Content.cfm?sPageName=Confidentiality_1 (accessed July 30, 2004).

30. Tracy Mitrano, comments at the teleconference, "Safeguarding Our Patron's Privacy: What Every Librarian Needs to Know About the USA Patriot Act & Related Anti-Terrorism Measures," Indiana University School of Library and Information Science, Bloomington, IN, December 11, 2002.

31. T. Trew, Indiana University School of Library and Information, SLIS Event News, "Satellite Teleconference Spotlights Patriot Act," http://www.slis.indiana.edu/news/story.php?story_id=532 (accessed July 30, 2004).

32. Ibid.

33. Gary Strong, Comments at the teleconference, "Safeguarding Our Patron's Privacy: What Every Librarian Needs to Know About the USA Patriot Act & Related Anti-Terrorism Measures," Indiana University School of Library and Information Science, Bloomington, IN, December 11, 2002.

34. Jones, "Academic Libraries and Intellectual Freedom," 41–53.

35. Ibid.

36. Ibid.

37. Ibid.

38. Ibid.

39. Ibid.

40. Ibid.

41. Neil Postman, *Technopoly: The Surrender of Culture to Technology* (New York: Alfred A. Knopf, 1992), xii.

42. Ernest A. Kallman and John P. Grillo, *Ethical Decision Making and Information Technology: An Introduction with Cases* (New York: McGraw Hill, 1996), 22.

43. Richard S. Rosenberg, *The Social Impact of Computers* (Boston: Academic Press, 1992), 340.

44. Richard A. Spinello, *Ethical Aspects of Information Technology* (Englewood Cliffs: Prentice Hall, 1995), 1.

45. Multnomah County Library, "Statements on Privacy and Confidentiality of Library Records," http://www.multcolib.org/about/pol-privacy.html (accessed August 13, 2004).

46. Ibid.

47. James G. Neal, comments at the teleconference, "Safeguarding Our Patron's Privacy: What Every Librarian Needs to Know About the USA Patriot Act & Related Anti-Terrorism Measures," Indiana University School of Library and Information Science, Bloomington, IN, December 11, 2002.

48. Pamela Jerskey, "The Privacy Audit: A Primer by Pamela Jerskey, Ivy Dodge and Sanford Sherizen," http://www2.bc.edu/~jerskey/privacy.htm (accessed July 30, 2004).

49. Trew, "Satellite Teleconference Spotlights Patriot Act."

50. Platform for Privacy Preferences (P3P) Project, http://xml.coverpages.org/p3p.html (accessed August 13, 2004).

51. MIT Distribution Center for PGP (Pretty Good Privacy), http://web.mit.edu/network/pgp.html (accessed August 13, 2004).

52. Tim Lewontin, conversation with Carol Gordon, at Boston University, June 30, 2003.

CHAPTER 7

Privacy Resources for Educators and Librarians

This chapter is a select bibliography of privacy resources. It is intended to be a starting place to provide you with opportunities to further explore privacy issues. It includes both web- and print-based resources, each with a short abstract. While monographs and journal articles are listed, as one would expect, the web is a good place to start and it is an excellent place to keep up-to-date on the latest news and views on privacy from a wide variety of perspectives. The references in this chapter start with general sites of interest and then follow the topics as presented in the preceding chapters.

Privacy-Related Organizations and Advocacy Groups

Below are organizations or groups that are advocates for privacy or have an interest in privacy issues.

- American Civil Liberties Union (ACLU). http://www.aclu.org
Among its many interests, the ACLU is one of the leading organizations promoting privacy and challenging governments at all levels regarding privacy issues. The privacy section of its web site (http://www.aclu.org/Privacy/PrivacyMain.cfm) has the latest news on privacy issues, Congressional actions, and the latest ACLU privacy reports.

- American Library Association (ALA) Office for Intellectual Freedom (OIF). http://www.ala.org/oif
The OIF is the ALA's primary unit that tracks the topic of privacy and advocates on library privacy issues. The OIF web site has considerable information related to privacy issues in libraries and schools, including information on the impact of the USA PATRIOT Act on libraries.

- beSpacific. http://www.bespacific.com
This site "focuses on the expanding resources in the public and private sector related to law and technology news. Daily postings provide updates on issues in-

cluding copyright, privacy, censorship, the Patriot Act, ID theft, and freedom of information." A well-vetted, reliable resource from law librarian Sabrina I. Pacifici of the legal web site LLRX.com.

• Center for Democracy and Technology (CDT). http://www.cdt.org
The center works to promote democratic values and constitutional liberties in the digital age. With an expertise in law, technology, and policy, the CDT web site has many resources related to enhancing free expression and privacy with an emphasis on how speech and privacy are impacted by technology. The CDT is especially valuable as a resource on governmental use or regulation of technology.

• Computer Professionals for Social Responsibility (CPSR). http://www.cpsr.org
The CPSR is one of the best-known computing organizations. The CPSR's Privacy and Civil Liberties page (http://www.cpsr.org/program/privacy/privacy.html) is always a good resource.

• Electronic Frontier Foundation (EFF). http://www.eff.org
One of the best organizations on privacy and First Amendment issues related to Internet use, the EFF is a nonprofit group working to protect digital rights. It covers a variety of issues including biometrics, surveillance, and financial privacy.

• Electronic Privacy Information Center (EPIC). http://www.epic.org
EPIC is one of the best sites on privacy in relation to technology. Its web site covers many areas including passenger profiling, RFID, and data mining. It is an especially good source for the latest news on privacy issues. Highly recommended.

• Freedom to Read Foundation (FTRF). http://www.ala.org/ala/ourassociation/
    othergroups/ftrf/freedomreadfoundation.htm
Incorporated in 1969, the FTRF promotes freedom of speech and of the press and supports libraries by supplying legal counsel to defend First Amendment rights. The organization often participates in litigation dealing with defense of civil liberties including privacy. The FTRF publishes the "Freedom to Read Foundation News" both in print and archived online.

• Libraryprivacy. http://www.libraryprivacy.org/
A site sponsored by the California Library Association and the ACLU of southern California. It provides links to many sites related to reading and privacy, the USA PATRIOT Act, and more.

• Privacy International (PI). http://www.privacyinternational.org/
Privacy International is a human rights group formed in 1990 as a watchdog on surveillance and privacy invasions by governments and corporations. PI has conducted research on a wide range of issues from wiretapping and national security to ID cards, video surveillance, and medical privacy.

• Privacy Rights Clearinghouse. http://www.privacyrights.org
A not-for-profit consumer education and research organization. The clearinghouse has excellent resources and many "fact sheets" on a wide variety of topics including identity theft, financial privacy, and more.

• Politech: Politics & Technology. http://www.politechbot.com/
A web site created and managed since 1994 by journalist Declan McCullagh. Besides privacy, it includes a broad range of technology topics. It has an email list

which is a good source of "what's hot this week" information on privacy, free speech, intellectual property rights, and other current issues related to technology and politics.

Legal Resources

• LibraryLaw. http://www.librarylaw.com
LibraryLaw was started by Mary Minow, a well-known librarian and attorney. The site focuses on legal issues of interest to librarians including copyright, privacy, and the First Amendment. Includes a LibraryLaw blog.

• Legal Information Institute: Right of Privacy. http://www.law.cornell.edu/topics/privacy.html
Cornell University's easy-to-navigate web site includes important legal topics and court decisions. The section on the Right of Privacy is a good starting place for those seeking to better understand how privacy law works and to review recent court cases on privacy issues.

• Federal Trade Commission (FTC) Privacy Initiatives. http://www.ftc.gov/privacy/index.html
The FTC is the federal government's chief agency on privacy issues. Its web site provides practical information on a variety of privacy topics, including children's privacy, the national "Do Not Call" list, security, spam email, financial privacy, and more. The focus is on educating and assisting individual consumers, although the FTC also hosts workshops oriented toward businesses and professionals. The web site also provides detailed information about current FTC proceedings and allows consumers to file complaints online.

• American Bar Association (ABA), Section on Individual Rights & Responsibilities, Winter 1999. http://www.abanet.org/irr/hr/winter99toc.html
This 1999 edition of the ABA's *Section* magazine remains an excellent resource on a wide range of privacy law topics.

Books on Privacy

• Amitai, Etzioni. *The Limits of Privacy.* New York: Basic Books, 1999.
This monograph focuses on flashpoint issues such as mandatory HIV testing of infants, encryption of electronic documents, national identification cards, and medical records. The book argues that some social needs should outweigh the right to privacy.

• Givens, Beth, with Dale Fetherling. *The Privacy Rights Handbook: How to Take Control of Your Personal Information.* New York: Avon Books, 1997.
The authors describe how to safeguard one's privacy and tell how to find out whether it has already been compromised. Topics include ways to become more assertive about privacy rights, how to find out the contents of medical and credit records, how to order a copy of one's Social Security file, and how to stop junk mail and telemarketing calls.

• Rosen, Jeffrey. *The Unwanted Gaze: The Destruction of Privacy in America.* New York: Random House, 2001.

A good book that examines the legal, technological, and cultural changes that have undermined our ability to control how much information about ourselves is communicated to others.

- Bielefield, Arlene. *Library Patrons and the Law*. New York: Neal-Schuman Publishers, 1995.

This book summarizes the legal issues regarding library patrons, for librarians and the general public. It covers constitutional, statutory, and other rights, addressing subjects such as the First Amendment, the right to receive information and ideas, the right to privacy, freedom of information laws, copyright, the Americans with Disabilities Act, and censorship. It has a section on common patron questions and suggested answers and the text of the U.S. Freedom of Information Act.

- Sykes, Charles J. *The End of Privacy: The Attack on Personal Rights at Home, On-Line, and in Court*. New York: St. Martin's Press, 2000.

Sykes explores how privacy has changed recently by citing examples of citizens who have had their privacy violated.

- Cate, Fred H. *Privacy in Perspective*. Washington, DC: AEI Press, 2001.

The author outlines the complexity of privacy issues and the stakes in the national debate, sets that debate in a practical context, defines key concepts and policy alternatives, and identifies likely ramifications.

- Cate, Fred H. *Privacy in the Information Age*. Washington, DC: Brookings Institution Press, 1997.

A detailed look at critical privacy issues in the context of computerized information, providing an overview of the technologies that are provoking the current privacy debate and the range of legal issues raised. It examines central elements of the definition of privacy, and compares regulations in Europe and the United States. It discusses questions that cut across the fields of business, communications, economics, and law.

- Torremans, Paul L. C. *Copyright and Human Rights: Freedom of Expression, Intellectual Property, Privacy*. The Hague: Kluwer Law International, 2004.

The author examines the collision of copyright and human rights and the changes in recent decades that include safeguarding the profits of corporate marketers of widely used media and software products.

- Agre, Philip E., and Marc Rotenberg. *Technology and Privacy: The New Landscape*. Cambridge, MA: MIT Press, 1998.

A collection of essays that address changes such as increases in communications bandwidths, the wide adoption of computer networking and public-key cryptography, new digital media that support a wide range of social relationships, a massive body of practical experience in the development and application of data-protection laws, the rapid globalization of manufacturing, culture, and policy making. It provides a new conceptual framework for the analysis and debate of privacy policy and for the design and development of information systems.

- Kuner, Christopher. *European Data Privacy Law and Online Business*. Oxford; New York: Oxford University Press, 2003.

A review of the legal concepts of data privacy law, and the application of European Union (EU) law to particular electronic commerce and online activities. Includes:

how to transfer personal data outside Europe to comply with EU law; a comprehensive analysis of how to deal with complex compliance challenges, including notification of databases, processing of employee data, privacy policies, codes of conduct, and web site compliance and standardization.

Chapter 1: An Overview of Privacy in the United States

Federal Protection on Disclosure of Financial Information

- "In Brief: The Financial Privacy Requirements of the Gramm-Leach-Bliley Act." Federal Trade Commission, http://www.ftc.gov/bcp/conline/pubs/buspubs/glbshort.htm

A very good, straightforward explanation of the privacy provisions in the Gramm-Leach-Bliley Act (GLBA).

- "Privacy of Consumer Financial Information; Final Rule." Federal Trade Commission, http://www.ftc.gov/os/2000/05/65fr33645.pdf

This is the detailed, final GLBA privacy rule as printed in the *Federal Register* (16 CFR Part 313).

- "Frequently Asked Questions for the Privacy Regulation." Federal Trade Commission, December 2001, http://www.ftc.gov/privacy/glbact/glb-faq.htm

While this FAQ, authored by FTC staff, is targeted at financial institutions, it has a wealth of information of interest to consumers too.

- Givens, Beth. "Financial Privacy: The Shortcomings of the Federal Financial Services Modernization Act." Privacy Rights Clearinghouse, September 15, 2000, http://www.privacyrights.org/ar/fin_privacy.htm

This paper covers not just some of the weak areas of the act but also the broader issue of the new mega-financial institutions and how much of your personally identifiable information (PII) they can now access.

Federal Protection on Disclosure of Health and Medical Information

- "Fact Sheet: Protecting the Privacy of Patients' Health Information." U.S. Department of Health and Human Services, April 14, 2003, http://www.hhs.gov/news/facts/privacy.html

A straightforward fact sheet targeted at both consumers and health care pro-viders.

- "Standards for Privacy of Individually Identifiable Health Information; Final Rule." U.S. Department of Health and Human Services, August 14, 2002, http://www.hhs.gov/ocr/hipaa/privrulepd.pdf

This is the detailed, final privacy rule of the Health Insurance Portability and Accountability Act (HIPAA) as printed in the *Federal Register* (45 CFR Parts 160 and 164).

- "Myths and Facts about the HIPAA Privacy Rule." Health Privacy Project, September 22, 2003, http://www.healthprivacy.org/info-url_nocat2303/info-url_nocat_show.htm?doc_id=173435

Very good document that addresses some of the myths and misconceptions about the privacy protections in HIPAA. It is targeted at consumers.

- "HIPAA: Privacy Essentials for the Physician's Office." OHIC Insurance Company and Ohio University College of Osteopathic Medicine, 2003, http://www.ouwb.ohiou.edu/hipaa/ohic-oucom/

Although developed for the physician's office, this is an excellent site for consumers too. It has questions and answers, such as "Use and Disclosure" and "Patient Access."

- "Medical Privacy." Electronic Privacy Information Center (EPIC), 2004, http://www.epic.org/privacy/medical

Like many EPIC sites, this is a good site to keep up-to-date with the latest legal cases and other news related to medical privacy issues. It includes advice to consumers on how to safeguard their medical records and has a good reference listing.

Privacy in the Workplace

- "Fact Sheet 7: Workplace Privacy." Privacy Rights Clearinghouse, September 2002, http://www.privacyrights.org/fs/fs7-work.htm

Written in an FAQ type of fashion, this is a good overview that covers various topics including telephone and computer monitoring by employers and employee use of email.

- "Workplace Privacy." Electronic Privacy Information Center, January 21, 2004, http://www.epic.org/privacy/workplace/

Another good EPIC site that includes a "latest news" section, relevant laws and court cases, and a list of further resources.

- Dixon, Rod. "With Nowhere to Hide: Workers Are Scrambling for Privacy in the Digital Age." *Journal of Technology Law & Policy*, Vol. 4, Issue 1, Spring 1999, http://journal.law.ufl.edu/%7Etechlaw/4/Dixon.html

A detailed article covering a wide variety of issues like the use of electronic tools to monitor employee activities and the scope of an employee's privacy rights versus those of the employer. It cites over fifty legal cases.

- Rogers, Amy. "You Got Mail But Your Employer Does Too: Electronic Communication and Privacy in the 21st Century Workplace." *Journal of Technology Law and Policy*, Vol. 5, Issue 1, Spring 2000, http://grove.ufl.edu/%7Etechlaw/vol5/emailfinal.htm

This article covers employee/employer rights in the workplace related to privacy and the use of technology resources. It includes background information on many legal cases on the subject.

Chapter 2: Privacy and Emerging Technologies

Federal Programs and Privacy Issues

- "Data Mining: Federal Efforts Cover a Wide Range of Users." General Accounting Office (GAO), May 2004, http://www.gao.gov/new.items/d04548.pdf

An in-depth report by the GAO that describes planned and operational federal data mining efforts. The report identifies 199 separate data mining efforts by 128 federal departments and agencies.

- Stanley, Jay. "The Surveillance-Industrial Complex: How the American Government Is Conscripting Businesses and Individuals in the Construction of a Surveillance Society." American Civil Liberties Union, August 2004, http://www. aclu.org/Files/OpenFile.cfm?id=16225

This ACLU report documents the federal government's efforts to recruit businesses and citizens in its attempts to increase security, and how such attempts often infringe on privacy rights.

Terrorism Information Awareness (TIA)

- "Safeguarding Privacy in the Fight Against Terrorism." Report of the Technology and Privacy Advisory Committee, Department of Defense, March 2004, http://www.cdt.org/security/usapatriot/20040300tapac.pdf

An extensive report from a committee appointed by Defense Secretary Donald Rumsfeld in February 2003. The charge to the committee was to examine the TIA program and to "ensure that the application of this or any like technology developed within DOD is carried out in accordance with U.S. law and American values related to privacy." The report also recommends more coordinated efforts in the federal government to address privacy issuses.

- "'Terrorism' Information Awareness (TIA)." Electronic Privacy Information Center, September 10, 2003, http://www.epic.org/privacy/profiling/tia/

A good starting point for information on the TIA project. This site provides background on TIA and includes a "Latest News" section and over 100 links to related sites and sources.

- "Report to Congress Regarding the Terrorism Information Awareness Program." Defense Advanced Research Projects Agency (DARPA), May 20, 2003, http://www.epic.org/privacy/profiling/tia/may03_report.pdf

This DARPA report on TIA, mandated by Congress, is probably the most extensive report on the program.

- "LifeLog." Defense Advanded Research Projects Agency, http://www.darpa.mil/ ipto/Programs/lifelog/index.htm

The DARPA site that has information on the LifeLog program including the program's objective, description, and references.

Novel Intelligence from Massive Data (NIMD)

- "Novel Intelligence from Massive Data," http://www.ic-arda.org/Novel_Intelli gence/

The official site of NIMD, it notes that the program is "aimed at focusing analytic attention on the most critical information found within massive data—information that indicates the potential for strategic surprise."

- "U.S. Still Mining Terror Data." *Wired News*, February 23, 2004, http://www.wired. com/news/conflict/0,2100,62390,00.html

This article is critical of the manner in which programs like NIMD are started and funded with often little Congressional oversight.

* "United States Intelligence Community." April 19, 2004, http://www.intelligence. gov/

The main site of the Intelligence Community, which consists of federal executive branch agencies that are responsible for protecting the country from foreign security threats.

Multistate Anti-TeRrorism Information eXchange (MATRIX)

* "Multistate Anti-TeRrorism Information eXchange (MATRIX)." March 24, 2004, http://www.matrix-at.org/

The official MATRIX site that includes a history of the program, an FAQ, and information on data sources.

* "Testimony of The Honorable Paula B. Dockery, Florida State Senator, Before the Subcommittee on Technology, Information Policy, Intergovernmental Relations and the Census Committee on Government Reform." March 25, 2003, http://reform.house.gov/UploadedFiles/Dockery.pdf

Testimony before the U.S. Senate Committee on Home Defense, Public Security and Ports that provides good background information on the MATRIX program.

* Ramasastry, Anita. "Why We Should Fear the Matrix." FindLaw's Legal Commentary, November 5, 2003, http://writ.news.findlaw.com/ramasastry/2003 1105.html

This article outlines the MATRIX program and other federal programs like TIA and highlights the dangers of data mining ensnaring innocent citizens.

Computer-Assisted Passenger Prescreening System II (CAPPS II)

* "CAPPS II: Myths and Facts." U.S. Department of Homeland Security, Transportation Security Administration, February 20, 2004, http://www.dhs.gov/ dhspublic/display?content=3163

A practical overview of the CAPPS II program written in an FAQ style. Many questions relate to how the program will impact the flying public.

* "CAPPS II: Government Surveillance via Passenger Profiling." Electronic Frontier Foundation, http://www.eff.org/Privacy/cappsii/

This includes a step-by-step review of how CAPPS II works and provides information on how the system can mistakenly identify an individual as a security risk.

* "Passenger Profiling." Electronic Privacy Information Center, April 26, 2004, http://www.epic.org/privacy/airtravel/profiling.html

A good review with the latest developments and links to over fifty other sites addressing CAPPS II.

DCS1000 (Also known as Carnivore)

* "Carnivore FOIA Documents." Electronic Privacy Information Center, http://www. epic.org/privacy/carnivore/foia_documents.html

This site includes a wealth of background information on the program with links to many reports and other studies often made public by an EPIC Freedom of Information Act request.

- "Independent Technical Review of the Carnivore System: Final Report." December 2000, http://www.usdoj.gov/jmd/publications/carniv_final.pdf
Very detailed report done under a Department of Justice contract. If you want to know the technical details on how DCS1000 really works, this is the document.

- "Authority to Intercept Voice Communications in Computer Hacking Investigations." U.S. Department of Justice, http://www.epic.org/privacy/terrorism/DOJ_guidance.pdf
A detailed (30 p.) review of the authority that the federal government has in relation to electronic surveillance. It includes changes made by the USA PATRIOT Act, such as the act's provision for nationwide search warrants.

The Internet

- "A Nation Online: How Americans Are Expanding Their Use of the Internet." National Telecommunications and Information Administration, 2002, http://www.ntia.doc.gov/ntiahome/dn/index.html
Like other NTIA reports, this one is very detailed and has considerable information on how the Internet is being used.

- "Broadband Penetration on the Upswing: 55% of Adult Internet Users Have Broadband at Home or Work." Pew Internet and American Life Project, April 2004, http://www.pewinternet.org/reports/pdfs/PIP_Broadband04.Data Memo.pdf
This report documents the dramatic rise of residential broadband access. It is just one of several Pew Trust studies on the Internet.

- "EPIC Online Guide to Practical Privacy Tools." Electronic Privacy Information Center, September 2003, http://www.epic.org/privacy/tools.html
This EPIC report contains over 100 links to sites and products (commercial and free/shareware) to protect your privacy. It is divided into a variety of sections covering email, cookie management, firewalls, and more.

- Garfinkel, Simson L. "5 Biggest Threats to Your Privacy Online." *MSN Money*, http://moneycentral.msn.com/articles/banking/online/5485.asp
A good, straightforward overview of common issues and threats, and recommendations on how to address or avoid them. Authored by Simson Garfinkel, a well-known privacy advocate.

- "Privacy in Cyberspace: Rules of the Road for the Information Superhighway." Privacy Rights Clearinghouse, August 2003, http://www.privacyrights.org/fs/fs18-cyb.htm
A first-rate review of the privacy threats online. Includes issues like how to surf anonymously, spyware, and privacy concerns when accessing the Internet in public locations (cybercafes, airports, etc.). Has links to many related sites.

- Edelman, Benjamin. "Methods and Effects of Spyware." March 19, 2004, http://www.ftc.gov/os/comments/spyware/040319edelman.pdf

A detailed report on how spyware works and how it can compromise your privacy and the security of your workstation. Authored by Benjamin Edelman, in response to a Federal Trade Commission forum on spyware. (Edelman is also well known for his research on Internet filters.)

- Scambusters.org. http://scambusters.com/
A good site with the latest information on scams and other fraudulent schemes.

Privacy and Technology

- "Who Goes There? Authentication Through the Lens of Privacy." National Research Council of the National Academy of Sciences, March 2003, http://books.nap.edu/html/whogoes/
This report provides an in-depth analysis of authentication technology and the privacy implications and concerns raised by any type of authentication technology. This is from the National Research Council and is an outstanding resource.

- "Radio Frequency Identification (RFID) Systems." Electronic Privacy Information Center, July 23, 2004, http://www.epic.org/privacy/rfid/
This is the usual, high quality, detailed information on the topic from EPIC. It includes a section on recent RFID news and developments related to privacy.

- "RFIDbuzz.com." http://www.rfidbuzz.com/
This site has a variety of news releases, and it documents the latest uses of RFID.

- "RFID Journal." http://www.rfidjournal.com
The web version of this journal is a good place to find the latest implementation of RFID in business, industry, and government.

See also the section below on RFID in libraries.

- Burrows, David. "Privacy Concerns and the future of GPS." http://www.pocketgps. co.uk/privacyfuture.php
A succinct article that outlines some of the privacy issues with GPS.

- "Landmark Ruling Says Police Need Warrant for GPS Surveillance." September 11, 2003, http://www.aclu-wa.org/ISSUES/privacy/GPSPolice.html
In an interesting court case from the Washington Supreme Court, the court ruled unanimously that police must obtain a warrant in order to track a person's movements by a GPS device.

- "IBG BioPrivacy Initiative." http://www.bioprivacy.org/
The International Biometric Group's (IBG) "BioPrivacy Initiative" defines best practices and technology guidelines related to PII in deploying biometric systems. The initiative is also designed to raise awareness of privacy issues for end users and deployers of biometric technology.

- Clark, Roger. "Biometrics and Privacy." April 15, 2001, http://www.anu.edu.au/ people/Roger.Clarke/DV/Biometrics.html
This article is a good overview on biometrics including how biometric technologies work and what are the privacy issues and concerns related to biometrics.

- "Privacy Code." Biometrics Institute. May 6, 2004, http://www.biometricsinstitute.
  org/bi/codeofconduct.htm
A detailed privacy code with the intent to help ensure that biometrics enhances
rather than threatens the privacy of individuals. The Biometrics Institute represents
fifty-two organizations in Australia. Its "Privacy Code" has been submitted to the
Australian Office of the Federal Privacy Commissioner. The code will have the effect of law if accepted by the privacy commissioner.

Chapter 3: Privacy and Libraries in a Changing World

- "State Privacy Laws Regarding Library Records." American Library Association,
  2003, http://www.ala.org/oif/stateprivacylaws
A valuable online resource archiving state confidentiality laws for forty-eight states
and the District of Columbia. Two states, Hawaii and Kentucky, do not have specific statutes; however, their attorneys general have opinions regarding the confidentiality of patron library records.

- "Privacy Tool Kit." American Library Association, http://www.ala.org/oif/
  iftoolkits/privacy.
Excellent resource. The tool kit is designed to help librarians understand privacy
and its relationship to information access in libraries. It includes links to various
ALA privacy statements, policies, and other documents including the "Guidelines"
document in the following reference.

- "Guidelines for Developing a Library Privacy Policy." American Library Association,
  August 2003, http://www.ala.org/ala/oif/iftoolkits/toolkitsprivacy/library
  privacy.htm
A very good, detailed guide that includes background on both ALA policy and privacy law, instructions on how to draft a privacy policy, guidance on special considerations for policies in academic libraries, school library media programs, and
public library service to minors, a checklist of basic questions about privacy and
confidentiality, information on conducting a privacy audit, and sample privacy and
confidentiality policies. Part of the ALA's "Privacy Tool Kit."

- "Conducting a Privacy Audit." American Library Association Office for Intellectual
  Freedom, http://www.ala.org/ala/oif/iftoolkits/toolkitsprivacy/libraryprivacy.
  htm#privacyaudit
This is Appendix 2 of the *Guidelines for Developing a Library Privacy Policy*. It contains
a brief definition and rationale for carrying out a privacy audit and the types of
records to be audited for personally identifiable information.

- "Code of Ethics of the American Library Association." American Library Association, June 28, 1995, http://www.ala.org/alaorg/oif/ethics.html
This is the principal document of the ALA that codifies the ethical principles that
guide the work of librarians.

- "Policy on Confidentiality of Library Records." American Library Association, 1986,
  http://www.ala.org/ala/oif/statementspols/otherpolicies/policyconfiden
  tiality.htm
This is the primary policy statement of the ALA on the issue of privacy and confidentiality of library records.

- "Policy Concerning Confidentiality of Personally Identifiable Information about Library Users." American Library Association, 1991, http://www.ala.org/ala/oif/statementspols/otherpolicies/policyconcerning.htm

This policy statement, while complementing the "Policy on Confidentiality of Library Records," is more detailed and provides good background on why the confidentiality of PII is important.

- "Privacy: An Interpretation of the Library Bill of Rights." American Library Association, 2002, http://www.ala.org/ala/oif/statementspols/statementsif/interpretations/privacy.htm

This statement addresses the issue of privacy in the broader context of the "Library Bill of Rights."

- "Task Force on Privacy and Confidentiality in the Electronic Environment: Final Report." American Library Association, Library and Information Technology Association (LITA), July 2000, http://www.ala.org/ala/lita/litaresources/taskforceonpriv/alataskforce.htm

A report by LITA on the impact of new technologies on patron privacy and the confidentiality of electronic records.

- "Confidentiality and Coping with Law Enforcement Inquiries Guidelines for the Library and Its Staff." American Library Association, 2002, http://www.ala.org/ala/oif/ifissues/guidelineslibrary.pdf

This document provides good, practical advice on procedures to address issues of requests from law enforcement officials related to patron activity and the use of the library's resources and services. It includes explanations of the three types of court orders—subpoena, search warrant, and search warrant issued by a Foreign Intelligence Surveillance Act (FISA) court.

- "ALA Privacy Tutorial." American Library Association, 2003, http://www.fontanalib.org/table%20of%20contents.htm

Online tutorial to help librarians learn about the wide range of privacy issues in all types of libraries. It especially demystifies those issues related to providing Internet access and electronic services.

- Winter, Kenneth A. "Privacy and the Rights and Responsibilities of Librarians." *The Katharine Sharp Review* (No. 4), Winter 1997, http://alexia.lis.uiuc.edu/review/winter1997/winter.html

The article's abstract states it best: "This article presents legal, ethical and professional arguments for the protection of patron privacy, discussing different ways in which librarians have dealt with specific privacy violations."

- Coyle, Karen. "Make Sure You Are Privacy Literate." *Library Journal*, 10/1/2002, Vol. 127, Issue 16, p. 55, 3p.

A basic and very readable introduction to the privacy audit process and the types of information—legal, policy, and data collection systems—that should be included.

- "Privacy Guidelines for Electronic Resources Vendors." International Coalition of Library Consortia, July 2002, http://www.library.yale.edu/consortia/2002privacyguidelines.html

A good, succinct statement that libraries should make certain is in any contract they sign with vendors.

- Minow, Mary, and Tomas A. Lipinski. *The Library's Legal Answer Book.* Chicago: American Library Association, 2003.

Following a lengthy chapter entitled "Library Records and Privacy," an appended chart on pages 200–210 contains State Library Confidentiality Statutes and includes the name of the state, number of the statute, protection granted under the law, and significant exceptions.

- Schneider, Karen G. "Privacy: The Next Challenge." *American Libraries,* August 1999, Vol. 30, Issue 7, p. 98.

A concise article that addresses some technology-related privacy issues, including references to authentication issues.

- Breeding, Marshall. "Marshall Protecting Personal Information." *Computers in Libraries,* April 2004, Vol. 24, Issue 4, pp. 22–25.

A good article that focuses on privacy and security issues related to integrated library systems.

USA PATRIOT Act Resources

- Foerstel, Herbert N. *Refuge of a Scoundrel: The Patriot Act in Libraries.* Westport, CT: Libraries Unlimited, 2004.

This monograph provides a thorough examination of government interest in patron use of libraries from the 1970s, how the Bureau of Alcohol, Tobacco & Firearms was interested in which patrons were reading material related to explosives or guerilla warfare to the 1980s, and the FBI's Library Awareness Program to the USA PATRIOT Act. It includes details on the fight to pass the USA PATRIOT Act.

- Privacy and Library Records Update: USA Patriot Act. http://www.librarylaw. com/Patriotbib.htm

Part of the LibraryLaw web site, this is an annotated list of over thirty resources divided into such areas as Law and Guidelines, Analysis, and the ALA.

- Estabrook, Leigh S. "Public Libraries' Response to the Events of September 11th, 2001." *Illinios Libraries,* Winter 2002, Vol. 84, No. 1, http://www.cyber driveillinois.com/publications/pdf_publications/illibrary_v84_n1.pdf

A survey of public library responses and actions taken in the aftermath of September 11, 2001. From the Library Research Center at the University of Illinois, Graduate School of Library and Information Science.

- Mart, Susan Nevelow. "Protecting the Lady from Toledo: Post-USA PATRIOT Act Electronic Surveillance at the Library." *Law Library Journal,* Vol. 96, No. 3, Summer 2004, 24 pp., http://www.aallnet.org/products/2004-27.pdf

An article from the legal perspective on how the USA PATRIOT Act has expanded the federal government's authority and the impact on libraries of using this expanded authority.

- Minow, Mary. "Library Records Post-Patriot Act (Federal Law)." http://www.llrx. com/features/libraryrecords.htm

In this work, published in September 2002, attorney and librarian Mary Minow has created a detailed chart on the ways in which the federal law enforcement agents may obtain library records under the USA PATRIOT Act. Information includes the type of order (i.e., subpoena), the type of information which may be requested, the legal standard, citation of the statute, and notes and sample orders.

- Minow, Mary. "The USA PATRIOT Act and Patron Privacy on Library Internet Terminals." February 15, 2002, http://www.llrx.com/features/usapatriotact.htm

Written in an FAQ type of style, this is a very readable article on this subject.

- Minow, Mary. "The USA Patriot Act." *Library Journal,* Oct. 1, 2002, Vol. 127, Issue 16, p.54, 4 pp.

Beginning with a description of the time period when the USA PATRIOT Act was passed, this article describes the extension of law enforcement powers under the amended Foreign Intelligence Surveillance Act, describes in detail types of court orders and subpoenas, and gives specific advice on what librarians should do when faced with a law enforcement request.

- Starr, Joan. "Libraries and National Security: An Historical Review." http://first monday.org/issues/issue9_12/starr/

This lengthy essay reviews the perceived threats to national security during World War I (1914 to 1919), World War II (1939 to 1945), the early cold war and McCarthyism (1946 to 1955), and the late cold war (the 1970s and 1980s) and how libraries and librarians were involved. It discusses the expanded law enforcement powers under the USA PATRIOT Act and how libraries were affected. Last, it compares the similarities and differences with the past and suggests appropriate actions.

- "USA Patriot Act of 2001." Washington Office of the American Library Association, http://www.ala.org/ala/washoff/WOissues/civilliberties/theusapatriotact /usapatriotact.htm, accessed June 19, 2004.

The ALA provides a brief explanation of this landmark legislation with numerous helpful links to understanding the legislation and preparing library staff to protect patron privacy.

- "USA PATRIOT Act." American Civil Liberties Union, http://www.aclu.org/Safe andFree/SafeandFreeList.cfm?c=262

This is the USA PATRIOT Act section of the ACLU web site. It includes summaries and analyses of the law, an audio archive, press releases, publications, letters and testimonies, news updates on legal actions by the ACLU against the act's provisions, and actions to be taken by concerned citizens.

Law Enforcement Surveillance and Libraries

- American Library Association. "FBI in Your Library," http://www.ala.org/Template. cfm? Section=Intellectual_Freedom_Issues&Template=/ContentManagement/ ContentDisplay.cfm&ContentID=21662#libraryawarenessprogram

This section of the ALA web site includes the ALA "Policy on Governmental Intimidation," the attorney general's guidelines allowing the FBI to search for records without probable cause, the Terrorism Information and Prevention System [TIPS], the Library Awareness Program, the Counterintelligence Program [Cointelpro], and news about the FBI in libraries.

- Foerstel, Herbert N. *Surveillance in the Stacks: The FBI's Library Awareness Program.* Westport, CT: Greenwood Press, 1991.

An academic science librarian, the author recounts in detail the FBI's Library Awareness Program from 1973 through the late 1980s in which federal law enforcement agents attempted to recruit librarians to report on foreign nationals using unclassified scientific information in public and academic libraries. Foerstel details the efforts of the American Library Association and the media and congressional response to the program which resulted in state laws guarding confidentiality of library patron records. While the book is currently out of print, a summary of the Library Awareness Program does appear in Foerstel's *Refuge of a Scoundrel: The Patriot Act in Libraries.*

Campaign for Reader Privacy

- American Booksellers Foundation for Free Expression. www.abffe.org

Founded by the American Booksellers Association in 1990, this organization promotes and protects the free exchange of ideas, participates in legal cases involving First Amendment rights, and has been an active participant in the fight to restore protections of bookseller and library records weakened under the USA PATRIOT Act. It is a co-sponsor of the Campaign for Reader Privacy with the American Library Association and the Pen American Center.

- Reader Privacy. http://www.readerprivacy.com/

This web site has information for librarians, booksellers, writers, and the general public on the petition campaign to amend Section 215 of the USA PATRIOT Act co-sponsored by the ALA, American Booksellers Foundation for Free Expression, and the Pen American Center. A copy of the petition and a poster of Uncle Sam can be downloaded from the site.

Privacy Audits

- Jerskey, Pamela, Ivy Dodge, and Sanford Sherizen. "The Privacy Audit: A Primer." http://www2.bc.edu/~jerskey/privacy.htm. Accessed June 14, 2004.

Defines privacy and discusses the areas for audit, including data security and access controls, password administration, database administration, wide-area network administration, local area networks and end user computing controls, and storage and disposal of output.

- "Privacy Audit and Guidelines." Systemwide Operations and Planning Advisory Group (SOPAG) Privacy Task Force, University of California, Draft August 13, 2001, http://libraries.universityofcalifornia.edu/sopag/privacytf/privacy_audit.html

A good audit checklist. While prepared for academic libraries, it can be easily adapted to any library. This document serves as a basis for the privacy audit in Appendix II.

RFID in Libraries

- "RFID in Libraries." http://libraryrfid.typepad.com

A very good place to keep up-to-date on news in this area, get background papers, and access other RFID resources.

- "RFID Implementation in Libraries." Presentations to ALA Intellectual Freedom Committee at the 2004 ALA Mid-Winter Conference, American Library Association. January 10, 2004, http://www.privacyrights.org/ar/RFID-ALA. htm

These are two useful presentations by Beth Givens from the Privacy Rights Clearinghouse and Lee Tien from the Electronic Frontier Foundation. The site has a good bibliography.

- "RFID Technology for Libraries." A PLA TechNote prepared by Richard W. Boss. May 14, 2004, http://www.ala.org/ala/pla/plapubs/technotes/rfidtech nology.htm

This TechNote reviews the technology including implementation processes and costs. Recommended.

- "RFID: A Brief Bibliography, ALA Library Fact Sheet Number 25." American Library Association, http://www.ala.org/ala/alalibrary/libraryfactsheet/ala libraryfactsheet25.htm

This is a comprehensive bibliography listing both ALA resources and those from the broader library world.

- Chachra, Vinod, and Daniel McPherson. "Personal Privacy and Use of RFID Technology in Libraries." October 31, 2003, http://www.vtls.com/documents/ privacy.pdf

A very good overview of RFID, both how it works and how it is used in libraries. Highly recommended.

- Schneider, Karen. "RFID and Libraries: Both Sides of the Chip." Testimony before the Committee on Energy and Utilities, California Senate, November 20, 2003, http://www.senate.ca.gov/ftp/SEN/COMMITTEE/STANDING/ ENERGY/_home/11-20-03karen.pdf

A good review of some common assumptions about library use of RFID and how some of those assumptions are of questionable validity.

- "Guidelines for Using RFID Tags in Ontario Public Libraries." The Information and Privacy Commissioner of Ontario, http://www.ipc.on.ca/docs/rfid -lib.pdf

Published in June 2004, this is one of the most extensive (15-page) guidelines on the subject. Includes a best practices section and covers other issues like disclosure, retention, and security.

- RFID_LIB.

An email list for libraries to discuss the uses and implications of using RFID in libraries. Send a request to listproc@listproc.sjsu.edu and in the body, type subscribe RFID_LIB YourFirstname YourLastname.

Chapter 4: Privacy Issues for Public Libraries

- Nolan, Christopher. "The Confidentiality of Interlibrary Loan Records." *Journal of Academic Librarianship*, May 1993, Vol. 19, Issue 2, pp. 81–87.

A good review of issues related to privacy and interloan. One of the few articles that covers this topic.

- Wiegand, Shirley A. "Lawmakers, Lawbreakers: The Problem of Library Record Destruction." *American Libraries*, January 1994, Vol. 25, Issue 1, pp. 102–105.

This article addresses the issue that some of the information collected by libraries regarding patron use of the library's resources may be a "public record" as defined by state statute and cannot be arbitrarily destroyed.

- Minow, Mary. "Could You Be Sued for Turning over an Internet User's Sign-up Information to Law Enforcement? A Cautionary Tale for Libraries and Other Internet Service Providers." April 26, 2004, http://www.llrx.com/ features/internetsignup.htm

This article outlines all the permutations on the complex issue of Internet sign-up sheets. It emphasizes the need for libraries to seek legal counsel and to have policies in place to address law enforcement requests for this information. See also Ms Minow's article "Sample of Search Warrant Procedures for Libraries" at http:// www.llrx.com/features/draftsearch.htm.

- "Some Elements of Library Privacy Policies." SOPAG Privacy Task Force. http:// libraries.universityofcalifornia.edu/sopag/privacytf/elements.html.

A good outline of issues to consider in developing a library privacy policy including why is the information collected, who has access to it, and other subjects. From the University of California's Systemwide Operations and Planning Advisory Group (SOPAG).

- Force, Pam. "Children's Privacy in the Library." *Library and Information Science News*, http://www.lisnews.com/article.php3?mode=flat&sid=20000921155048

A detailed article on the library profession's responsibilities toward children and their privacy. It addresses the cognitive development of children and how this impacts privacy issues for young people.

Chapter 5: Privacy Issues in K–12 School Library Media Centers

General Privacy as an Intellectual Freedom

- Intellectual Freedom Committee of the American Association of School Librarians. "Intellectual Freedom and the School Library Media Center Q & A." Tri-fold brochure, 2004.

Following a definition of intellectual freedom, the brochure addresses current issues of importance to school library media specialists including the USA PATRIOT Act, the Children's Internet Protection Act (CIPA), filtering, sources of assistance with materials challenges, and a concise definition of the difference between selection and censorship.

- American Library Association, Office for Intellectual Freedom. *Intellectual Freedom Manual.* 6th edition. Chicago: American Library Association, 2002.

While the entire volume is the "Bible of Intellectual Freedom," of special interest is the chapter "The Buckley Amendment: Student Privacy versus Parents' Right to Know," pp. 319–322.

- Vandergrift, Kay E. "Privacy, Schooling, and Minors." *School Library Journal* Vol. 37, No. 1 (January 1991): 26–31.

An excellent article on the many aspects of student privacy from required testing to counseling sessions to facets of library service which impact a student's right of privacy.

- Kniffel, Leonard. "Children's Access: Protection or Preparation?" *American Libraries*, Vol. 30, Issue 10 (November 1999): 59–62.

Although the article primarily focuses on access to information by youth in libraries, the issue of privacy enters the dialog in an indirect way.

Confidentiality of Student Library Records

- Family Educational Rights and Privacy Act (FERPA) of 1974. http://www.ed.gov/policy/gen/guid/fpco/ferpa/index.html

This federal law protects the privacy of student education records and grants parents specified rights to their children's educational records. The law applies to all schools that receive funds under an applicable program of the U.S. Department of Education.

- Gerhardt, Lillian N. "Ethical Back Talk: III." *School Library Journal* Vol. 36, No. 6 (June 1990): 4.

The longtime editor of *School Library Journal* discusses the third point in the ALA's Code of Ethics and the view that privacy is often reserved only for adults in the United States.

- Torrans, Lee Ann. *Law for K–12 Libraries and Librarians*. Westport, CT: Libraries Unlimited, 2003.

Written by a Texas-based lawyer with a degree in library science, Chapter 9, "Patron Privacy and Filtering in the School Library: Guarding Outgoing Data-Monitoring Incoming Data," pp. 141–164, is of special interest. It discusses FERPA and school library records, state confidentiality laws, subpoenas and court orders, library policies, and the USA PATRIOT Act.

- Simpson, Carol, ed. *Ethics in School Librarianship: A Reader*. Worthington, OH: Linworth Publishing, Inc., 2003. Chapter 4, pp. 45–63, by Harry Willems.

Discusses the ethics of confidentiality in the school library covering posting overdue notices and nonautomated circulation systems to the student names and photos on district web sites.

- "Forum Guide to Protecting the Privacy of Student Information." National Center for Educational Statistics. http://nces.ed.gov/pubsearch/pubsinfo.asp?pubid=2004330

Published by the National Center for Educational Statistics in both print and online format in early 2004, the document gives a general overview of federal privacy laws and recent changes to some, provides background on the key principles and concepts in student privacy, and suggests data management practices for schools.

- Willard, Nancy. "Capturing the 'Eyeballs' and 'E-wallets' of Captive Kids in School: Dot.com Invades Dot.edu." Center for Advanced Technology in Education, University of Oregon, Eugene, OR, 2000, http://responsiblenetizen.org/onlinedocs/documents/eyeballs.html

This lengthy article discusses commercial partnerships between schools and companies.

- Willard, Nancy. "Safe & Responsible Use of the Internet: A Guide for Educators." Responsible Netizen Institute, 2002–2003, http://responsiblenetizen.org/onlinedocs/pdf/srui/sruilisting.html

This is an excellent online guide. Of most interest to readers would be Part II, "Safe and Responsible Internet Use Plan," Section 7: "Supervision, Monitoring, and Privacy," and Part III, "Legal Issues—Internet Use in School," Section 4: "Student and Staff Privacy Issues" including a discussion of the expectation of privacy. The guide also contains sample district and student AUPs.

Chapter 6: Privacy Issues for Academic Libraries

Web Sites

- "Intellectual Freedom Principles for Academic Libraries: An Interpretation of the Library Bill of Rights." American Library Association, Adopted July 12, 2000, http://www.ala.org/alaorg/oif/ifprinciplesacademiclibraries.html, accessed July 29, 2004.

An interpretation that is specifically directed at the needs and services of academic libraries.

- Cain, Charlene C. "Intellectual Freedom Manual: Intellectual Freedom Issues in Academic Libraries." http://www.llaonline.org/fp/files/pubs/if_manual/twelve.pdf, accessed July 30, 2004.

Brief but good overview addressing a variety of subjects, like addressing the copyright issue and addressing institutional support and use of student email.

- "Privacy and Confidentiality Issues in Today's Academic Library." University of Northern Iowa. http://www.library.uni.edu/cmss/web_sites_related_to_privacy_and_confid_issues.htm

A bibliography of more than twenty web sites related to academic libraries and the issue of privacy. Includes links to academic library privacy policies and statements.

- "Information Privacy Principles under the [Australian] Privacy Act 1988." Office of the Australian Federal Privacy Commissioner, http://www.privacy.gov.au/publications/ipps.html

These are the eleven privacy principles incorporated into the Australian Privacy Act of 1988.

Journal Articles

- Hafner, A. W., and J. J. Keating, III. "Supporting Individual Library Patrons with Information Technologies: Emerging One-to-One Library Services on the College or University Campus." *Journal of Academic Librarianship* 28, no. 6 (November 2002): 426–29.

This article analyzes an approach to mass marketing that applies technologies for targeted marketing and the implications for one-to-one library services.

- Jones, B. M. "Academic Libraries and Intellectual Freedom." *Intellectual Freedom Manual.* 6th ed. Chicago: American Library Association, 2000, 41–53.
The author discusses the practical considerations of privacy protection for academic librarians, including policy procedures with regard to library collections, services, and electronic access.

- Smith, B., B. T. Fraser, and C. R. McClure. "Federal Information Policy and Access to Web-Based Federal Information." *Journal of Academic Librarianship* 26, no. 4 (July 2000): 274–81.
A good article that relates how federal agencies exploit the web environment, chronicling those government policies that have a bearing on web development, and discusses how privacy has been affected by government access to information and information security.

- Releya, H. C. "E-Gov: The Federal Overview." *Journal of Academic Librarianship* 27, no. 2 (March 2001): 131–48.
The article traces thirty years of conditions contributing to the e-government phenomenon, legislation regarding privacy protection, and the digital divide.

Releya, H. C. "Legislating Personal Privacy Protection: The Federal Response." *Journal of Academic Librarianship* 27, no. 1 (January 2001): 36–51.
An article that describes threatening new technologies and the legislation of privacy protection, including the Privacy Act, Crime Control Act, Fair Credit Reporting Act, FERPA, and other legislation.

- Shuler, J. A. "Privacy and Academic Libraries: Widening the Frame of Discussion." *Journal of Academic Librarianship* 30, no. 2 (March 2004): 157–59.
The author discusses the balance between academic freedom and privacy and "mutually assured anonymity" as a tool for academic librarians.

- Hernon, P., and R. E. Dugan. "GIS and Privacy." *Journal of Academic Librarianship* 23 (November 1997): 515–16.
A good article that describes how GIS technology and geo-coded data could create profiling, computer matching, and database linkage that raise privacy concerns.

- Heckart, R. J. "Imaging the Digital Library in a Commercialized Internet." *Journal of Academic Librarianship* 25, no. 4 (July 1999): 274–80.
This article discusses how current trends, including Internet commercialization, user self-sufficiency, personalized service, artificial intelligence, and electronic book technology, will affect future information access.

CHAPTER 8

The Future of Privacy in Libraries

Introduction

There is an often repeated quote by Sun Microsystems' CEO Scott Mc-Nealy: "You have zero privacy anyway. Get over it."[1] While a shocking statement, there is an element of truth in it. The loss of personal privacy includes surveillance cameras watching our actions in public places, spyware tracking our mouse clicks on the Internet, and law enforcement agents legally requesting individuals' bookstore or library records. Civil libertarians continue to be concerned about state and federal legislation that steadily encroaches on the rights of individual citizens. This trend, begun after September 11, 2001, must be reversed, and citizens are beginning to realize that privacy cannot be traded for security. As Benjamin Franklin wrote in 1759, "They that can give up essential liberty to obtain a little temporary safety deserve neither liberty nor safety."[2] So, where are the country and its libraries headed with respect to privacy and confidentiality? Will library patrons enjoy some degree of privacy in the future?

The Future of Privacy in Public Libraries

In part because of their broad mission, public libraries will continue to be at the forefront of privacy issues in the library community. Besides the more general issues of privacy, legislative actions at the federal and state levels will continue to pose privacy challenges in public libraries. And from the federal perspective, the USA PATRIOT Act continues to be of concern to all libraries. It is probably of most concern to public libraries because they offer a more open environment than any other type of library.

Public libraries must now comply with the Children's Internet Protection Act (CIPA). Most of the focus of this act has been on its filtering mandate, but it will also have direct privacy implications. To better manage filtering, there will be an increasing trend in public libraries to implement Internet time management systems. To allow patrons to access the Internet, these systems require some form of authentication, which most often is the patron's library card. Even if a public library does not comply with CIPA, such programs will continue to be installed in many libraries. Libraries will increasingly need to develop policies to address what patron data are collected and retained that are associated with Internet use. Related to this is the need to make certain your state's library privacy statute ensures patron privacy when using the Internet. If it does not, the public library community needs to work to change the law to provide such protection.

While technology has had a dramatic impact on the use of print resources in academic libraries, the circulation of both print and audiovisual titles in public libraries is still a very important and a very popular service. In this regard, the protection of basic circulation data remains a critical concern. This concern increases as more public libraries join regional, shared Integrated Library Systems. Membership in such systems increases the number of staff who have access to a patron's record of library use. The larger wide area networked environment also leads to greater security and privacy risks. Security is the first line of defense in maintaining patron privacy in a networked environment. As threats and attacks on computer networks continue to multiply, there is a parallel rise in the threats and attacks on patron privacy.

The trend toward outsourcing library services and the offer by the library or the vendor community of personalized library information portals will continue to increase. Similar to networked services, librarians must work closely within the profession and with the vendor community to ensure the highest degree of privacy when patrons create and use their portal.

Educating library staff and trustees about privacy rights and responsibilities, and the privacy rights of their patrons, continues to be a high priority. It must be incorporated as a regular part of any staff or trustee inservicing. On a parallel track is the need to educate local law enforcement authorities and legal staff (e.g., city attorney) on the legal rights that patrons have when they use the library. Another area that librarians must address more than they currently do is the need to educate their patrons on privacy issues. This need incorporates a wide variety of topics from explaining the legal protections afforded to patrons when they use the library's services to educating them on the dangers of Internet and email consumer fraud schemes.

Public libraries will continue to be at the vanguard of protecting patron privacy and there will be a continuing need for staff and trustees to maintain a high degree of attention to privacy issues. At the same time the public library community must be more prepared than in the past to confront continuing threats to its privacy policies and the underlying statutes that give such policies their legitimacy and authenticity.

The Future of Privacy in School Library Media Centers

Except for administrators and guidance counselors, few staff in schools have as much responsibility for student privacy as school library media specialists. Yet, the topic has been slower in being recognized in the professional community. Nationally, the question of whether the Family Educational Rights and Privacy Act applies to school library records has not been clarified. In several states, the confidentiality of school library patron records is not legally protected by state confidentiality statutes, and there is a disturbing legislative trend toward parents gaining access to library records of minor children.

Until recently many school library media specialists may have considered privacy only in relationship to patron circulation records. Teaching the youth of America to protect their privacy while online is a major issue for school library professionals as physical library use diminishes. Additionally, authentication of patrons for remote use of resources and the concern about collection and possible use of personally identifiable information about patrons by electronic resources vendors continue to show how technology has the potential to impact student patron privacy.

To ensure the right of student library patrons to privacy and confidentiality, certain management policies and practices must be in place. Examples of public and academic library privacy audits abound, but none have been linked to use in school library media centers. It is hoped that as the broader concept of privacy in school library programs takes root, media professionals will begin to conduct privacy audits of their practices and procedures. Many districts had confidentiality of library records policies; but unlike public and academic libraries, there have been no privacy policies spelling out for patrons their privacy protections within the school library. This must also change, with privacy policies becoming as universal as materials selection policies.

As Kay Vandergrift, an Associate Professor at Rutgers University, acknowledged over a decade ago, "students often accept . . . violations of privacy without even a conscious awareness that they are being violated. Thus they enter adult society having learned to give up their right to privacy without question."[3] Just as school librarians are recognized for their fight against censorship, it is expected that they will also become vocal privacy advocates for their students. These efforts, as well as legal protection for school library records, is critical if students are to recognize and claim their right to privacy.

The Future of Privacy in Academic Libraries

Academic librarians are witnessing the shift from traditional library use to computer-based information use. " 'We can't pretend people will go back to walking into a library and talking to a reference librarian,' said Kate Wittenberg, director of the Electronic Publishing Initiative at Columbia University. . . . 'We have to respond to these new ways,' Ms. Wittenberg said, 'and come up with a way to make better research material available on-line.' "[4]

The transition from paper to electronic modes of information delivery has profound implications for academic libraries that are already affecting the way they do business. A higher level of personalized service will mean a higher level of privacy risk as patrons divulge personally identifiable information as a trade-off for information access and delivery that may not be optional.

As new technologies are introduced in academic libraries, the onus for privacy risk will be placed on the user. Although privacy statements abound on web sites and in electronic information products, patrons really do not have a choice to reject access in light of their academic and research needs. For academic libraries these issues culminate in the relationship with electronic publishers. The collection of personal information through subscription database use and the library's loss of control over the use of that information are two of many issues that threaten the autonomy of academic libraries to direct privacy policy. The alarming rate of mergers among electronic publishers is limiting the options academic libraries have for information access, particularly in the case of research journals, and will also limit options libraries will have to control privacy policy. User self-sufficiency and expectations for personalized service may also threaten the control that academic library institutions have with regard to privacy. As decisions for privacy risks fall to the individual patron, library policy may become a moot point. Library patrons may accept the loss of privacy as an acceptable consequence of better information services.

Technology will continue to bring both problems and solutions to privacy issues. It is likely that the gathering of information by cookies on web servers may be replaced by a more centralized collection of user information. In the cookie scenario, because the information is stored locally, web browsers can alert users to an imminent cookie download and offer a choice. "But because the information is most useful if it is readily available for ongoing analysis and manipulation, there is no doubt that customer information will continue to be found in centralized files."[5] This raises the privacy concern of informed consent. "In the digital library context, there is the problem of where 'cookies' would be stored when the client computer is a public workstation."[6] There is another dimension to the collection and use of personal information.

On the other hand, academic libraries may become the bastions of privacy protection: in the academic setting threats to privacy are seen as threats to academic freedom and inquiry, copyright, and intellectual property rights that are highly prized values vital to scholarship and teaching in academia. In addition, technology itself may present the solutions in the privacy-enhancing tools that are already emerging and promise to become more instrumental in placing not only the onus but also the power for privacy protection in the hands of patrons.

Complicating this future scenario will be the role of government and its concerns of terrorism and subversion. An example of federal intervention is the government's attempt to block Pretty Good Privacy (PGP), a product developed by Phil Zimmerman that protects the privacy of Internet users by allowing patrons to set their privacy preferences.[7] The rationale was not unlike that used for the USA PATRIOT Act, that is, to protect national security, and may be a harbinger of stronger government restrictions on privacy-enhancing tools and weaker privacy legislation.

There are more questions than answers when we speculate on the future of privacy in academic libraries. Will the commercial sector set the technological agenda and shape user expectations about what the web is and what web sites can do?[8] Will artificial intelligence and knowledge systems replace the one-to-one relationship between librarians and patrons? Will traditional professional values of confidentiality and free inquiry survive in the policies and procedures of academic libraries?

Laws and the Future of Privacy

Privacy will continue to be a hot legal issue for the foreseeable future— at least for the next decade. But few laws protecting privacy are likely to pass, and Americans should not place much faith in the idea that laws are the most effective way to protect their privacy.

The privacy issues certain to be debated by Congress in the near future are all those related to the sections of the USA PATRIOT Act scheduled to expire on December 31, 2005, including Section 215, which is the section impacting library records. In 2003–2004, members of Congress introduced at least a dozen bills addressing this issue, some intending to correct the privacy invasion, others intending to permanently award law enforcement officers these powers. Librarians and booksellers nearly won a floor vote in the U.S. House of Representatives, over an amendment that would have corrected the privacy invasion created by the USA PATRIOT Act. While it is encouraging that there is so much support for libraries and librarians, the Department of Justice and other law enforcement agencies will continue fighting for expanded, permanent power. Librarians will need to be equally vocal and more persuasive, developing relationships with sympathetic members of Congress and persuading them to consider protecting libraries.

Beyond the USA PATRIOT Act fixes, privacy will stay a hot topic for legislators because technology, business, and law enforcement will continue to erode historical expectations of privacy. As computerized records become easier and less expensive to create, retain, and search, as new technologies like global positioning systems (GPS) and spyware reduce our expectations of privacy, and as businesses use new technology to target marketing efforts with ever-greater efficiency, there will be high profile breakdowns where consumer privacy is dramatically compromised. Lawmakers will introduce legislation and hold hearings to "do something."

But most of these legislative efforts to protect privacy will fail for one of three reasons:

First, legal efforts will take place at the wrong level of government. States and localities that try to protect privacy rights in their communities, especially individual privacy rights against businesses, will find themselves embroiled in expensive litigation. The U.S. Constitution prohibits states from making laws that interfere with interstate commerce—and nearly all Internet commerce is interstate commerce.

Second, legal efforts will be too narrow. They will focus on what can or cannot be done via the Internet or other online technology. Businesses will react that it is unfair to treat a transaction that is carried out using the Internet differently from how the same transaction would be treated if it were done face to face or over the telephone. Many privacy advocates are persuaded that the data processing power of millions of computers connected via the Internet, combined with the ability to retain and track personally identifiable information in such transactions, make Internet transactions very different from a privacy perspective. However, Congress has been persuaded by the business unfairness argument, and they are very likely to continue being persuaded by that argument.

Third, legal efforts will be too broad. If there is the political will to seriously address a privacy issue in Congress, privacy advocates and members of Congress are likely to see only one opportunity to address all of their privacy concerns. In the past, Congress has successfully passed targeted privacy protections, such as children's privacy (COPPA), banking record privacy (GLBA), health information privacy (HIPPA), and educational record privacy (FERPA). But the only broad privacy law Congress has passed was thirty years ago: the Privacy Act of 1974.

That said, it is possible that the law and the legal system will be used to protect privacy. What would be required for the legal system to effectively protect privacy is a significant shift in political will, and an even more significant shift in the resources available for government enforcement of privacy protections. As long as privacy rights are only protected by individuals bringing a private legal action against someone (or some business) that has caused them damage through loss of their privacy, those rights will not be enforced with much impact. Most individuals never even know that their privacy has been invaded, and when they do know, proving that the loss of privacy has hurt them in any measurable way is almost impossible. Only when the government can step in and bring action against companies or other government agencies for violating people's privacy rights will there be enforcement with the potential to effectively deter future violations.

Individuals concerned with protecting their privacy in the workplace, at home, and in libraries will be better served by limiting disclosure of their own personally identifiable information to the best of their ability. For example, individuals may want to use encryption software when they send or receive email. The best way for a person to protect their own privacy is to consider carefully what information is being provided, to whom, for what purpose, and whether or not they trust those answers to remain enforced over time. Then, individuals can make informed decisions about providing or refusing to provide personally identifiable information.

The Final Word on Privacy

Many citizens, the media, representatives of governmental agencies, members of Congress, and the President are engaged in a public discussion over Section 215 of the USA PATRIOT Act. Richard Clark, former Bush administration special adviser for Cyberspace Security within the National Security Council, stated during his address at the American Library Association in June 2004 that in twenty years of fighting terrorism, he never experienced a need to look at library records. Clark said, "If we give up our civil rights to fight the Jihadists, they will have won."[9]

Part of the debate over retaining civil liberties resides in America's libraries—school, public, and academic. It is significant that over 330 communities and four states have adopted resolutions or other expressions of concern about provisions of the USA PATRIOT Act relating to access to individuals' "business records including library, bookstore, financial, and records."[10] Equally important is the fact that the staff in libraries across the country are actively defending the right of their patrons to use library resources without any oversight or inquiry.

As observed earlier, debates on privacy of library patrons are not new; neither is the reality of diminishing privacy. Reporter Mark Maremont wrote in the *Wall Street Journal* on the eve of the year 2000, also known as Y2K,

> For all the power of public outrage and for all the technology power marshaled by individuals, we will never be as private in the future as we are now. Just as we're not as private now as we were a century ago. The question is not whether we can retain privacy, but what we can do to keep it from disappearing entirely.[11]

The authors of this book challenge *you* the reader to take action to protect the privacy of public, school, and academic library patrons.

Notes

1. Stephen Manes, "Private Lives/Not Ours!" *PC World*, June 2000, Vol. 18, Issue 6, p. 312.

2. *Bartlett's Familiar Quotations*, 10th ed., #3929, Bartleby.com, http://www.bartleby.com/100/245.1.html (accessed July 4, 2004).

3. Kay E. Vandergrift, "Privacy, Schooling, and Minors," *School Library Journal* 37, no. 1 (January 1991): 26–30, http://search.epnet.com/login.aspx?direct=true&db=aph&an=12689568 (accessed July 27, 2004).

4. K. Hefner, "Old Search Engine, the Library, Tries to Fit Into a Google World," *New York Times*, June 21, 2004.

5. Ibid.

6. Ibid.

7. *The Ethical Spectacle*, "The Zimmerman Case" (July 1995), http://www.spectacle.org/795/zimm.html (accessed August 9, 2004).

8. R. J. Heckert, "Imagining the Digital Library in a Commercialized Internet," *Journal of Academic Librarianship* 25, no. 4 (July 1999), 274–80.

9. Richard Clark, keynote address, American Library Association Conference, Orlando, Florida, June 26, 2004.

10. Timothy Egan, "Sensing the Eyes of Big Brother, and Pushing Back," *New York Times*, August 8, 2004, http://www.nytimes.com/2004/08/08/national/08patriot.html (accessed August 13, 2004).

11. Mark Maremont, "The Wall Street Journal Millennium (A Special Report): Money & Markets—We'll Be Watching You: Can Anything Be Done to Protect Your Privacy in Cyberspace? Perhaps; But Disaster Might Have to Strike First," *Wall Street Journal*, Easter Edition, December 31, 1999, R, 26: 1.

Core Documents Relating to Privacy in Libraries

The following are core documents from the American Library Association (ALA) that address privacy issues and concerns. All documents reprinted by permission of the American Library Association. More background information and related resources are often found on the ALA web site where the latest versions of these documents reside.

1. Code of Ethics of the American Library Association
   http://www.ala.org/alaorg/oif/ethics.html
2. ALA Policy on Confidentiality of Library Records
   http://www.ala.org/ala/oif/statementspols/otherpolicies/policyconfidential ity.htm
3. ALA Policy Concerning Confidentiality of Personally Identifiable Information about Library Users
   http://www.ala.org/ala/oif/statementspols/otherpolicies/policyconcerning. htm
4. Privacy: An Interpretation of the Library Bill of Rights
   http://www.ala.org/ala/oif/statementspols/statementsif/interpretations/priva cy.htm
5. Resolution Reaffirming the Principles of Intellectual Freedom in the Aftermath of Terrorist Attacks
   http://www.ala.org/ala/oif/statementspols/ifresolutions/resolutionreaffirm ing.htm
6. Resolution on the USA PATRIOT Act and Related Measures That Infringe on the Rights of Library Users
   http://www.ala.org/ala/oif/statementspols/ifresolutions/resolutionusa.htm

Code of Ethics of the American Library Association (1995)

As members of the American Library Association, we recognize the importance of codifying and making known to the profession and to the general public the ethical principles that guide the work of librarians, other professionals providing information services, library trustees and library staffs.

Ethical dilemmas occur when values are in conflict. The American Library Association Code of Ethics states the values to which we are committed, and embodies the ethical responsibilities of the profession in this changing information environment.

We significantly influence or control the selection, organization, preservation, and dissemination of information. In a political system grounded in an informed citizenry, we are members of a profession explicitly committed to intellectual freedom and the freedom of access to information. We have a special obligation to ensure the free flow of information and ideas to present and future generations.

The principles of this Code are expressed in broad statements to guide ethical decision making. These statements provide a framework; they cannot and do not dictate conduct to cover particular situations.

I. We provide the highest level of service to all library users through appropriate and usefully organized resources; equitable service policies; equitable access; and accurate, unbiased, and courteous responses to all requests.

II. We uphold the principles of intellectual freedom and resist all efforts to censor library resources.

III. We protect each library user's right to privacy and confidentiality with respect to information sought or received and resources consulted, borrowed, acquired or transmitted.

IV. We recognize and respect intellectual property rights.

V. We treat co-workers and other colleagues with respect, fairness and good faith, and advocate conditions of employment that safeguard the rights and welfare of all employees of our institutions.

VI. We do not advance private interests at the expense of library users, colleagues, or our employing institutions.

VII. We distinguish between our personal convictions and professional duties and do not allow our personal beliefs to interfere with fair representation of the aims of our institutions or the provision of access to their information resources.

VIII. We strive for excellence in the profession by maintaining and enhancing our own knowledge and skills, by encouraging the professional development of co-workers, and by fostering the aspirations of potential members of the profession.

Adopted by the ALA Council, June 28, 1995.

ALA Policy on Confidentiality of Library Records (1986)

The Council of the American Library Association strongly recommends that the responsible officers of each library, cooperative system, and consortium in the United States:

1. Formally adopt a policy which specifically recognizes its circulation records and other records identifying the name of library users to be confidential in nature. (Note: See also ALA Code of Ethics, point III: "We protect each library user's right to privacy and confidentiality with respect to information sought or received, and resources consulted, borrowed, acquired or transmitted.")

2. Advise all librarians and library employees that such records shall not be made available to any agency of state, federal, or local government except pursuant to such process, order, or subpoena as may be authorized under the authority of, and pursuant to, federal, state, or local law relating to civil, criminal, or administrative discovery procedures or legislative investigative power.

3. Resist the issuance or enforcement of any such process, order, or subpoena until such time as a proper showing of good cause has been made in a court of competent jurisdiction. (Note: Point 3 means that upon receipt of such process, order, or subpoena, the library's officers will consult with their legal counsel to determine if such process, order, or subpoena is in proper form and if there is a showing of good cause for its issuance; if the process, order, or subpoena is not in proper form or if good cause has not been shown, they will insist that such defects be cured.)

Adopted by the ALA Council, January 20, 1971; revised July 4, 1975, July 2, 1986.

ALA Policy Concerning Confidentiality of Personally Identifiable Information about Library Users (1991, 2004)

"In a library (physical or virtual), the right to privacy is the right to open inquiry without having the subject of one's interest examined or scrutinized by others. Confidentiality exists when a library is in possession of personally identifiable information about users and keeps that information private on their behalf" (*Privacy: An Interpretation of the Library Bill of Rights*). The ethical responsibilities of librarians, as well as statutes in most states and the District of Columbia, protect the privacy of library users. Confidentiality extends to "information sought or received and resources consulted, borrowed, acquired or transmitted" (*ALA Code of Ethics*), and includes, but is not limited to, database search records, reference interviews, circulation records, interlibrary loan records and other personally identifiable uses of library materials, facilities, or services.

The First Amendment's guarantee of freedom of speech and of the press requires that the corresponding rights to hear what is spoken and read what is written be preserved, free from fear of government intrusion, intimidation, or reprisal. The American Library Association reaffirms its opposition to "any use of governmental prerogatives that lead to the intimidation of individuals or groups and discourages them from exercising the right of free expression as guaranteed by the First Amendment to the U.S. Constitution" and "encourages resistance to such abuse of governmental power" (ALA Policy 53.4). In seeking access or in the pursuit of information, confidentiality is the primary means of providing the privacy that will free the individual from fear of intimidation or retaliation.

The American Library Association regularly receives reports of visits by agents of federal, state, and local law enforcement agencies to libraries, asking for personally identifiable information about library users. These visits, whether under the rubric of simply informing libraries of agency concerns or for some other reason, reflect insensitivity to the legal and ethical bases for confidentiality, and the role it plays in the preservation of First Amendment rights, rights also extended to foreign nationals while in the United States. The government's interest in library use reflects a dangerous and fallacious equation of what a person reads with what that person believes or how that person is likely to behave. Such a presumption can and does threaten the freedom of access to information. It also is a threat to a crucial aspect of First Amendment rights: that freedom of speech and of the press include the freedom to hold, disseminate and receive unpopular, minority, extreme, or even dangerous ideas.

The American Library Association recognizes that law enforcement agencies and officers may occasionally believe that library records contain information that would be helpful to the investigation of criminal activity. The American judicial system provides the mechanism for seeking release of such confidential records: a court order, following a showing of *good cause* based on *specific facts*, by a court of competent jurisdiction.

The American Library Association also recognizes that, under limited circumstances, access to certain information might be restricted due to a legitimate national security concern. However, there has been no showing of a plausible probability that national security will be compromised by any use made of unclassified information available in libraries. Access to this unclassified information should be handled no differently than access to any other information. Therefore, libraries and librarians have a legal and ethical responsibility to protect the confidentiality of all library users, including foreign nationals.

Libraries are one of the great bulwarks of democracy. They are living embodiments of the First Amendment because their collections include voices of dissent as well as assent. Libraries are impartial resources providing information on all points of view, available to all persons regardless of origin, age, background, or views. The role of libraries as such a resource must not be compromised by an erosion of the privacy rights of library users.

Adopted by the ALA Council, July 2, 1991; amended June 30, 2004.

Privacy: An Interpretation of the Library Bill of Rights (2002)

Introduction

Privacy is essential to the exercise of free speech, free thought, and free association. The courts have established a First Amendment right to receive information in a publicly funded library. Further, the courts have upheld the right to privacy based on the Bill of Rights of the U.S. Constitution. Many states provide guarantees of privacy in their constitutions and statute law. Numerous decisions in case law have defined and extended rights to privacy.

In a library (physical or virtual), the right to privacy is the right to open inquiry without having the subject of one's interest examined or scrutinized by others. Confidentiality exists when a library is in possession of personally identifiable information about users and keeps that information private on their behalf.

Protecting user privacy and confidentiality has long been an integral part of the mission of libraries. The ALA has affirmed a right to privacy since 1939. Existing ALA policies affirm that confidentiality is crucial to freedom of inquiry. Rights to privacy and confidentiality also are implicit in the *Library Bill of Rights'* guarantee of free access to library resources for all users.

Rights of Library Users

The *Library Bill of Rights* affirms the ethical imperative to provide unrestricted access to information and to guard against impediments to open inquiry. Article IV states: "Libraries should cooperate with all persons and groups concerned with resisting abridgement of free expression and free access to ideas." When users recognize or fear that their privacy or confidentiality is compromised, true freedom of inquiry no longer exists.

In all areas of librarianship, best practice leaves the user in control of as many choices as possible. These include decisions about the selection of, access to, and use of information. Lack of privacy and confidentiality has a chilling effect on users' choices. All users have a right to be free from any unreasonable intrusion into or surveillance of their lawful library use.

Users have the right to be informed what policies and procedures govern the amount and retention of personally identifiable information, why that information is necessary for the library, and what the user can do to maintain his or her privacy. Library users expect and in many places have a legal right to have their information protected and kept private and confidential by anyone with direct or indirect access to that information. In addition, Article V of the *Library Bill of Rights* states: "A person's right to use a library should not be denied or abridged because of origin, age, background, or views." This article precludes the use of profiling as a basis for any breach of privacy rights. Users have the right to use a library without any abridgement of privacy that may result from equating the subject of their inquiry with behavior.

Responsibilities in Libraries

The library profession has a long-standing commitment to an ethic of facilitating, not monitoring, access to information. This commitment is implemented locally through development, adoption, and adherence to privacy policies that are consistent with applicable federal, state, and local law. Everyone (paid or unpaid) who provides governance, administration, or service in libraries has a responsibility to maintain an environment respectful and protective of the privacy of all users. Users have the responsibility to respect each others' privacy.

For administrative purposes, librarians may establish appropriate time, place, and manner restrictions on the use of library resources. In keeping with this principle, the collection of personally identifiable information should only be a matter of routine or policy when necessary for the fulfillment of the mission of the library. Regardless of the technology used, everyone who collects or accesses personally identifiable information in any format has a legal and ethical obligation to protect confidentiality.

Conclusion

The American Library Association affirms that rights of privacy are necessary for intellectual freedom and are fundamental to the ethics and practice of librarianship.

Adopted by the ALA Council, June 19, 2002.

Resolution Reaffirming the Principles of Intellectual Freedom in the Aftermath of Terrorist Attacks

WHEREAS: Benjamin Franklin counseled this nation: "They that can give up essential liberty to obtain a little temporary safety deserve neither liberty nor safety"; and

WHEREAS: "The American Library Association believes that freedom of expression is an inalienable human right, necessary to self-government, vital to the resistance of oppression, and crucial to the cause of justice, and further, that the principles of freedom of expression should be applied by libraries and librarians throughout the world" (Policy 53.1.12, "Universal Right to Free Expression"); now, THEREFORE BE IT

RESOLVED: that the American Library Association reaffirms the following principles, and:

Actively promotes dissemination of true and timely information necessary to the people in the exercise of their rights (Policy 53.8, "Libraries: An American Value");

Opposes government censorship of news media and suppression of access to unclassified government information (Policy 53.3, "Freedom to Read;" Policy 53.5, "Shield Laws");

Upholds a professional ethic of facilitating access to information, not monitoring access (Policy 53.1, "Library Bill of Rights;" Policy 53.1.17, "Intellectual Freedom Principles for Academic Libraries");

Encourages libraries and their staff to protect the privacy and confidentiality of the people's lawful use of the library, its equipment, and its resources (Policy 52.4, "Policy on Confidentiality of Library Records");

Affirms that tolerance of dissent is the hallmark of a free and democratic society (Policy 53.1.12, "Universal Right to Free Expression");

Opposes the misuse of governmental power to intimidate, suppress, coerce, or compel speech (Policy 53.4, "Policy on Governmental Intimidation;" Policy 53.6, "Loyalty Oaths"); and, BE IT FURTHER

RESOLVED: that this resolution be forwarded to the President of the United States, to the Attorney General of the United States, and to both Houses of Congress.

Adopted by the ALA Council, January 23, 2002.

Resolution on the USA PATRIOT Act and Related Measures That Infringe on the Rights of Library Users

WHEREAS, The American Library Association affirms the responsibility of the leaders of the United States to protect and preserve the freedoms that are the foundation of our democracy; and

WHEREAS, Libraries are a critical force for promoting the free flow and unimpeded distribution of knowledge and information for individuals, institutions, and communities; and

WHEREAS, The American Library Association holds that suppression of ideas undermines a democratic society; and

WHEREAS, Privacy is essential to the exercise of free speech, free thought, and free association; and, in a library, the subject of users' interests should not be examined or scrutinized by others; and

WHEREAS, Certain provisions of the *USA PATRIOT Act*, the revised Attorney General Guidelines to the Federal Bureau of Investigation, and other related measures expand the authority of the federal government to investigate citizens and non-citizens, to engage in surveillance, and to threaten civil rights and liberties guaranteed under the United States Constitution and Bill of Rights; and

WHEREAS, The USA PATRIOT Act and other recently enacted laws, regulations, and guidelines increase the likelihood that the activities of library users, including their use of computers to browse the Web or access e-mail, may be under government surveillance without their knowledge or consent; now, therefore, be it

RESOLVED, That the American Library Association opposes any use of governmental power to suppress the free and open exchange of knowledge and information or to intimidate individuals exercising free inquiry; and, be it further

RESOLVED, That the American Library Association encourages all librarians, library administrators, library governing bodies, and library advocates to educate their users, staff, and communities about the process for compliance with the USA PATRIOT Act and other related measures and about the dangers to individual privacy and the confidentiality of library records resulting from those measures; and, be it further

RESOLVED, That the American Library Association urges librarians everywhere to defend and support user privacy and free and open access to knowledge and information; and, be it further

RESOLVED, That the American Library Association will work with other organizations, as appropriate, to protect the rights of inquiry and free expression; and, be it further

RESOLVED, That the American Library Association will take actions as appropriate to obtain and publicize information about the surveillance of libraries and library users by law enforcement agencies and to assess the impact on library users and their communities; and, be it further

RESOLVED, That the American Library Association urges all libraries to adopt and implement patron privacy and record retention policies that affirm that "the collection of personally identifiable information should only be a matter of routine or policy when necessary for the fulfillment of the mission of the library" (ALA *Privacy: An Interpretation of the Library Bill of Rights*); and, be it further

RESOLVED, That the American Library Association considers sections of the USA PATRIOT Act are a present danger to the constitutional rights and privacy rights of library users and urges the United States Congress to:

1. provide active oversight of the implementation of the USA PATRIOT Act and other related measures, and the revised Attorney General Guidelines to the Federal Bureau of Investigation;
2. hold hearings to determine the extent of the surveillance on library users and their communities; and
3. amend or change the sections of these laws and the guidelines that threaten or abridge the rights of inquiry and free expression; and, be it further

RESOLVED, That this resolution be forwarded to the President of the United States, to the Attorney General of the United States, to Members of both Houses of Congress, to the library community, and to others as appropriate.

Adopted by the ALA Council, January 29, 2003.

Center for Democracy and Technology Standards for Government Access to Papers, Records, and Communications, 2004

What Information Can the Government Get About You, and How Can They Get It?

	For real-time interception or immediate seizure, does government need a warrant issued on a HIGH PROBABLE CAUSE STANDARD?	Can government use a subpoena or court order under a LOWER STANDARD?	At time of search / subpoena, must government give the customer / subscriber to whom the information pertains NOTICE?	What are the standards for FOREIGN INTELLIGENCE?
☐ = STRONG PRIVACY PROTECTION				
☐ = MODEST OR INTERMEDIATE PRIVACY PROTECTION				
☐ = LITTLE OR NO PRIVACY PROTECTION				
PAPERS Papers in your home or office (record subject = record holder)	YES 4th Amendment	YES Subpoena	YES "Sneak and peek" under USA PATRIOT Act § 213, codified at 18 USC § 3103a	Probable cause-foreign power or agent of foreign power. No notice. 50 USC §§ 1824-25
DATA Electronic data on your hard drive or disks at home or office (record subject = record holder)	YES 4th Amendment	YES Subpoena	YES "Sneak and peek" under USA PATRIOT Act § 213, codified at 18 USC § 3103a	Probable cause-foreign power or agent of foreign power. No notice. 50 USC §§ 1824-25

RECORDS IN YOUR POSSESSION

Version 3.0, August 2004, The Center for Democracy & Technology, Washington, DC 20006, www.cdt.org

COMMUNICATIONS: REAL-TIME

TELEPHONE / VOICE Real-time interception of face-to-face conversations, phone calls, faxes	**YES** 18 USC § 2518 Various exceptions: 18 USC §§ 2510(5)(a), 2511(2)-(3)	NO	NO Always delayed 18 USC § 2518	Probable cause-foreign power or agent of foreign power. No notice. 50 USC §§ 1805-06
EMAIL / INTERNET Real-time interception of electronic communications in transit (grabbing bits off the wire)	**YES** 18 USC § 2518 Various exceptions: 18 USC §§ 2510(5)(a), 2511(2)-(3)	NO	NO Always delayed 18 USC § 2518	Probable cause-foreign power or agent of foreign power. No notice. 50 USC §§ 1805-06
TELEPHONE / VOICE (NON-CONTENT) Real-time interception of dialed numbers by pen register / trap & trace device	NO	YES, Court order 18 USC §§ 3122-23	NO Not even delayed 18 USC § 3123(d)(2)	Relevance standard. No notice. 50 USC §§ 1842, 1845
EMAIL / INTERNET (NON-CONTENT) Real-time interception of routing information of electronic communications in transit by pen register / trap & trace device	NO	YES, Court order 18 USC §§ 3122-23 USA PATRIOT Act § 216 confirmed application of pen/trap to Internet	NO Not even delayed 18 USC § 3123(d)(2)	Relevance standard. No notice. 50 USC §§ 1842, 1845

Version 3.0, August 2004, The Center for Democracy & Technology, Washington, DC 20006, www.cdt.org

INFORMATION STORED BY 3RD PARTY: ELECTRONIC COMMUNICATIONS

EMAIL, UNOPENED, <= 180 DAYS OLD Unopened email in storage for 180 days or less with provider of service to the public	YES 18 USC § 2703(a) Provider can voluntarily disclose in emergencies 18 USC § 2702	NO	NO 18 USC § 2703(a)	FISA is unclear. If it is considered an interception, probable cause-foreign power or agent. No notice. 50 USC §§ 1805-06
EMAIL, OPENED Opened email held by provider of service to the public	NO 18 USC § 2703(a)-(c)	YES, Subpoena or voluntary disclosure in emerg. 18 USC §§ 2702, 2703(b), 2703(d)	NO if warrant; otherwise, can be delayed 18 USC §§ 2703(b), 2705	If it is a record, "sought for" std. Notice prohibited. 50 USC § 1861(a), (d)
EMAIL, UNOPENED, > 180 DAYS OLD Unopened email in storage for more than 180 days with provider of service to the public	NO 18 USC § 2703(a)-(c)	YES, Subpoena or voluntary disclosure in emerg. 18 USC §§ 2702, 2703(b), 2703(d)	NO if warrant; otherwise, can be delayed 18 USC §§ 2703(b), 2705	If it is a record, "sought for" std. Notice prohibited. 50 USC § 1861(a), (d)
SUBSCRIBER INFORMATION Records identifying subscribers and telephone toll records	NO 18 USC § 2703(c)(2)	YES, Subpoena or voluntary disclosure in emerg. 18 USC §§ 2702, 2703(c)(2)	NO 18 USC § 2703(c)(3)	"Relevant to" & "sought for" stds. Notice prohibited. 18 USC § 2709(b), (c) 50 USC § 1861(a), (d)
EMAIL / INTERNET LOGS Internet transactional records (e.g., to/from lines of email headers)	NO 18 USC § 2703(c)(1)	YES, § 2703(d) order or voluntary disclosure in emerg. 18 USC §§ 2702, 2703(c)(1), 2703(d)	NO 18 USC § 2703(c)(3)	"Relevant to" & "sought for" stds. Notice prohibited. 18 USC § 2709(b), (c) 50 USC § 1861(a), (d)

INFORMATION STORED BY 3RD PARTY: OTHER RECORDS

Category				
CABLE Cable television subscription information	YES 18 USC § 2518 Clear & convincing 47 USC § 551(h)(1)	Where cable company provides Internet access, see 18 USC § 2703	YES 47 USC § 551(h) Where cable company provides Internet access, see 18 USC § 2703	"Sought for" standard. Notice prohibited. 50 USC § 1861(a), (d)
FINANCIAL Records in possession of bank or other financial institution	NO 12 USC §§ 3405-06	YES, Subpoena 12 USC §§ 3405, 3407-08	NO Can be delayed 12 USC § 3409	"Relevant to" & "sought for" stds. Notice prohibited. 12 USC § 3414(a)(5)(A) 15 USC §§ 1681u, 1681v 50 USC § 1861(a), (d)
CREDIT HISTORY	NO	YES, Grand jury subpoena 15 USC § 1681b(a)(1)	15 USC § 1681g	
EDUCATION Educational records	NO	YES 20 USC §§ 1232g(b)(1)(J)(i), 1232g(j)(2). 9007(c)	NO Prohibited 20 USC § 1232g(b)(1)(J)(i). 1232g(j); 34 CFR 99.31	"Relevant to" & "sought for" stds. Notice prohibited. 20 USC § 1232g(j) 50 USC § 1861(a), (d)
OTHER RECORDS Store purchases, library, travel, and other records not protected by a specific privacy law	NO Video rental & sale records require probable cause & notice 18 USC § 2710(b)	YES Plus voluntary disclosure	NO	"Sought for" standard. Notice prohibited. 50 USC § 1861(a), (d)
INTERNATIONAL Voice, email, or data intercepted in transit or seized from storage medium overseas	Title III & the 4th Amendment warrant clause have no extraterritorial effect	N/A	NO	FISA, NSLs have no extraterritorial effect

Version 3.0, August 2004, The Center for Democracy & Technology, Washington, DC 20006, www.cdt.org

APPENDIX II

Privacy Audit Documents

Privacy Audit and Guidelines for Libraries*

This guide is intended to assist library staff in conducting a privacy audit by listing the location and type of personally identifiable information, and then suggesting the requisite actions needed to protect that information. Not all of the information will be relevant to all libraries.

Protecting the privacy of our users is both a core professional value of librarianship and, in most states, a requirement by law for libraries using public funds. Protecting privacy is an increasing challenge to the library profession because in many situations the more services we provide to patrons the more Personally Identifiable Information (PII) we must collect and the more places PII is located. Overall, the library community can meet its ethical and legal obligations to protect the privacy of library users by adhering to the following basic principles:

- Know what PII the library collects and for what purposes that information is used.
- Keep only the minimum PII necessary to meet the library's program needs. Be cautious about collecting any PII "just in case" it may be used at some future date.
- Keep PII related to use of the library's services and resources only as long as necessary.

*This Model Privacy Audit and Guidelines is based on the guidelines developed by the University of California Libraries' Systemwide Operations and Planning Advisory Group (SOPAG) Privacy Policy Task Force (http://libraries.universityofcalifornia.edu/sopag/privacytf/). This material is used with permission of the University of California and copyright of the source material is held by the Regents of the University of California.

- Restrict access to PII based on a need-to-know basis.
- Inform users what PII the library collects and why. Tell patrons they have the right to review what PII the library has about them and they can correct errors in their PII.
- Be certain staff know exactly what PII is protected under state or federal law and the extent or limitations of such protections.
- Be certain staff know exactly what policies and procedures the library has to protect PII. (This is based on position or responsibility. For example, not all staff need know the intimate details of network security measures that, in part, protect privacy.)
- Be certain staff know exactly what actions to take when anyone requests access to PII that is not their own.
- Be certain to know how the library's privacy policy relates to any privacy or related policies of the library's parent body (e.g., school district, academic institution, city or county government).

Location or use of PII: **Integrated Library Systems and related services**	**Actions to Consider**
Circulation-related processes, including: • Patron registration records • Circulation transaction logs • Overdue and related billing records (e.g., lost or damaged items) • Document delivery and interlibrary loan transactions • Records of access to electronic reserves and items on hold	• Restrict access to staff who have a legitimate need (1) to access any records and logs revealing what a patron borrowed, and (2) to access patron registration records. • Do not allow access to the above by nonlibrary personnel without written authorization from the patron, by court order, or by other procedures as stated in appropriate statutes. • Delete individual patron identity when a transaction has been completed (e.g., when the item has been returned, fines are paid, etc.). • Delete patron registration records after expiration of borrower privileges or after a specified period of inactivity. • For analysis on collection use, only retain data (e.g., category of user) that cannot be traced back to a particular patron. • Review retention policies of backup or archival files. • Keep billing information only as long as required by financial record policies. • If outsourcing the collection of fines or related debts, make certain the collection agency adheres to library privacy policies and state library privacy statutes.

- Post on the library web site:
  - ○ What patron PII is collected
  - ○ What PII is retained about borrowing histories, how long it is retained, and who has access to it
  - ○ Patron privacy rights under library policy and state statute.

Records to support personalized services, including: • Search histories saved after a session • Saved searches and result sets • Personal profiles (these are often created by the patron) • Files/logs of previous electronic reference queries and answers	• Notify patrons whenever their PII (e.g., name, email, etc.) is requested and will be stored on the system. • Restrict access to patron PII to staff who have a legitimate need for such access. • Do not allow access to patron PII by nonlibrary personnel without written authorization from the patron, by court order, or by other procedures per state statute. • Offer patrons the option of limited personalized services that do not require their PII. • Regularly purge unused personalized services records with PII. • Delete patron personalized services records after expiration of privileges or after a specified period of inactivity. • If reference answers are saved by the library for future use, disaggregate any patron PII before saving. • If outsourcing personalized services, make certain the vendor adheres to library privacy policies and any state library privacy statutes. • Advise patrons (e.g., post on library web site) of privacy issues involved in their providing PII to support personalized services.
OPAC search logs (see also web server logs below)	• Restrict access to search logs to staff who have a legitimate need for such access. • If patron PII is logged, delete it as soon as possible. • For analysis on OPAC use, only retain data (e.g., category of user) that cannot be traced back to a particular patron. • If patron PII is logged, advise patrons (e.g., post on library web site) that such records exist and the privacy of such records will be maintained per library policy and any state statute.

Online displays of patron borrower records, patron-initiated renewals, and the like via the ILS	• Ensure that a patron's borrowing records are only accessible to staff who have a legitimate need for such access and to the patron. • Have prominently displayed signage and screen messages instructing patrons to close out their session before leaving any public access workstation. • After a period of inactivity, set time outs for any displays of patron information. • Allow patrons to opt-out of having their borrowing record displayed when they access the ILS.

Location or use of PII: **Library Servers**	**Actions to Consider**
Library web server logs, including proxy servers	• If access to some resources is authenticated by patron card number or user ID, notify users that their number or ID will be stored in web server logs. (Note: workstation IP addresses are routinely logged for any web use and may be used to determine user identity.) • Restrict access to server logs to staff who have a legitimate need for such access. • Review state library privacy statutes to determine if logs are covered. • Do not provide server logs to a third party without permission of the patron or by proper court order. • Routinely purge log files, keeping only aggregate data for statistics tracking. For analysis on web use and publication of statistics, only retain data that cannot be traced back to a particular patron.
Email servers and message files (most relevant when the library or parent institution provides patrons or students with email)	• Implement necessary procedures to ensure email security. • Restrict access to email servers (messages, logs, etc.) to authorized staff who have a legitimate need for such access. • Capture and log email messages only if needed to investigate a specific incident of possible abuse. • Limit inspection of email messages by systems staff to the minimum needed for proper functioning and security of the system. • Get proper authorization before inspecting any email messages, or allowing anyone else to inspect email messages.

- Notify the user if any email messages are inspected. Unless it is an emergency, notify the user before inspection.

- Advise users to carefully review the privacy provisions and policies of any other email provider (e.g., Yahoo, Google) they use.

- Advise users that there is no expectation of privacy for email sent beyond the library.

- Advise users to delete their emails on a regular basis and to empty their trash or delete folders.

- Email administrators should purge deleted messages and email logs from the server on a regular basis.

- For staff, be certain they are aware of any public records retention policies and any appropriate policies or laws related to retaining, archiving and deleting email.

Location or use of PII: **Public Workstations**	**Actions to Consider**
Browser temporary files (e.g., cache, history, cookies, certificates)	• Implement necessary procedures to keep all logs and web-related user files (e.g., cache, cookie and certificate files) secure including prevention of public access.
	• Restrict access or inspection of logs and related files to authorized staff who have a legitimate need for access, such as the proper functioning and security of the system.
	• Do not provide logs or files to a third party without permission of the patron, by legitimate administrative procedure or proper court order.
	• Make cookie files read-only.
	• Allow only authorized staff to create and edit bookmark files. Don't allow personal bookmarks on public workstations.
	• Advise users of the privacy exposures involved in using cookies.
	• Advise users to always use nontrivial passwords when needed to enter a restricted site or to access restricted content or services.
	• Advise users on web security and of the risks of entering PII on the web, especially on nonsecured sites.
	• Purge all public workstation temporary files (caches, cookies, etc.) frequently, such as upon closing of the browser.

Operating system logs	• If logs include PII, such as login IDs, implement necessary procedures to keep logs secure. • Restrict access to logs to authorized staff who have a legitimate need for such access, such as the proper functioning and security of the system. • Do not provide logs to third parties without permission of the patron, by legitimate administrative procedure, or proper court order. • Purge logs with PII frequently. • Advise users about logging and retention policies for shared workstations.
Public display monitors	• Install privacy screens or recessed monitors. • Position workstations so monitors cannot easily be seen from neighboring workstations or from long distances.
Workstation behavior	• Advise patrons about the library's policy regarding the viewing of possibly obscene images or text. • Advise patrons that obscenity is not protected by the Constitution and such viewing is not protected by the library's privacy policy or state privacy statute. • Advise patrons that inappropriate or illegal behavior is not protected by privacy policy or library privacy statutes.
Internet use registration	• Restrict access to sign-up sheets or logs of the Internet access management program, to authorized staff who have a legitimate need for such access. • Do not have sign-up sheets publicly posted next to a workstation. • Allow patrons to sign up with a nickname or pseudonym. • Destroy sign-up sheets or logs of the Internet access management program on a regular basis. • Review state library privacy statutes to determine if sign-up sheets and user files are covered.
Location or use of PII: **Network Services**	**Actions to Consider**
Router/switch logs	• Implement necessary procedures to ensure that any traffic logs are secure. • Restrict access to logs to authorized staff who have a legitimate need for such access, such as the proper functioning and security of the system.

- Do not provide logs to third parties without permission of the patron, by legitimate administrative procedure, or proper court order.
- For libraries in wide-area networks (WANs), verify that network partners all adhere to the same network traffic review policies.
- Alert users to library policies related to monitoring of network traffic.

Location or use of PII: **Licensed (external, outsourced) services**	**Actions to Consider**
Remote web sites, including content providers, outsourced web hosting, proxy servers, etc.	• Advise users of limits to library privacy protection when they use remote sites. • Reference privacy provision in the contract. For example, the vendor will 　○ Not pass patron/staff emails or search requests to third parties 　○ Provide for the confidentiality of users and ensure proper and secure logging practices 　○ Provide for usage statistics in aggregate.
Personalized portals and services beyond the library	• Advise users of the privacy exposures involved in providing PII to support personalized services. • Advise users that the library is not responsible for their use of services not directly supported by the library. • Advise users to carefully review the privacy policies posted by the entity providing the service and to look for adherence to self-regulatory codes (e.g., Health on the Net [HON]).

Privacy Audit Guidelines for Academic Libraries

Privacy Concerns	Sources of Data
Are patrons informed of the library's practices to protect privacy and risks to their privacy?	Up-to-date library policy statement posted on the web site. The use of dialog boxes that transition patrons from the world wide web to an encrypted page.
Do policies and procedures observe legalities?	Internet Security and Privacy Act Freedom of Information Law Personal Privacy Protection Law Federal laws State law Local ordinances
Do current library policies align with professional policies?	ALA Policy on Confidentiality (ALA Code of Ethics 54.15 pt.3) ACRL's Library Bill of Rights and Intellectual Freedom principles for Academic Libraries University policies Information Technology Policies
Is access to library systems data and network restricted to staff with legitimate needs to know?	Circulation records Patron registration Circulation transaction logs Overdue, billing, and payment records Institutional network
Should circulation records be deleted from a patron's file after items are returned? Should patron registration records be deleted after expiration of borrower's privileges? How long should information gathered be kept?	Circulation records Transaction logs Interlibrary loan records
Does data gathering by the library serve administrative purposes such as analyzing use of resources and improving services?	Circulation records Database use statistics Patron surveys

Privacy Concerns	Sources of Data
Are library records vulnerable via the world wide web?	World wide web access
Does the system require users to login to access the Internet?	
Does the system personalize desktop terminals to the personal settings of the user?	
Do email features subject the patron to vulnerability?	
Does the system keep web-server logs of patron Internet activities?	
Is authentication and/or IP authorization needed to access electronic indices?	Subscription databases
Do remote systems pose privacy risks?	Automated interlibrary loan transactions that involve personal information needed to process requests
Are users advised of limits to privacy protection when using remote sites?	
Are proper and secure logging practices and procedures negotiated in contracts?	Policies of database vendors
	Licensing agreements and contracts
Which data will be retained?	System rules
How are user data stored on the system protected from unauthorized use?	
Who has access to the data?	
How long are the data retained?	
Are users notified when personally identified information is stored on the system?	System data
Are time limits set for data storage?	
Are data removed from dormant accounts? How is the system secured?	
Are aggregate, rather than individual, statistics collected?	
Is there a privacy officer?	Staffing
Is staff educated about privacy?	Training procedures
Is the library web site certified by a creditable organization to observe its privacy policy as stated on the web site and to be generally trustworthy?	Better Business Bureau Online TRUSTe

Privacy Concerns	Sources of Data
Are students and instructors educated about ethical issues of information use?	University policies Library instruction program Inservice program for instructors

Privacy Audit Guidelines for School Library Media Programs

Task	Source(s) of Information	Special Considerations
1) Review federal[1] and state laws related to student records and library records.	a) Family Educational Rights and Privacy Act b) State Library Confidentiality Laws c) Public records laws d) State pupil records retention laws or guidelines	a) Who does and does *not* have legal access to student library records in public schools? b) To whom may student library records be released legally, and what types of libraries are covered by the state law?[22] Note: School library records are confidential IF schools are covered under the state confidentiality law. c) What library records may be covered under public records laws? [Example Internet history logs] d) Are there state guidelines for how long Internet logs, staff email, etc. must be archived?
2) Examine policies related to privacy and confidentiality.	a) District student confidentiality policies b) Library media program policies	a) Consider legality of local policies. b) Weigh library policy against ALA policy statements including Policy Concerning Confidentiality of PII
3) Assess data collected, data handling, and retention practices in the library manually or via automated system(s).	a) Patron registration and circulation/ reserve records in an automated system b) Overdue notices c) Backup tapes of circulation system transactions d) Internet sign-up sheets or network login logs e) Interlibrary loan records with patron name, paper or automated records	a) System set to retain links between patron and specific item? Who may access records? b) Overdue notices publicly posted? Paper notice to patron? Delivery method? Who handles notices? c) Time period for overwriting records? Who has access to the tapes? d) Time period retained? Who has access? Electronic or paper? Shredded? e) Time period retained? Who has access? Shredded or deleted?

Task	Source(s) of Information	Special Considerations
	f) Oral or electronic reference assistance records, paper notes or email queries g) OPAC search histories	f) Formal record including PII ? Who has access? Time period kept? Shredded? Purged? Check OPAC activity logs. Logs retained or purged on schedule?
4) Assess network access and security.	a) Records of personal network logins by students and staff b) Security evaluation by technology staff	a) Restrict access to server logs to specified library and technology staff. b) Obtain outside assistance if needed.
5) Assess Internet use vulnerability by patrons.	a) Login record of users b) Web-server logs of patron searches c) Cache records at end of patron session, history files, cookies file, certificates d) Email server logs (local) or remote host logs e) Router log files, firewall files f) Internet security evaluation	a) Is a login required to use the Internet? b) Restrict access to specified library and technology staff. c) Are tools used to clear cache automatically? d) Check confidentiality policy of remote host. e) Check retention time. f) Obtain outside assistance if needed.
6) Assess remote access to subscription databases.	a) Vendor contracts b) ICOLC Privacy Guidelines for Electronic Resources Vendors	a) Language of contract forbids collection of PII but allows anonymous aggregate use statistics b) Privacy with respect to information seeking is protected.
7) Determine library staff knowledge of privacy and confidentiality as applies to the school library media center.	a) Examination of training records. b) Local library policies	a) Include *all staff* (professional staff, adult assistants, student assistants, volunteers).
8) Name a privacy officer for the school or district.	a) ALA Office for Intellectual Freedom resources b) ALA Office for Information Technology Policy resources	a) Responsibilities include keeping current on privacy as it relates to school library media programs.

9) Analyze data, determine parameters for securing patron data, and modify current practice.	a) Data and informal staff observations from audit steps no. 1–6.	a) Develop plan for determining patron PII information needed, record retention time, process for aggregating data, who has access, security measures. b) Develop or revise Record Retention Policy and procedures for the gathering, use, handling, transferring, and removal of each type of patron PII data. c) Develop/revise library privacy policy.
10) Train the staff on privacy-protected data collection, retention, expunging, and handling law enforcement requests.	a) Plan including parameters for data collection, retention, access, and security. b) ALA Confidentiality and Coping with Law Enforcement Inquiries: Guidelines for the Library and its Staff.	a) Training done by privacy officer. Training covers *all library staff* (professional, paraprofessional, student staff and volunteers) and *IT staff.* b) Train *all library staff* on the library's procedure for handling law enforcement requests. c) Provide staff development for *all* K–12 staff on library policies relating to intellectual freedom.
11) Implement the procedures for PII patron information.	a) Plan including parameters for data collection, retention, access, and security	a) Monitor the plan for modifications to ensure highest level of patron privacy and confidentiality of data.
12) Inform patrons of the types of data collected and the staff's commitment to protecting patron PII.	a) Privacy policy	a) Post the board-approved privacy policy in areas where PII is collected and library webpages. b) Plan for regularly scheduled library audit every three years.

Note: These guidelines are based on information obtained from the American Library Association, Office for Information Technology Policy, "Online Privacy Tutorial #27: Conducting a Privacy Audit," 2002; Karen Coyle, "Make Sure You Are Privacy Literate," *Library Journal* 127, no. 16 (October 1, 2002), 55–57; and Mairi McFall and Karen G. Schneider, "The USA Patriot Act, and What You Can Do," California Library Association, http://www.cla-net.org/resources/articles/us_patriot_act.php (accessed May 9, 2004). See Chapter 5, "Privacy Issues in K–12 School Library Media Centers" for more detailed information on privacy, confidentiality, and retention policies and a library privacy audit.

Notes

1. It is unclear whether library records are considered "education records" under the Federal Educational Rights and Privacy Act (FERPA). More information may be found about the varying interpretations as to whether FERPA applies to school library records may be found in Chapter 5 in the FERPA and School Libraries section.

2. Wisconsin State Confidertiality Law, http://www.ala.org/ala/oif/ifgroups/stateifcchairs/atateifcinaction/stateprivacy.htm, accessed July 14, 2004. State library records laws vary in coverage of school libraries and the types of records or information covered. For example, Wisconsin's state confidentiality law covers "records of any library which is supported by public funds indicating the identity of any individual who borrows or uses the library's documents or other materials, resources, or services may not be disclosed except by court order." According to a State Library opinion, the law protects patron registration information; circulation records; use of the Internet including email, Internet logs, temporary files, and Internet sign-up sheets; and use of in-house databases. State Confidentiality laws for 48 states and the District of Columbia may be found on the American Library Association Office for Intellectual Freedom web site: http://www.ala.org/alaorg/oif/stateprivacylaw.html/.

Privacy and Confidentiality Policies

Sample Public Library Policy: Privacy of Library Records and Library Use*

This document is not a recommended policy; rather it is intended to be a starting point for development of a local library policy. This sample policy was originally developed for Wisconsin public libraries by the Wisconsin Division for Libraries, Technology, and Community Learning, the state library agency. However, other types of libraries in other jurisdictions will find it helpful too, with obvious changes needed to the statutory citations and any other changes needed to accommodate local circumstances. This sample policy is designed to be an internal, staff-oriented policy. Ideally any such policy will be developed with the full participation of the library board, with assistance from legal counsel, and with input from the community.

The _____ Public Library protects the privacy of library records and the confidentiality of patron use of the library as required by relevant laws of the State of Wisconsin. In addition, the _____ Public Library Board supports the principle of freedom of inquiry for library patrons, and has adopted this policy to protect against any unwarranted or unlawful invasion of the personal privacy of library users. The library board supports the intellectual freedom and privacy principles articulated by the American Library Association.

---

*Written by Mike Cross, director, Wisconsin Division for Libraries, Technology, and Community Learning, Public Library Development Team.

Legal Requirements

The relevant Wisconsin laws concerning the confidentiality of library records are Wisconsin Statutes, Section 43.30 and the Wisconsin Personal Information Practices Act (Sections 19.62 to 19.80).

Under section 43.30 of the statutes, library records which indicate the identity of any individual who borrows or uses the library's documents or other materials, resources, or services may *only* be disclosed:

1. with the consent of the library user
2. by court order
3. to staff acting within the scope of their duties in the administration of the library
4. to other libraries (under certain circumstances) for interlibrary loan purposes, or
5. to custodial parents upon request for records of any minor children under age sixteen.

Wisconsin's Personal Information Practices Act (Sections 19.62 to 19.80) requires all state and local government organizations, including public libraries, to develop procedures to protect the privacy of personal information kept by the organization. Libraries (and all other government organizations) are required to develop rules of conduct for employees involved in collecting, maintaining, using, and providing access to personally identifiable information (PII). Libraries are also required to ensure that employees handling such records "know their duties and responsibilities relating to protecting personal privacy, including applicable state and federal laws." Records indicating the identity of library users include a library user's name, library card number, Social Security number, telephone number, street address, post-office box number, or 9-digit extended zip code.

Records held by the library that include personally identifiable information about library users may also contain information that must be provided to those who request that information, under Wisconsin's open public records law. Personally identifiable information about library users must be redacted from any records that are publicly disclosed, except as the records are disclosed under one of the five exceptions provided by Section 43.30 (see the preceding text).

Procedures to Be Followed by Library Staff

1) As required by state law, library staff may only disclose library records indicating the identity of library users under the following conditions:
   a) disclosure to staff members of the _____ Public Library, and the staff of other libraries and library systems only according to written pro-

cedures that comply with the laws cited above and that are approved by the director

b) disclosure as authorized by the individual library user

c) disclosure pursuant to court order (see the following for handling of different types of court orders)

2) Library staff must refer all requests for library records and all requests for information about particular library patrons to the library director or the supervisor in charge.

3) Library staff are not allowed to share information about use of library resources and services by identified library patrons except as necessary for the performance of their job duties and in accordance with procedures approved by the library director and/or board.

Procedures to Address Court Orders

Note: All search warrants are court orders, but *not* all subpoenas are court orders. Library staff may not disclose library records in response to a subpoena that is not a court order if those records indicate the identity of library users.

If a law enforcement officer (or anyone else) brings a *subpoena*[†] directing library staff to produce library records:

1. Notify the library director, or if the director is not available, notify the highest-ranking staff person on duty.

2. The library director or the highest-ranking staff person should ask the municipal attorney (or library counsel) to review the subpoena.

3. If the subpoena has any legal defects, require that the defects be cured before records are released.

4. If appropriate, ask legal counsel to draft a protective order to be submitted to the court keeping the requested information confidential and limiting its use to the particular case.

5. Follow legal counsel's advice for compliance with the subpoena.

If law enforcement officers bring a court order in the form of a *search warrant*[‡]:

[†]A subpoena is a call to come before a court, and may include a direction to bring specified records. Not all subpoenas are court orders. Your municipal attorney (or library counsel) can determine if a particular subpoena is a court order. A subpoena normally indicates that a response is required within a certain number of days. Library staff may not disclose library records in response to a subpoena that is not a court order if those records indicate the identity of library users.

[‡]A search warrant is an order signed by a judge directing a law enforcement officer to conduct a search of a designated person, a designated object, or a designated place for the purpose of seizing designated property or kinds of property.

1. A search warrant is executable immediately, unlike a subpoena. The law enforcement officers may begin a search of library records as soon as they enter the library.
2. Request that the law enforcement officers wait until the municipal attorney (or library counsel) is present before the search begins in order to allow counsel an opportunity to examine the search warrant and to assure that the search conforms to the terms of the search warrant. (The law enforcement officials are *not* required to accede to your request to delay the search.)
3. Cooperate with the search to ensure that only the records identified in the warrant are produced and that no other users' records are disclosed.

   If federal agents bring a court order in the form of a search warrant issued under the *Foreign Intelligence Surveillance Act (FISA)*[§]:

1. A search warrant is executable immediately, unlike a subpoena. The law enforcement officers may begin a search of library records as soon as they enter the library.
2. Request that the law enforcement officers wait until the municipal attorney (or library counsel) is present before the search begins in order to allow counsel an opportunity to examine the search warrant and to assure that the search conforms to the terms of the search warrant. (The law enforcement officials are *not* required to accede to your request.)
3. Cooperate with the search to ensure that only the records identified in the warrant are produced and that no other users' records are disclosed.
4. It is illegal to disclose to any other person (other than those persons necessary to produce the tangible things sought in the warrant) that the federal authorities have sought or obtained records or other items under the Foreign Intelligence Surveillance Act (FISA).

[§]The USA PATRIOT Act amended the Foreign Intelligence Surveillance Act (FISA) to allow the FBI to apply for a court order requiring the "production of any tangible things (including books, records, papers, documents, and other items) for an investigation to protect against international terrorism or clandestine intelligence activities, provided that such investigation of a United States person is not conducted solely upon the basis of activities protected by the first amendment."

Sample School Library Media Program Privacy Policy[1]

The American Library Association defines privacy in a library as "the right to open inquiry without having the subject of one's interest examined or scrutinized by others."[2] Privacy is a key concept of student intellectual freedom and fundamental to free and open inquiry for all students in school library media programs.

The NAME School District Library Media Program is dedicated to protecting the privacy of its students and staff while they use library resources, services, and facilities. NAME School District Library Media Program staff are further committed to maintaining the confidentiality of patron personally identifiable information and records of their library usage.

School library media program staff are legally obligated to comply with valid legal process, as mandated by state and federal law.[3] STATE NAME AND NUMBER OF STATUTE/SECTION prohibit the release of personally identifying records kept by a library except under specified circumstances. These exceptions vary by state, but often include release to the individual account holder, to library staff in pursuit of their duties, or by court order. Some states also require that the library release the information in response to a valid subpoena.[4] *Alternate Language* to be used in states where state library records confidentiality laws grant parents and guardians access to their child's library records: "Library staff are required to disclose to ADD PERSON[5] [for example, a custodial parent or guardian] of a child under the age of ADD AGE records relating to that child's library records."[6]

The NAME School District Library Media Program collects the following personally identifiable information for registration purposes from its patrons: name, address, telephone number. *Add other local information as required.* Circulation data maintained for each patron may include: items currently checked out, items on reserve, overdue materials, and fines. Requests for items on interlibrary loan may include the patron's name, the name of the item, and the lending institution. To use the public access computers or access the Internet, library staff require *Insert other local information as desired e.g., the name of the student, date, and time of use for paper records; network login; or other information. Additional optional language may include the next two sentences.* The district's AUP prohibits students from supplying personally identifiable information about themselves or others while using the Internet or school email. The library web site will comply with district policy stating only group photos of students will be included on the web site, and individual students will not be identified.

The NAME School District Library Media Program's web pages contain links to other Internet sites. Sites visited may have different privacy policies relating to personally identifiable information, and the library media program is not responsible for protecting personal information gathered by other web sites. Commercial web sites are required to get parental permission before gathering personal information about children under 13.[7]

Library patrons have the right to request access to their library circulation records during regular library media center hours.

Information collected by the NAME School District Library Media Program is used solely for management purposes and is not shared with any person, agency or organization except as required by law. Procedures have been put in place to secure the data and assure their integrity. Patron personally identifiable information is retained only as long as needed and regularly purged, shredded, or otherwise destroyed by library staff following the schedule in the DISTRICT School Library Media Program Records Retention Policy.

Instruction will be provided to patrons on protecting their personal privacy. NAME Library Media Program patrons who believe their privacy and confidentiality have been violated should report their complaints to the library media specialist, principal, guidance counselor, or other proper authority. Formal complaints will be forwarded to the principal and handled following the school or district's due process procedures.

Legal Reference:	STATE Library Confidentiality Statute[8] located at http://www.ala.org/alaorg/oif/stateprivacylaws.html
	STATE Public Records Law[9]
	FEDERAL Family Educational Rights and Privacy Act (FERPA) 20 U.S.C. § 1232g; 34 CFR Part 99[10]
	FEDERAL Children's Online Privacy Protection Act of 1998 (COPPA) 16 U.S.C. § 6501 et seq.; 16 CFR Part 312[11]
Cross Reference:	NAME School District Confidentiality of School Library Media Program Records Policy
	LOCAL School District Records Retention Policy
	NAME School District Acceptable Use Policy
	NAME School District Web Site Policy and Guidelines
Related Documents:	American Library Association "Privacy: An Interpretation of the Library Bill of Rights" (2002) http://www.ala.org/ala/oif/statementspols/statementsif/interpretations/privacy.htm
	American Library Association "Policy on Confidentiality of Library Records" (1986) http://www.ala.org/ala/oif/statementspols/otherpolicies/policyconfidentiality.htm

American Library Association "Policy Concerning Confidentiality of Personally Identifiable Information about Library Users" (2004) http://www.ala.org/ala/oif/statementspols/otherpolicies/policyconcerning.htm

American Library Association "Confidentiality and Coping with Law Enforcement Inquiries: Guidelines for the Library and Its Staff" (2002) http://www.ala.org/ala/oif/ifissues/guidelineslibrary.pdf

Note: The policy was created by Helen Adams and is based on information obtained from the American Library Association "Guidelines for Developing a Library Privacy Policy" and from policies of the following libraries: Cleveland Heights–University Heights Public Library (OH), Madison Public Library (WI), Mill Valley Public Library (CA), Santa Clara City Library (CA), Seattle Public Library (WA), the Spokane County Library District (WA), and Mary Minow at LibraryLaw.com.

Notes

1. Privacy policies are aimed at patrons, not library staff, and let student patrons know their privacy rights in a school media center.

2. American Library Association Office for Intellectual Freedom, "Questions and Answers on Privacy and Confidentiality," http://www.ala.org/ala/oif/statementspols/statementsif/interpretations/questionsanswers.htm (accessed July 26, 2004).

3. Although it is unclear whether library records are considered "education records" under the Federal Educational Rights and Privacy Act (FERPA), some parents may argue that it does apply. Until this issue is clearly delineated by legislation or by the courts, a local interpretation should be sought from the school or district's legal counsel and the policy worded accordingly.

4. Since state library confidentiality laws vary, school district legal counsel should be consulted to properly cite the instances in which designated school library records may legally be released. Generally, a subpoena will give the library time to respond, for example, five days. This is in contrast to a search warrant, which is a type of court order and executable immediately.

5. The person(s) to whom designated library use records may be disclosed varies among the states.

6. The states allowing parents or guardians to legally access library records of minor children include Alaska, Alabama, Colorado, Florida, Georgia, Louisiana, Ohio, New Mexico, South Dakota, Utah, Virginia, West Virginia, Wisconsin, and Wyoming. The type of library records accessible may vary, and library staff should review their state's statute. Additionally, Oklahoma Statutes, Section 65-1-105. Disclosure of Records, grants this exception: "B. The requirements of this section shall not prohibit middle and elementary school libraries from maintaining a system of records that identifies the individual or group to whom library materials have been loaned even if such system permits a determination, independent of any disclosure of such information by the library, that documents or materials have been loaned

to an individual or group." "State Laws on the Confidentiality of Library Records," maintained by Paul Neuhaus, Carnegie Mellon University, updated December 31, 2004, http://www.library.cmu.edu/People/neuhaus/state_laws.html (accessed January 27, 2005).

7. The Children's Online Privacy Protection Act of 1998 (COPPA) requires obtaining parental permission before gathering personal information about children under age 13.

8. State library confidentiality laws vary as to whether school libraries are included; therefore, it is wise to check your state's confidentiality statute on ALA's web site http://www.ala.org/alaorg/oif/stateprivacylaws.html and verify that it is the latest version by checking your state codes. A "State Laws on the Confidentiality of Library Records," web site is also maintained by Paul Neuhaus, Carnegie Mellon University and updated frequently http://www.library.cmu.edu/People/neuhaus/state_laws.html. In some cases, library records are listed as an exception in the state public records law. In others, it is a separate confidentiality law, and will "trump" or override a public records law in the area of library records. Some state confidentiality laws are more inclusive than others protecting more types of records. For example, New York's law safeguards a wide range of library records, while the California and Pennsylvania statutes provide confidentiality for only registration and circulation records. For more information on state confidentiality laws see the "State Library Records Confidentiality Laws" section in Chapter 5.

9. State public records laws generally encompass ALL records, including electronic records with specified exceptions. Such exceptions may be found in specific language relating to library records within the public records law or in a separate library confidentiality statute.

10. As noted in Chapter 5, it is unclear whether K–12 school library records are considered "education records" under FERPA.

11. Information on the Children's Online Privacy Protection Act of 1998 is available for teachers, parents, web site operators, and children at the Kidz Privacy web site maintained by the Federal Trade Commission at http://www.ftc.gov/bcp/conline/edcams/kidzprivacy/index.html/. Information on COPPA directed specifically to school librarians may be found at http://www.ala.org/ala/washoff/WOissues/civilliberties/coppa/coppalibrarians.htm#School/.

Sample Confidentiality of School Library Media Program Records Policy

The NAME School District recognizes the right of patrons to read and use library materials and services without fear that others will intrude on their personal privacy. Confidentiality of library use records containing personally identifying information is fundamental to free and open inquiry for young children, preteens, and teenagers in school library media programs. The American Library Association states "confidentiality exists when a library is in possession of personally identifiable information about users and keeps that information private on their behalf."[1]

School library media program staff are legally obligated to comply with valid legal process, as mandated by state and federal law.[2] STATE NAME AND NUMBER OF STATUTE/SECTION[3] prohibit the release of personally identifying records kept by a library except under specified circumstances. These exceptions vary by state, but often include release to the individual account holder, to library staff in pursuit of their duties, or by court order. Some states also require that the library release the information in response to a valid subpoena.[4] *Alternate Language* to be used in states where state library records confidentiality laws grant parents and guardians access to their child's library records: "Library staff are required to disclose to ADD PERSON[5] [for example, a custodial parent or guardian] of a child under the age of ADD AGE records relating to that child's library records."[6]

Information collected by the NAME School District Library Media Program is used solely for management purposes and is not shared with any person, agency, or organization except as required by law. School library staff will develop rules and procedures to ensure the confidentiality of library records, secure the data, and assure their integrity. Patron personally identifiable information is retained only as long as needed and regularly purged, shredded, or otherwise destroyed by library staff following the schedule in the DISTRICT School Library Media Program Records Retention Policy.

Legal Reference: STATE Library Confidentiality Statute located at
                    http://www.ala.org/alaorg/oif/stateprivacylaws.html

                    STATE Public Records Law[7]

                    FEDERAL Family Educational Rights and Privacy Act
                    (FERPA) 20 U.S.C. § 1232g; 34 CFR Part 99[8]

Cross Reference: NAME School District School Library Media Program Privacy Policy

                    LOCAL School District Records Retention Policy

Related Documents: American Library Association "Privacy: An Interpretation of the Library Bill of Rights" (2002)
http://www.ala.org/ala/oif/statementspols/statementsif/interpretations/privacy.htm

American Library Association "Policy on Confidentiality of Library Records" (1986)
http://www.ala.org/ala/oif/statementspols/otherpolicies/policyconfidentiality.htm

American Library Association "Policy Concerning Confidentiality of Personally Identifiable Information about Library Users" (2004)
http://www.ala.org/ala/oif/statementspols/otherpolicies/policyconcerning.htm

The policy was created by Helen Adams.

Notes

1. American Library Association Office for Intellectual Freedom, "Questions and Answers on Privacy and Confidentiality," http://www.ala.org/ala/oif/statementspols/statementsif/interpretations/questionsanswers.htm (accessed July 26, 2004).

2. Although it is unclear whether library records are considered "education records" under the Federal Educational Rights and Privacy Act (FERPA), some parents may argue that it does apply. Until this issue is clearly delineated by legislation or by the courts, a local interpretation should be sought from the school or district's legal counsel and the policy worded accordingly.

3. Forty-eight states and the District of Columbia have laws relating to the confidentiality of library patron and use records. State Library Confidentiality laws vary as to whether school library records are covered; therefore, it is wise to check your state's confidentiality statute on ALA's web site http://www.ala.org/alaorg/oif/stateprivacylaws.html and verify that it is the latest version by checking your state codes. If school library records are protected, the extent of coverage also varies from broad coverage such as New York which includes but is not limited to "records related to the circulation of library materials, computer database searches, interlibrary loan transactions, reference queries, requests for photocopies of library materials, title reserve requests, or the use of audio-visual materials, films or records, . . ." ARTICLE 45—EVIDENCE, S 4509 New York State Consolidated Laws Civil Practice Law & Rules, http://assembly.state.ny.us/leg/?cl=16&a=36 (accessed July 22, 2004). In other states, the law has a more narrow scope. For example, Pennsylvania covers only circulation records. Paul Neuhaus, "Privacy and Confidentiality in Digital Reference," *Reference & User Service Quarterly* 43, no. 1 (Fall 2003): 32 (accessed July 22, 2004).

4. Since state library confidentiality laws vary, school district legal counsel should be consulted to properly cite the instances in which designated school library records may legally be released. Generally, a subpoena will give the library time to respond for example, five days. This is in contrast to a search warrant, which is a type of court order and executable immediately.

5. The person(s) to whom designated library use records may be disclosed varies among the states.

6. The states allowing parents or guardians to legally access library records of minor children include Alaska, Alabama, Colorado, Florida, Georgia, Louisiana, Ohio, New Mexico, South Dakota, Utah, Virginia, West Virginia, Wisconsin, and Wyoming. The type of library records accessible may vary, and library staff should review their state's statute. Additionally, Oklahoma Statutes, Section 65-1-105. Disclosure of Records grants this exception: "B. The requirements of this section shall not prohibit middle and elementary school libraries from maintaining a system of records that identifies the individual or group to whom library materials have been loaned even if such system permits a determination, independent of any disclosure of such information by the library, that documents or materials have been loaned to an individual or group." "State Laws on the Confidentiality of Library Records," maintained by Paul Neuhaus, Carnegie Mellon University, updated December 31, 2004, http://www.library.cmu.edu/People/neuhaus/state_laws.html (accessed January 27, 2005).

7. State public records laws generally encompass *all* records, including electronic records with specified exceptions. Such exceptions may be found in specific language relating to library records within the public records law or a separate library confidentiality statute.

8. As noted in Chapter 5, it is unclear whether K–12 school library records are considered "education records" under FERPA.

Sample School Library Media Program Records Retention Policy

To protect the privacy of its patrons and the confidentiality of their library records and their library usage and to prevent their unauthorized disclosure, the NAME School District will regularly purge, shred, or otherwise destroy records containing personally identifiable information of library media center patrons. This will include, but is not limited to, circulation records, interlibrary loan records, public access computer/Internet signup lists or automated signups, temporary files, cookies, and use records created during Internet searching, reference interviews and email queries, and server logs. Library and technology staff will develop a schedule and guidelines to ensure nonessential personally identifying data or files are not retained and programs are configured to remove personally identifiable information. Disposal of records must follow the NAME School District retention schedules, which are adopted/modified from the STATE Records Retention Schedule for School Districts.[1] NAME School District contracts with vendors will require vendors to adhere to local, state, and federal laws protecting student and library records. NAME School District will also require adherence to the International Coalition of Library Consortia (ICOLC) "Privacy Guidelines for Electronic Resources Vendors," whenever possible.[2]

Legal Reference: LOCAL School District Records Retention Policy[3]

STATE Public Records Law[4]

FEDERAL Family Educational Rights and Privacy Act (FERPA) 20 U.S.C. § 1232g; 34 CFR Part 99[5]

Cross Reference: STATE Education Records Retention Schedule

STATE Library Confidentiality Statute located at http://www.ala.org/alaorg/oif/stateprivacylaws.html[6]

Related Documents: International Coalition of Library Consortia (ICOLC) "Privacy Guidelines for Electronic Resources Vendors," located at http://www.library.yale.edu/consortia/2002priva cyguidelines.html

American Library Association "Privacy: An Interpretation of the Library Bill of Rights" (2002) http://www.ala.org/ala/oif/statementspols/statementsif/ interpretations/privacy.htm

American Library Association "Policy on Confidentiality of Library Records" (1986) http://www.ala.org/ala/oif/statementspols/otherpolicies/ policyconfidentiality.htm

American Library Association "Policy Concerning Confidentiality of Personally Identifiable Information About Library Users" (2004)
http://www.ala.org/ala/oif/statementspols/otherpolicies/policyconcerning.htm

American Library Association "Guidelines for Developing a Library Privacy Policy" (2003) located at http://www.ala.org/Template.cfm?Section=toolkitsprivacy&Template=/ContentManagement/ContentDisplay.cfm&ContentID=43556

Guidelines for Retention of School Library Records[7]

1. Circulation Records: Patron electronic circulation and reserve records will be retained until the item is returned and fines are paid. [*Alternative wording*: or until the item is checked out to the next borrower, or thirty days elapse].[8]

2. Database Records: Personally Identifying Information (PII) is not generally required for database searches performed onsite. When PII is required for authentication to use databases, that information is deleted, if possible, by the library after the search is completed. If the PII is retained by third party vendors, LOCAL DISTRICT must ensure by contract that vendors will comply with local, state, and federal confidentiality laws as well. Vendor contracts will include reference to the ICOLC "Privacy Guidelines for Electronic Resources Vendors" whenever possible.

3. Library Server Records: Backup tapes are overwritten [*time period options*: after thirty days or up to ninety days].[9]

4. Internet History Logs: Server security software will overwrite the logs [*time period options*: after every session ends, daily, or every thirty days].[10]

5. Public Access Library Computer or Internet Use Sign-Up: Paper sign-up logs are retained for [*time period options*: one day, five days, ten days, for three months] until usage statistics are aggregated for reporting purposes. [*Optional language*: If students access the Internet and local servers using their student ID and password, the records will be purged on the schedule of library server records and Internet history logs.]

6. Interlibrary Loan Records: Paper or electronic interlibrary loan records for books are retained for [*time period options*: one semester, one school year]. Records relating to interlibrary loan requests for magazine articles will be retained for three years to comply with copyright guidelines.[11]

7. Oral Reference Interviews: No record is made of oral reference queries between students, staff, or others using the school library media centers unless necessary to follow-up on a request. Records or PII relating to the request are destroyed as soon as the transaction is completed.

8. Electronic Reference Queries: Messages are deleted [*time period options*: daily, weekly, biweekly].[12]

9. Data, logs, or other records hosted offsite will be managed/administered according to this policy as enforced through contracts with, including local, state, and federal law as well as with the ICOLC Privacy Guidelines.

Note: The policy was created by Helen Adams are based on information obtained from the American Library Association "Guidelines for Developing a Library Privacy Policy," the Madison (WI) Public Library Records and the USA PATRIOT Act (http://www.madisonpubliclibrary.org/about/patriot.html), and from Mary Minow at LibraryLaw.com.

Notes

1. The titles vary within the 50 states.

2. In 2002, the International Coalition of Library Consortia (ICOLC), an informal, international group of over 160 library consortia in North America, Europe, Australia, Asia, and Africa announced its "Privacy Guidelines for Electronic Resources Vendors" to serve as the basis for vendor practices in relation to ensuring the privacy of library users in their information seeking activities. http://www.library.yale.edu/consortia/2002privacyguidelinespressrelease.html (accessed January 5, 2005).

3. In some states, a school district has the latitude to adopt wholly, partially, or modify its state's records' retention schedule for school districts as part of local district policy on record retention. For example, the State of Wisconsin's "Record Retention Schedule for School Districts" states districts can make modifications to the schedule; however, it should also be noted that the State of Wisconsin asserts, "For records to be retained less than seven years, the district may not adopt a retention period shorter than that indicated in the Schedule without the approval of the Public Records and Forms Board," http://www.doa.state.wi.us/docs_View2.asp?docid=195 (accessed January 5, 2005). The Archives Resource Center, "Information Resources on Archives and Records Administration for State and Local Governments," provides links to resources on state archives and records program web sites at http://www.coshrc.org/arc/states/res_sch_genlst.htm. This may be a useful starting point if you are unfamiliar with your state's guidelines on school district record retention. While there may be no specific references to school library records, it will give an overview of what types of records must be retained and insight into creating a library record retention policy.

4. State public records laws generally encompass *all* records, including electronic records with specified exceptions. Such exceptions may be found in specific language relating to library records within the public records law or a separate library confidentiality statute.

5. As noted in Chapter 5, it is unclear whether K–12 school library records are considered "education records" under FERPA. However, a March 2003 article in the *North Carolina Law Review* makes a case that the logs produced when students log in to a college campus computer network should be protected under FERPA. Jennifer C. Wasson, "FERPA in the Age of Computer Logging: School Discretion at the Cost of Student Privacy?" *North Carolina Law Review*, March 2003, LexisNexis™ Academic (accessed January 6, 2005).

6. State library confidentiality laws vary as to whether school libraries are included; therefore, it is wise to check your state's confidentiality statute on ALA's web site, http://www.ala.org/alaorg/oif/stateprivacylaws.html, and verify that it is the latest version by checking your state codes. One may also check with district legal counsel regarding under what circumstances records may legally be released. In some cases, library records are listed as an exception in the state public records law. In others, it is a separate confidentiality law, and will "trump" or override a

public records law in the area of library records. Some state confidentiality laws are more inclusive than others protecting more types of records. For example, New York's law safeguards a wide range of library records, while the California and Pennsylvania statutes provide confidentiality for only registration and circulation records. For more information on state confidentiality laws see the "State Library Records Confidentiality Laws" section in Chapter 5.

7. Whether school libraries may destroy records is determined by state and local district records retention schedules. It the type of record is not specifically noted and there is no broad language which might include the record, the library may presumably dispose of it. Retention periods for records are a matter of local policy or preference unless dictated by local, state, or federal law, state records retention schedules, or contracts. A shorter retention period results in less exposure to liability for the school library and less potential for violating the privacy of patrons. If a school library receives a request for records and the library has no record to produce, the matter ends there. If records exist, a district should *never* destroy them after receiving the records request. Library staff and administrators, in conjunction with district legal counsel, will determine the next step. Within these guidelines, time periods are *suggested* with the shortest period of retention preferred.

8. Alternate policy language is provided to give libraries an option. Some school libraries may opt to purge the circulation records upon return of the item or payment of an outstanding related fine. Others may want to retain the record until the item is checked out again in case damage is discovered later.

9. While it is recommended that record retention periods be as limited as possible, it is necessary to consider some record retention from an IT point of view. At times errors are not found within a thirty day period; therefore, it is wise to consider retaining server records for collection and other data for a longer period of time.

10. A New Hampshire court ruled that Internet history logs are public records. "Exeter Internet Ruling, Complete Ruling," *Portsmouth Herald*, January 8, 2001, http://www.seacoastonline.com/2001news/1_8special.htm (accessed January 6, 2005). This ruling is valid only in that jurisdiction; however, other jurisdictions faced with a similar situation will likely consider the reasoning involved in the New Hampshire case. In Utah, the State Records Committee decided the Utah Education Network's Internet history filtering logs were public records and should be turned over to Michael Sims, who sought them to analyze the use of filtering systems. Pamela Mendels, "State's Filtering Effort Comes Under Critical Eye," September 16, 1998, Technology, *New York Times*, http://www.nytimes.com/library/tech/98/09/cyber/articles/16filter.html (accessed January 6, 2005). More information on Internet history or use logs as public records may be found in Chapter 5 under "Internet Use Logs as Public Records."

11. Magazine article requests through interlibrary loan should be retained for three years to comply with CONTU copyright guidelines known as the "Rule of 5." The National Commission on New Technological Uses of Copyright Works (CONTU) "Guidelines on Photocopying under Interlibrary Loan Arrangements," located at http://www.cni.org/docs/infopols/CONTU.html, "were developed to assist librarians and copyright proprietors in understanding the amount of photocopying for use in interlibrary loan arrangements permitted under the copyright law."

12. Personally identifiable information about patrons may be removed and queries retained for creating knowledge bases for future reference work.

Glossary

Anonymizer "An Anonymizer is an intermediary which prevents web sites from seeing a user's Internet Protocol (IP) address. An anonymizer, also called a web anonymizer, is a privacy service that allows a user to visit web sites without allowing anyone to gather information about which sites they visit and without allowing a visited web site to gather information about them."[1]

Authentication "(1) [T]he process of verifying identity, origin, or lack of modification of a subject or object. Authentication of a user is generally based on something the user knows, is, or has. The use of some kind of system to ensure that a file or message which purports to come from a given individual or company actually does. Many authentication systems are now looking towards public key encryption, and the calculation of a check based upon the contents of the file or message as well as a password or key. Related concepts are change detection and integrity."[2]

Biometrics A general term for technology that identifies people by their physical characteristics, for example, fingerprints, retina or iris scans, hand geometry, facial and voice recognition, or force profiles based on how one walks.

CALEA Communications Assistance for Law Enforcement Act of 1994. The law regulating wiretaps.

CAPPS II Computer Assisted Passenger Prescreening System II. A computerized air passenger prescreening system to identify possible criminal or terror suspects.

CIPA "The Children's Internet Protection Act requires libraries and schools to install filters on their Internet computers to retain federal funding and discounts for computers and computer access. Because this law directly affected libraries and their ability to make legal information freely available to their patrons, the American Library Association and the Freedom to Read Foundation filed a lawsuit to overturn CIPA, but the Supreme Court on June 23, 2003, in a 6–3 decision, upheld the constitutionality of the Children's Internet Protection Act (CIPA)."[3]

Confidentiality "Confidentiality exists when a library is in possession of personally identifiable information about users and keeps that information private on their behalf."[4]

Confidentiality policy   A policy aimed at library staff and focused on their responsibility to keep patron personally identifiable information (PII) about library
materials checked out and services used confidential.

Cookie   A text file placed on a computer's hard-drive by web sites visited while online and used for a number of purposes, including identifying a user as a return
visitor to a site, aggregating items for purchasing online, and holding a log-in
code and password for sites which require membership to enter or are fee-based.

Cookie cutter software   Software products that protect online privacy and security
by erasing unwanted tracks left on the computer from surfing the Internet, such
as history, typed URLs (the drop down address list), AutoComplete, cookies,
temporary files, recent document list, and recycle bin.[5]

**CONTU (National Commission on New Technological Uses of Copyright Works)
"Guidelines on Photocopying under Interlibrary Loan Arrangements"**   Also
known as the "Rule of 5," the guidelines assist librarians in determining the legal
amount of photocopying of periodical articles permitted under copyright law.
Libraries should not request or acquire more than five articles from the same
journal within five years of an interlibrary loan request.[6]

COPA   Children's Online Protection Act. "COPA passed in October 1998, treated
activity involving the publishing (for commercial purposes) of communications
or content (particularly sexual in nature) that includes material harmful to minors, but that also does not restrict access to minors. Under COPA, violators
could expect up to a $50,000 fine, six months in jail, and/or additional civil
fines."[7] The legal status of COPA is unclear at this time; it has already been reviewed by the Supreme Court twice, and is currently back in the lower court.

COPPA   Children's Online Privacy Protection Act. Passed by Congress in 1998 to
protect the privacy of children online up through the age of twelve. "COPPA is
enforced by the U.S. Federal Trade Commission. It requires U.S.-based web sites
that collect personal information from people under the age of 13 to obtain
permission from parents or guardians before asking for such data. It prohibits
web sites from requiring the collection of personal information as a prerequisite
for accessing online interactive services (such as chat rooms), and allows parents
to determine, review (and delete) any data on kids that is provided to online services, and block any further data collection.

   "It also spells out requirements and guidelines for site and content design to
accommodate privacy protections, such as the link to a privacy statement, and
easily understood privacy guarantees. In order to comply with the law, web sites
must either receive email verification of age or parental permission if the data
was only for internal purposes, or have written permission (regular mail or fax),
telephone verification (like a call to a toll-free 800 number), or a 'digital signature' (similar to credit card verification) if the site in question will either give or
sell the information it collects to a third party. Sites violating COPPA can face a
potential fine of $11,000 for each violation."[8]

Court order   A decision or instruction issued by a court. This term is not generally used to describe a final judgment of a court, but rather, requirements of the
court at an earlier stage in a legal proceeding. A court order must either be complied with or formally challenged by an attorney representing the person or organization receiving the order. See Subpoena.

CPPA The Child Pornography Prevention Act prohibited both actual depictions of children engaged in explicit sexual activity and computer-generated or "morphed" images that appeared to be children engaged in explicit sexual activity.[9] This law was found unconstitutional by the Supreme Court in 2002. In 2003, Congress passed another law against "morphed" child pornography, known as the Prosecutorial Remedies and Tools Against the Exploitation of Children Today, or PROTECT Act.

Data mining "Analysis of data in a database using tools which look for trends or anomalies without knowledge of the meaning of the data."[10]

DCS1000 (also known as Carnivore) A federal program that consists of hardware and software that is typically installed in an ISP's facilities. The system can intercept Internet packets using specific filtering parameters based on the type of information referenced in a court order.

ECPA Electronic Communications Privacy Act of 1986. The federal government's first major legislation attempting to translate telephone wiretap laws to cover computer, wireline, and wireless network communications.

Encryption "Any procedure used in cryptography to convert plain text into ciphertext (encrypted message) in order to prevent any but the intended recipient from reading that data."[11]

FERPA The Family Education Rights and Privacy Act of 1974 defines what is considered "education records" and protects the confidentiality of those records for students in any school receiving federal funds. The law gives parents and/or guardians the right to inspect and review their minor student's education records and the right to request correction of records they believe to be incorrect or misleading. This right to access a student's education record transfers to the student at the age of eighteen.

FIPPS Fair Information Practice Principles. Four principles of privacy that the Federal Trade Commission encourages be included, when relevant, in any privacy policy. The principles are targeted at any entity that collects PII. They are (1) Notice: consumers should have clear notice of the entity's information practices; (2) Choice: consumers should have a choice on how their PII is used; (3) Access: consumers should have access to their PII; and (4) Security: consumer PII must be protected and kept secure from any unauthorized access or use.

Firewall "A security device built into many Internet servers. Firewalls help prevent unauthorized activity on the server. On networks, firewalls are used to prevent Internet users from accessing files other than public Internet material."[12]

First Amendment "Amendment I to the United States Constitution, ratified in 1791, which guarantees freedom of speech: 'Congress shall make no law respecting an establishment of religion, or prohibiting the free exercise thereof; or abridging the freedom of speech, or of the press; or the right of the people peaceably to assemble, and to petition the government for a redress of grievances.' The Freedom to Read Statement and the Library Bill of Rights of the American Library Association are based on this constitutional protection."[13]

Foreign Intelligence Surveillance Act (FISA) This law gave the federal government authority and procedures to conduct wiretaps in investigations of potential threats from foreign governments or their agents. It also created a special

"FISA court" to oversee these investigations. The USA PATRIOT Act made a number of changes to existing FISA rules.

Fourth Amendment   Amendment IV to the U.S. Constitution, ratified in 1791, which is the foundation of citizens' right to privacy against the government: "The right of the people to be secure in their persons, houses, papers, and effects, against unreasonable searches and seizures, shall not be violated, and no warrants shall issue, but upon probable cause, supported by oath or affirmation, and particularly describing the place to be searched, and the persons or things to be seized."

Freedom of Information Act (FOIA)   This law, first passed by Congress in 1966 and amended in 1974, outlines the procedures by which individuals may obtain copies of records held by most federal agencies.

Gag order   A court order prohibiting a person or organization from making public statements about a legal proceeding. Gag orders may be very broad, but do not prohibit the right to consult an attorney.

Geographic information system (GIS)   "A computer system for capturing, storing, checking, integrating, manipulating, analyzing and displaying data related to positions on the Earth's surface."[14]

In loco parentis   Latin for "in place of a parent," usually a person who temporarily assumes parental authority.[15] In K–12 schools, educators serve in place of the parent or guardian while the child is within the school.

International Coalition of Library Consortia (ICOLC) "Privacy Guidelines for Electronic Resources Vendors"   In 2002, the International Coalition of Library Consortia (ICOLC), an informal, international group of over 160 library consortia in North America, Europe, Australia, Asia, and Africa announced its "Privacy Guidelines for Electronic Resources Vendors" to serve as the basis for vendor practices in relation to ensuring the privacy of library users in their information seeking activities.[16]

Multistate Anti-TeRrorism Information eXchange (MATRIX)   This program combines information about individuals from government and private-sector data repositories to allow searching through millions of records to judge if a resulting response identifies possible terrorist or other criminal activity.

Mutually assured anonymity (MAA)   Institutional interventions of academic libraries and their communities to balance academic freedom with privacy protection.[17]

NCIPA   Neighborhood Children's Internet Protection Act. Passed as part of the Children's Internet Protection Act (CIPA), it requires schools and libraries receiving E-rate discounts to have Internet policies addressing the unauthorized disclosure, use, and dissemination of personal identification information.

Network traffic logs   Software programs to monitor network traffic, identify unauthorized access or access to nonpublic information and monitor the performance of the institution's network.

Novel Intelligence from Massive Data (NIMD)   A Department of Defense program focusing on avoiding "strategic surprise" such as unforeseen events that impact national security, like the terrorist attacks of September 11, 2001.

Opt-in The term commonly used where you have the choice on whether and how any of your personally identifiable information will be used. In other words, you are in control of your PII and anyone wanting to use it must ask your permission. This is the current European Union's standard for the protection of its citizen's PII.

Opt-out The opposite of opt-in is opt-out; where any PII you make available on paper or via the web can be used in any manner stated, unless you specifically "opt-out" and request that it not be used. Unfortunately, it may not be clearly stated how your PII will be used, and opt-out provisions may not be available on a web site or paper form where you are entering PII.

Oral request for information by law enforcement agent A request is different from a court order. A library is not required to comply with an oral or written request for information from a law enforcement agent. State library confidentiality laws may make it inadvisable for a library to provide information to a law enforcement agency without a court order or subpoena.

P3P (Platform for Privacy Preferences) "The Platform for Privacy Preferences Project (P3P), developed by the World Wide Web Consortium, is emerging as an industry standard providing a simple, automated way for users to gain more control over the use of personal information on web sites they visit. At its most basic level, P3P is a standardized set of multiple-choice questions, covering all the major aspects of a web site's privacy policies."[18]

Pen/trap orders "Pen/trap" is an abbreviation of "pen register and trap and trace authority," which reflects the early technology used in wiretapping. A pen/trap order is an order from a court that permits use of a device that records transactional data only, about the communications made to or from a particular phone or computer, for example, telephone numbers.

Personally identifiable information (PII) Full name, home address, email address, telephone number, or other information that would allow someone to identify an individual.

PGP (Pretty Good Privacy) "A technique developed by Philip Zimmerman for encrypting messages. PGP is one of the most common ways to protect messages on the Internet because it is effective, easy to use, and free. PGP is based on the public-key method, which uses two keys—one is a public key that you disseminate to anyone from whom you want to receive a message. The other is a private key that you use to decrypt messages that you receive."[19]

Phishing A type of email or web-based criminal or malicious activity designed to get people to reveal their PII or unwittingly participate, and thus become a victim. These emails and web sites often look authentic and request password or bank account information. Legitimate commercial web businesses will almost never send you an email requesting such sensitive information.

Privacy The right of an individual to determine when, how, and what personal information may be shared with others and for what purpose.

Privacy (library context) "In a library, the right to privacy is the right to open inquiry without having the subject of one's interest examined or scrutinized by others."[20]

Privacy audit A systematic review and evaluation of an organization's current policies and procedures regarding privacy of information whereby data are collected, reviewed, and classified to determine the amount of security required to protect privacy of information in the organization.[21]

Privacy policy (library) Aimed at library patrons, the policy describes what types of personally identifiable information the library collects, how it is used, who has access to the information, how long it is retained before expunging, and what recourse patrons have if they feel their privacy has been compromised. The policy should be adopted by the library's governing board and posted publicly for patrons.

Privacy policy (web site) A web site's written statement describing data collection, use, and security of the data.

Privacy seal organization An organization that certifies the compliance of a business, institution, or other organization with their stated privacy policy in areas such as notice, choice, access, security, and redress with regard to personal information.[22]

Probable cause A legal standard used in criminal law, probable cause means there are facts that would lead a reasonable person to believe it is more likely than not that a crime has been committed and the suspect is involved. In criminal cases, law enforcement officers must demonstrate probable cause to obtain a search warrant from a judge.

Push- and pull-technologies Pull-technologies are characterized by the user clicking on links to pull information to the browser; push-technologies are characterized by pushing information based on a personal user profile. Using push web technologies, the library can send information selected on the basis of patron research interests.[23]

Radio Frequency Identification (RFID) Uses a small integrated circuit affixed to an object which contains data identifying the object, like a book. In libraries RFID tags are used to replace barcodes. A radio frequency transponder is used to "read" the data on the tags. Library tags are passive. They contain no embedded power and can usually be read from only several feet. Privacy issues arise when the tags contain data besides just the ID number identifying the item.

Reasonable suspicion A legal standard used in criminal law, reasonable suspicion means that before a person can be stopped and questioned by law enforcement officers, the officers must have a "reasonable suspicion" that the person being stopped is engaged in criminal activity. This is a lower standard than probable cause.

Records Retention Policy A policy that protects the privacy and confidentiality of school library media center patrons by specifying what types of library nonessential personally identifying data or files will not be retained and determines a schedule to purge, shred, or otherwise destroy those records and/or configure programs to remove personally identifiable information.

Seal programs Attempts by businesses or professions to self-regulate adherence to privacy principles and practices.

Search warrant A court order giving law enforcement agents permission to enter a home or business and search for evidence related to specific illegal activity.

Selective Dissemination of Information (SDI) Services that deliver customized, personalized information based on user-supplied profiles.[24]

Subpoena A subpoena is a court order which specifically requires a person to provide evidence in a legal proceeding.

Terrorism Information Awareness (TIA) A U.S. Defense Department program with the goal of accumulating, managing, and analyzing vast quantities of information to identify threats to national security and to detect and defeat terrorist networks.

USA PATRIOT Act Passed in the wake of the September 11, 2001, terrorist attacks, the act makes significant changes to many of the privacy protections formerly in place in law enforcement investigations. The act makes it easier to get a warrant to search or obtain information, including library use records.

Virtual personal network (VPN) Also called virtual private network. "A virtual private network (VPN) connection is a secure 'tunnel' formed between a private network and a remote machine connected anywhere on the Internet."[25]

Notes

1. Small Business Solutions, http://www.residual-rewards.com/anonymizer-definition.html (accessed August 1, 2004).

2. Rob Slade, "Glossary of Communication, Computer, Data, and Information Security Terms," http://sun.soci.niu.edu/~rslade/secgloss.htm (accessed August 1, 2004).

3. American Library Association, Office for Intellectual Freedom, "CPPA, COPA, CIPA: Which Is Which?" http://www.ala.org/ala/oif/ifissues/issuesrelated links/cppacopacipa.htm (accessed August 10, 2004).

4. American Library Association, Office for Intellectual Freedom, "Questions and Answers on Privacy and Confidentiality," http://www.ala.org/ala/oif/state mentspols/statementsif/interpretations/questionsanswers.htm (accessed July 26, 2004).

5. Cookie Cutter Software, http://www.cutedownloads.com/two/COOKIE-CUTTER.htm (accessed August 1, 2004).

6. James S. Heller, "Where Have You Gone, Fair Use: Document Delivery in the For-Profit Sector," January 2000, http://www.unc.edu/~unclng/copy-corner17.htm (accessed January 5, 2005).

7. "CIPA, COPA, COPPA, CPPA: Child Online Protections Explained," Ryan Turner, http://www.ombwatch.org/article/articleview/593/2/96/ (accessed August 10, 2004). See also "Primer: Children, the Internet, and Pornography," Robert MacMillan, http://www.washingtonpost.com/wp-dyn/articles/A39748-2002 May31.html (accessed August 10, 2004).

8. Ibid.

9. Neither this bill nor COPA is discussed in this book; however, many people have a difficult time keeping track of the differences between COPA, COPPA, CPPA, and CIPA. As this book refers to both COPPA and CIPA, we wanted to be clear.

10. FOLDOC (Free On-line Dictionary of Computing), http://foldoc.doc.ic.ac.uk/foldoc/foldoc.cgi?query=data+mining&action=Search (accessed August 1, 2004).

11. FOLDOC (Free On-line Dictionary of Computing), http://foldoc.doc.ic.ac.uk/foldoc/foldoc.cgi?query=encryption (accessed August 1, 2004).

12. B. F. Brent and Dan Scott, "Microcomputer Glossary: ASI Microcomputer Applications," http://www.oznet.ksu.edu/ed_asi490/Glossary/cgw.htm#F (accessed August 1, 2004).

13. Joan M. Reitz, "First Amendment," ODLIS (Online Dictionary for Library and Information Science), http://lu.com/odlis/odlis_f.cfm (accessed August 2, 2004).

14. FOLDOC (Free Online Dictionary of Computing), http://foldoc.doc.ic.ac.uk/foldoc/foldoc.cgi?query=geographic+information+system (accessed August 1, 2004).

15. Joan M. Reitz, "ODLIS: Online Dictionary for Library and Information Science," http://lu.com/odlis/odlis_i.cfm (accessed November 14, 2004).

16. "Privacy Guidelines for Electronic Resources Vendors" Press Release and "About the International Coalition of Library Consortia (ICOLC)," http://www.library.yale.edu/consortia/2002privacyguidelinespressrelease.html (accessed January 5, 2005).

17. John A. Shuler, "Privacy and Academic Libraries: Widening the Frame of Discussion," *Journal of Academic Librarianship* 30, no. 2 (March 2004): 157–59.

18. "Platform for Privacy Preferences Initiative," http://www.w3.org/P3P/#what (accessed August 10, 2004).

19. *Webopedia Computer Dictionary*, http://www.webopedia.com/TERM/P/Pretty_Good_Privacy.html (accessed August 1, 2004).

20. American Library Association, "Questions and Answers on Privacy and Confidentiality."

21. Pamela Jerskey, Ivy Dodge, and Sanford Sherizen, "The Privacy Audit: A Primer by Pamela Jerskey, Ivy Dodge and Sanford Sherizen," http://www2.bc.edu/~jerskey/privacy.htm (accessed July 30, 2004).

22. Arthur W. Hafner and John J. Keating III, "Supporting Individual Library Patrons with Information Technologies: Emerging One-to-One Library Services on the College or University Campus," *Journal of Academic Librarianship* 18, no. 6 (November 2002): 426–29.

23. Ibid.

24. Ronald J. Heckart, "Imagining the Digital Library in a Commercialized Internet," *Journal of Academic Librarianship* 24, no. 4 (July 1999): 274–80.

25. Virtual Private Network, http://www.utexas.edu/its/vpn/about.html#general (accessed August 1, 2004).

Index

Titles of legal cases and literary works are italicized.

About the Authors

HELEN R. ADAMS is a retired School Library Media Specialist.

ROBERT F. BOCHER is a State Public Library Consultant in Wisconsin.

CAROL A. GORDON is Head of Pickering Educational Resources Library and Associate Professor of Education, Boston University.

ELIZABETH BARRY-KESSLER is an Attorney specializing in privacy and First Amendment issues.